PSYCHOBIOLOGICAL PROCESSES IN HEALTH AND ILLNESS

PSYCHOBIOLOGICAL PROCESSES IN HEALTH AND ILLNESS

KATE HAMILTON-WEST

Los Angeles | London | New Delhi
Singapore | Washington DC

SAGE Publications Ltd
1 Oliver's Yard
55 City Road
London EC1Y 1SP

SAGE Publications Inc.
2455 Teller Road
Thousand Oaks, California 91320

SAGE Publications India Pvt Ltd
B 1/I 1 Mohan Cooperative Industrial Area
Mathura Road, Post Bag 7
New Delhi 110 044

SAGE Publications Asia-Pacific Pte Ltd
33 Pekin Street #02-01
Far East Square
Singapore 048763

1006286537

Library of Congress Control Number: 2010938029

British Library Cataloguing in Publication data

A catalogue record for this book is available from the British Library

ISBN 978-1-84787-243-2
ISBN 978-1-84787-244-9 (pbk)

Typeset by C&M Digitals Pvt Ltd, Chennai, India
Printed and bound in Great Britain by TJ International Ltd, Padstow, Cornwall
Printed on paper from sustainable resources

MIX
Paper from
responsible sources
FSC
www.fsc.org   FSC® C013056

To Tim, Honor and Phoebe

CONTENTS

PREFACE

Conceptualisations of health, illness and disease have changed considerably over the past few decades. These changing conceptualisations have influenced (and been influenced by) the development of new fields of study, many of which span traditional disciplinary boundaries.

Perhaps the most important boundary to be bridged in health research is that between the study of the mind (psychology) and the study of the body (biology). The emergence of disciplines such as health psychology, behavioural medicine and psychoneuroimmunology reflects a growing recognition that while particular psychological and biological processes can be isolated for research purposes, this isolation can distort the processes we aim to understand. To understand the nature of biological processes and their implications for health, we must also consider the influence of psychological processes; to understand the nature of psychological processes and their implications for health, we must also consider the influence of biological processes.

This integration between psychological and biological approaches is essential if we are to tackle the health challenges facing us today. Take, for example, the rise in chronic illness associated with behaviours such as drinking, smoking and overeating. How do we get to the root cause of this problem?

Explaining the causes of human behaviour has traditionally been the domain of psychologists, and there are numerous theories within this field to explain why individuals may engage in behaviours that are apparently self-defeating. These theories, however, tend to explain health-related behaviour in terms of consciously accessible beliefs, attitudes and expectations. It is becoming increasingly evident that explanations at this level cannot fully account for behaviour. People who want to follow a healthy diet, quit smoking or cut down on alcohol frequently fail, despite their best intentions, and recent research suggests that biological processes may be to blame. 'Will power' apparently relies on limited resources, and the energy required to constantly resist temptation may simply 'run out'. Such resources may be even more limited during stressful periods or periods of illness as the organism must redirect resources towards dealing with more immediate threats. Research also suggests that behaviours such as drinking, smoking and overeating may function in a similar manner to the body's own homeostatic mechanisms, allowing the individual to maintain normal functioning during challenging periods.

So, while psychologists still play a key role in explaining health-related behaviours, there is now increasing recognition that theories must be expanded to incorporate a role for psychobiological processes and that these processes may not necessarily be accessible to conscious awareness or self-report.

Other bodies of research are also important to this endeavour. Genetic research, for example, has important implications when considering to what extent health (and health-related behaviour) is 'written in the genes'. Perhaps the risk of disease is genetically predetermined. If so, does behaviour really matter? Perhaps some people are predestined to become obese or addicted to alcohol or cigarettes. If so, can we really do anything to change these outcomes?

Alternatively, perhaps it is the environment that is truly to blame. For example, epidemiological research highlights marked social gradients in health, both between and within countries. How do we account for these gradients? Why should life expectancy and the risk of disease depend on the country we live in or our occupation?

If we really want to tackle global health issues, should we be trying to change people's attitudes, genes or environments? It is clear that no one discipline can provide a complete answer to the health challenges that face us today. Scientists across a number of health-relevant disciplines will need to work together more closely, and we will need to train more scientists to work at the interface of psychology, biology and medicine.

THE AIMS OF THIS BOOK

While integration of the disciplines is important if we are to further understand, prevent and treat disease, it is not necessarily easy to achieve.

Differences in terminology exist between relevant disciplines and these render much research inaccessible to readers from other disciplinary backgrounds. Differences in research methods also present barriers to integration. For example, the process of defining and measuring psychological constructs may appear mysterious to researchers who are more accustomed to studying biological processes. This means that, outside the discipline of psychology, psychological constructs can appear 'woolly' or difficult to apply. Researchers with a pure psychology background may find immune or endocrine processes just as mysterious. While the discoveries arising from the Human Genome Project undoubtedly have important implications for all disciplines concerned with understanding the causes of disease and illness, scientists outside the genetic field may not be aware of the methods used to differentiate environmental and genetic contributions to disease or identify disease genes.

The purpose of this book, then, is to begin to break down some of these barriers and provide an accessible introduction to psychobiological processes relevant to health and illness, summarising key findings across a number of disciplines. Research methods within these disciplines are also discussed and key terms are defined as we proceed (these are also listed in the Glossary at the back of this book). Since the literature summarised in the following chapters is both vast and diverse, we have not attempted to cover it all, but instead provide a useful entrée. The structure of the book is described in greater detail below.

THE STRUCTURE OF THIS BOOK

CHAPTER 1

The first chapter invites you to take a step back and consider what we mean by commonly used terms such as 'health', 'illness' and 'disease', as well as what it means to be 'normal' (or 'abnormal'). In this chapter we also explain what we mean by 'psychobiological processes'; we consider disciplines concerned with these processes and discuss the methods used to define and measure theoretical constructs.

CHAPTER 2

In this chapter we summarise research focusing on stress – a concept that has been defined and measured in a number of ways and is therefore often viewed as particularly 'woolly'. Despite problems of definition, the stress concept is critical to an understanding of how changes in the external environment may influence processes within the body. Research focusing on psychobiological responses to stress also requires us to consider how the health effects of toxic environments should be measured – how do we quantify changes across multiple physiological systems, for example?

CHAPTER 3

Here we turn our attention to positive processes in health and illness. If negative emotions can damage our health, do positive emotions have the power to cure? Why is it that some people appear relatively resilient to life's challenges? How do patients find positive meaning in their experiences of illness? Are happier people healthier (or vice versa)? This chapter also aims to highlight trends in the psychological research literature – particularly the growing body of research focusing on promotion of positive psychological outcomes (as opposed to amelioration of psychopathology).

CHAPTER 4

In this chapter we consider the role that our genes play in determining personality, behaviour, health and well-being and how the Human Genome Project has contributed (and continues to contribute) to our understanding of the determinants of health and illness. You are invited to consider the opportunities and challenges presented by predictive genetic testing – is it useful, desirable or even ethical to predict an individual's risk of disease months or even years before symptoms appear? Would you want to know your risk? What are the implications of predictive genetic testing for the prevention and treatment of illness?

CHAPTER 5

Here we discuss an aspect of human experience in which psychological and biological processes are particularly closely interrelated – the experience of pain. Like stress, pain has proved difficult to define and measure, and a number of theories have been presented over the years to account for our experience of it. Nonetheless, pain is a very real and a very common problem. We consider how pain may influence and be influenced by psychological and biological processes and how understanding of psychobiological interactions may help to develop more effective treatments.

CHAPTER 6

While the research reviewed in Chapters 1 to 5 highlights implications of psychobiological processes for health and illness at an individual level, it is also important to consider to what extent these processes may account for variations in the risk of disease at the group level. For example, do we see higher rates of infectious illness or heart disease in groups exposed to chronic stress over a number of years (the stress associated with long-term caregiving or economic hardship, for example)? If not, we need to question whether associations between psychological and biological processes observed in the laboratory have any relevance in the real world. In this chapter, then, we take a look at a number of 'at risk' populations and consider the extent to which real-world evidence supports the findings of laboratory research.

CHAPTER 7

Next, we shift our attention from theory to intervention. In this chapter we consider to what extent psychobiological research has resulted in changes in the way we treat or prevent illness and disease. We discuss a wide range of approaches, including both coping-based interventions for patients with chronic illness and cognitive behavioural therapies for patients with chronic illness or pain. You are asked to consider the relative strengths and limitations of alternative approaches and the extent to which intervention effects may be explained by the theories and processes described in previous chapters.

CHAPTER 8

We focus here on methodological issues. We consider what kind of evidence is needed to demonstrate that psychological processes *actually* produce alterations in physical functioning, or that psychobiological processes *actually* produce changes in health outcomes. We describe the principles of experimental design and discuss alternative research designs, considering the relative advantages and disadvantages of each. The methods available for evaluating the effects of intervention are also discussed and we consider the complexities involved in developing and applying theory-based interventions.

CHAPTER 9

The final chapter presents a summary of the research discussed in previous chapters, highlighting themes that cut across disciplines and present opportunities for interdisciplinary collaboration. We draw some tentative conclusions regarding the nature of 'toxic' and 'optimal' conditions in relation to social, psychological and biological functioning and take a look into the future in order to consider how psychobiological research could benefit from recent technological advances. These include advances in information and communication technologies, brain imaging technologies and virtual reality applications. In this chapter we also consider how psychobiological research could be expanded to include a role for macro-level influences, those related to religion, culture and community.

NOTES ON FEATURES OF THIS BOOK

KEY TERMS AND THE GLOSSARY

Key terms are highlighted in bold the first time they appear and are listed at the end of each chapter. They are also listed in the Glossary at the end of this book, together with a brief definition or explanation – for a more detailed explanation please refer to the chapter.

BOXES

Some points require a more detailed explanation than is practicable within the main body of the text. These are therefore explained in greater detail in boxes. Some boxes summarise controversies in the research literature – for example, 'Can stress shrink your brain?', 'Does coping influence cancer survival?'

While research findings are summarised throughout this book, it is also important to take a detailed look at individual studies – what methods did the researchers use, what did they find and what conclusions did they draw? The 'Research in focus' boxes provide detailed descriptions of key studies in relation to the topics discussed in each chapter.

DISCUSSION QUESTIONS AND FURTHER READING

Each chapter ends with a list of discussion questions and further reading. These are to encourage you to delve further into the literature and relate the research discussed in each chapter to your own experience – clinical, research-based or real life.

ABOUT THE AUTHOR

I completed a PhD in health psychology in 2003 and have since qualified as a chartered psychologist and practising health psychologist. I have a very long-held interest in health and have previously worked in medical education and training, in health and social care research and in health psychology education and training. I am now a lecturer in health psychology at the University of Kent. My research focuses on relationships between emotions and health and the psychological implications of living with chronic illness. Much of my current research is multidisciplinary and I enjoy collaborating with colleagues (both academics and clinicians) across a range of health-related disciplines.

ACKNOWLEDGEMENTS

I would like to thank a number of people who have contributed to the process of writing this book: Chris Bridle, Christina Chryssanthopoulou, Aileen McGettrick, Katja Rudell and Derek Rutter for reading and commenting on early drafts, and Sarah Hotham for her work on the References section.

PUBLISHER'S ACKNOWLEDGEMENTS

The author and publisher wish to thank the following for permission to use copyright material:

We thank the American Psychiatric Association for permission to use Figure 1.1 Hierarchy of Natural Systems. From Engel, G. L. (1980). The Clinical Application of the Biopsychosocial Model. *American Journal of Psychiatry,* 137, 535–544. Reprinted with permission from the American Journal of Psychiatry, (Copyright 1980). American Psychiatric Association.

We thank the American Psychological Association for permission to use Table 3.1 Components of subjective well-being. From Diener, E., Suh, E. ., Lucas, R. & Smith, H. (1999). Subjective well-being: Three decades of progress. *Psychological bulletin,* 2, 276–302.

We thank BioMed Central for permission to use Figure 4.2 Diagram Showing Inheritance in Hybrid Pea Plants. From Porteous, J.W. (2004). We still fail to account for Mendel's observations. *Theoretical Biology and Medical Modelling,* 1, 1–4.

We thank BMJ Publishing Group for permission to use:

Figure 5.1. From Holdcroft, A. & Power, I. (2003) 'Recent Developments: Management of Pain'. *British Medical Journal*, 326, 635-9.

Figure 8.2 Sequential Phases of Developing Randomised Controlled Trials of Complex Interventions. Campbell, M., Fitzpatrick, R., Haines, A., Kinmonth, A.L., Sandercock, P., Spielgelhalter, D., & Tyrer, P. (2000) 'Framework for Design and Evaluation of Complex Interventions to Improve Health'. *British Medical Journal, 321, 694–696.*

We thank Elsevier for permission to use:

An excerpt from Slagboom, P.E. & Meulenbelt, I. (2002) 'Organisation of the Human Genome and our Tools for Identifying Disease Genes'. *Biological Psychology*, 61, 11–31.

Figure 1.2 An Integrative Model of Psychoneuroimmunology and Health Psychology. From Lutgendorf and Costanzo (2003) 'Psychoneuroimmunology and Health Psychology: An Integrative Model'. *Brain and Behavior and Immunity,* 17, 225–315.

Figure 1.4 Social Readjustment Rating Scale. From: Holmes, T. H. & Rahe, R H. (1967) 'The Social Readjustment Rating Scale'. *Journal of Psychosomatic Research*, 11, 213–18.

Figure 2.5 Theoretical Model of the Coping Process. From Folkman, S. (1997) 'Positive Psychological States and Coping with Severe Stress'. *Social Science and Medicine, 45*, p1207–1221.

Figure 2.6 The Cognitive Activation Theory of Stress. From Ursin, H., & Eriksen, H. R. (2004) 'The Cognitive Activation Theory of Stress'. *Psychoneuroendocrinology, 29*, 567–592.

Table 2.1 From Homeostasis to Pathology. From LeMoal, M.L. (2007) 'Historical Approach and Evolution of the Stress Concept: A Personal Account'. *Psychoneuroendocrinology, 32.* S3–S9.

Figure 3.1 Theoretical Model of the Coping Process and Figure 3.2. Revised theoretical Model of the Coping Process. From Folkman, S. (1997) 'Positive Psychological States and Coping with Severe Stress. *Social Science Medicine, 45*, 1207–1221.

Figure 4.5 Causal Model of Emotional Dysregulation as a Candidate Endophenotype of Alcohol Dependence. From Lesch, K. P. (2005) 'Alcohol Dependence and Gene X Environment Interaction in Emotion Regulation: Is Serotonin the Link? European Journal of Pharmacology, 526, 113–124.

Table 5.1 Definitions of Pain. From Summers, S. (2000) 'Evidence-based Practice Part 1: Pain Definitions, Pathophysiologic Mechanisms, and Theories'. Journal of PeriAnaesthesia Nursing, 15, 357–365.

Figure 5.3 The Gate Control Theory of Pain and Figure 5.4 The body-self Neuromatrix. From Melzack, R. (1999) 'From the Gate to the Neuromatrix'. *Pain, 82*, S121–S126.

Figure 5.5. Site of Endogenous Opioid Receptors. From Pleuvry, B. J. (2005). Opioid Mechanisms and Opioid Drugs. *Anaesthesia and Intensive Care Medicine, 6, 30–34.*

Figure 6.1 Life expectancy plotted against GDP per head. From Marmot, M. (2006) 'Health in an Unequal World'. *Lancet, 368*, 2081–2094.

Figure 6.4 from Spolentini, I., Gianni, W., Repetto, L., Bria, P., Caltagirone, C., Bossu, P., & Spalletta, G. (2008) 'Depression and Cancer: An unexplored and unresolved Emergent Issue in Elderly Patients. *Critical Reviews in Oncology/Hematology, 65,* 143–155.

Figure 6.5 from Gilley, D., Herbert, B-S., Huda, N., Tanaka, H., & Reed, T. (2008) 'Factors Impacting Hman Tlomere Hmeostasis and Age-related Disease'. *Mechanisms of Aging and Development, 129,* 27–34.

Figure 7.1 Diagram Showing Relationships between Placebo Treatment, Internal Regulatory Processes, and Outcomes. Wager, T. D. & Nitschke, J. B. (2005) 'Placebo Effects in the Brain: Linking Mental and Physiological Processes. *Brain, Behavior, and Immunity, 19*, 281–282.

Table 8.1 Hierarchy of Scientific Evidence for Inferring Causality. From Ketterer, M. W., Mahr, G., & Goldberg, A. D. (2000) 'Psychological Factors Affecting a Medical Condition: Ischemic Coronary Heart Disease'. *Journal of Psychosomatic Research, 48*, 357–367.

Table 8.2 from Glasgow, R. E., McKay, H. G., Piette, J. D., & Reynolds, K. D. (2001) 'The RE-AIM Framework for Evaluating Interventions: What can it tell us about Approaches to Chronic Illness Management?' *Patient Education and Counselling, 44*, 119–127.

We thank Merck & Co. for permission to use Figure 5.2 Referred Pain. From The Merck Manual of Medical Information – Home Edition, edited by Robert S. Porter. Copyright 2007 by Merck & Co., Inc., Whitehouse Station, NJ. Available at: http://www.merck.com/mmhe. Accessed on 2/5/2008.

We thank the National Heart, Lung, and Blood Institute (NHLBI), part of the National Institutes of Health and the U.S. Department of Health and Human Services for permission to use Figure 6.2 Coronary Atherosclerosis.

We thank Nature Publishing Group for permission to use Figure 4.4 from Boomsma, D., Busjahn, A., & Peltonen, L. (2002) 'Classical Twin Studies and Beyond'. *Nature, 3*, 872–882.

We thank Oxford University Press for permission to use:

Figure 2.1 The Autonomic Nervous System. From "Dictionary of Psychology" by Coleman Andrew (2006). By permission of Oxford University Press.

Fig 2.2 The Endocrine System. From 'The Oxford Companion to the Body' by Colin Blakemore and Sheila Jennett. By permission of Oxford University Press.

We thank Taylor and Francis for permission to use Figure 3.3. Schematic representation of Leventhal et al.'s (1980) Common Sense Model of Illness Representations. From Hagger, M.S. & Orbell, S. (2003) 'A Meta-analytic Review of the Common-sense Model of Illness Representations. *Psychology and Health, 18*, p141–184.

We thank the Public Library of Science (PLoS) for permission to use Figure 4.6 Waddington's epigenetic landscape. From Mitchell, K.J. (2007) 'The Genetics of Brain Wiring: From Molecule to Mind. PLoS Biology, 5, e113–115

We thank Wiley-Blackwell for permission to use Figure 2.7 Four Types of Allostatic Load. From McEwen, B.S. (1998) 'Stress, Adaptation, and Disease: Allostasis and Allostatic Load' *Annals of the New York Academy of Sciences, 840,* 33–44.

THE MIND–BODY CONNECTION

1

OVERVIEW

This chapter presents some key concepts relevant to an understanding of psychobiological and psychosocial processes in health and illness. Although the focus of this book is on psychobiological processes, the two are very closely related, so it is important to acknowledge the role of psychosocial processes before proceeding further.

   The biopsychosocial model of health is introduced and contrasted with the biomedical model of health. This discussion is set in the context of changing conceptualisations of mind and body and the emergence of 'new' fields of enquiry, including health psychology, behavioural medicine and psychoneuroimmunology. In so doing, we consider how advances in research are helping us to uncover the true complexity of links between psychological, social and biological processes with respect to their implications for health and how such advances may inform the development of new approaches to the treatment and prevention of illness.

LEARNING OUTCOMES

By the end of this chapter you should be able to:

- explain what is meant by 'psychobiological processes'

- explain what is meant by the terms 'health', 'illness' and 'disease'

- explain what is meant by 'normality'

- discuss global trends in disease, mortality rates and the causes of ill health

- describe the biopsychosocial model of health and compare it with the biomedical model

- discuss the influence of the biopsychosocial model on the development of new disciplines

- describe and differentiate between these disciplines

- describe the process of defining and measuring a psychological construct

- explain why psychobiological processes are important for understanding, preventing and treating disease and illness.

CHANGING CONCEPTUALISATIONS OF MIND AND BODY

1.1 This book is entitled *Psychobiological Processes in Health and Illness*, so, before proceeding further, it is useful to begin by considering what exactly we mean by the terms 'psychobiological', 'health' and 'illness'. While the latter two terms may *seem* intuitive, there has been considerable debate over the years regarding the definition of both 'health' and 'illness', and the distinction between **health, illness** and **disease**. Further, to explain the term 'psychobiological', we need to break the word down into its two constituent parts – 'psycho-' 'and 'biological'. In this chapter, then, we also consider why both psychological and biological processes are relevant to an understanding of health and illness and how these two types of processes have come to be combined into a single term.

1.1.1 DEFINING HEALTH, ILLNESS AND DISEASE

What does it mean to be healthy? Well, we could start by considering that health indicates a lack of illness or a lack of disease – you are not ill, therefore you are healthy. This is a difficult starting point, though, since both illness and disease themselves are poorly defined (as discussed further below). Also, are you in optimum health if you are not diseased or is health something more than absence of illness?

The World Health Organisation, for example, has defined health as 'a state of complete physical, mental and social well-being and not merely the absence of disease or infirmity' (WHO, 1946: 100). According to this definition, though, we would probably *all* be considered unhealthy. For example, you may not consider yourself completely healthy because you get out of breath walking up stairs or are unable to complete a marathon. At what point is our well-being less than complete?

Perhaps what really matters is the individual's ability to perform daily functions, such as continuing to go to work, raise a family or drive a car. Disease does not necessarily preclude normal daily functioning, so what about a patient with a terminal illness who is still able to go to work – is this person healthy or ill?

Perhaps you could consider yourself to be a healthy person even if you are, from time to time, afflicted with a runny nose, headache or sore throat. If so, why do these symptoms not constitute a lack of health? Maybe, then, we should overlook symptoms that are highly prevalent in the population and consider whether or not the individual experiences symptoms that are abnormal.

This, too, raises problems. First, how do we define 'abnormal' and, second, is 'abnormal' necessarily unhealthy? In relation to the former point, what is 'normal' in terms of physical, social and mental functioning depends on a wide range of factors, including the individual's age, gender, social status and culture. In relation to the latter point, it is clear that an individual can fall outside the range of **statistical normality** without necessarily being ill. For example, Veatch (1981) points out that the seven foot tall basketball player is not considered ill, nor are people with freckles, although both can be considered to be statistically abnormal (see Box 1.1).

BOX 1.1

Statistical normality

Many human characteristics follow a **normal distribution**. This means that most individuals will be at or around the average value for the group (such as being the average height for a man or woman). The frequency of a particular measurement decreases as the distance from the average value increases (there are few very short or very tall people, but many people are of roughly average height). If measurements are plotted on a graph, with the measurement scale on the X axis and frequency on the Y axis, this results in a bell-shaped curve, or 'Gaussian function'.

Individuals falling at the tail ends of the distribution are considered statistically abnormal. The cut-off value used most commonly is 95 per cent – that is, scores outside of the 95 per cent range (the top 2.5 or bottom 2.5 per cent) are abnormal.

It is important, however, to consider the 'reference group' used to calculate the normal range. For example, many people will appear abnormal if compared against norms for a different cultural group or age group or gender.

Many indicators of health (such as the level of glucose or cholesterol in the blood) follow a normal distribution. Individuals with values outside the normal range (for healthy individuals) are considered abnormal, although this does not necessarily indicate that these individuals are unhealthy. Many measures of psychological characteristics (such as intelligence, aggression) yield scores that are approximately normally distributed – that is, there are lots of people of roughly average intelligence, but few individuals with exceptional genius. As with indicators of physical health, abnormal scores on psychological measures do not necessarily indicate a need for treatment.

Perhaps, then, we should consider the individual's evaluation of his or her apparent symptoms. Are they abnormal for the individual and a source of distress or are they typical, tolerable? Thus, being unable to run a marathon could constitute evidence of ill health if the individual is normally able to run the marathon very easily and experiences distress in relation to this loss of physical fitness. Is this person really ill, though, or do they simply need to adapt their training routine?

It is clear, then, that although we may know in very general terms what we mean by the word 'health', providing a precise definition for this concept is far from straightforward. Further, it is evident that the related constructs of 'illness' and 'disease' are similarly ambiguous.

Engelhardt (1981: 39) writes that 'the concept of disease is an attempt to correlate constellations of signs and symptoms for the purposes of explanation, prediction and control', while Boorse (1977) proposes that a disease is only an 'illness' if it is serious enough to be incapacitating and therefore undesirable for the bearer, a title to special treatment and a valid excuse for normally criticisable behaviour. Thus, 'the concept of disease acts not only to describe and explain, but also to enjoin to action. It indicates a state of affairs as undesirable and to be overcome' (Engelhardt, 1981: 33).

In general, then, although these constructs are very difficult to define, a number of conclusions can be drawn:

- *health* is essentially an evaluative notion, based on adherence to physical, social and mental 'normality', although what is normal depends on a range of factors, including age, gender, culture and social status
- *illness* can be considered as a deviation from 'normality' that is perceived by the patient as distressing and entitling them to special treatment
- *disease* can be considered as an organising construct for explaining and responding to constellations of symptoms
- while health is a positive state of affairs, to be promoted and aspired to, both illness and disease are considered as negative states, to be treated or otherwise overcome.

1.1.2 THE ROLE OF PSYCHOLOGICAL PROCESSES

Thoughts, feelings and behaviours affect our health and well-being. Recognition of the importance of these influences on health and disease is consistent with evolving conceptions of mind and body and represents a significant change in medicine and the life sciences.

Baum & Posluszny, 1999: 138

It should be evident from the preceding discussion that psychological processes (thoughts, feelings and behaviours – also known as cognitions, emotions and actions) play an important role in health. First, as health is an evaluative notion, the same symptoms may be interpreted in different ways by different people. The individual's interpretation of these symptoms will influence behaviours such as seeking medical help, over-the-counter remedies or alternative therapies, and these behaviours are likely to influence health outcomes.

Further, the very causes of ill health in humans are often psychological in nature, setting us apart from other animals. As Kass (1981: 19) points out, 'other animals do not overeat, undersleep, knowingly ingest toxic substances, or permit their bodies to fall into disuse through sloth, watching television and riding about in automobiles, transacting business, or writing articles about health.'

The way we respond to stress as a species also highlights the role of psychological variables in the aetiology of illness. For example, Sapolsky (2002) explains that, while lions or zebras mobilise a stress response when faced with a physical threat, humans have a unique propensity to worry themselves sick by dwelling on antici-pated stressors, such as what to say in a job interview.

The recognition that health is the result of a combination of biological, social and psychological factors, is often referred to the **biopsychosocial model of health** (Engel, 1977), where the term 'model' indicates a 'complex integrated system of meaning used to view, interpret and understand a part of reality' (Veatch, 1981: 523). Engel (1977) contrasted this model to the (then dominant) **biomedical model**, which assumes disease to be fully explained by deviations from the norm of biological (somatic) variables.

These two models not only provide very different frameworks for interpreting and understanding illness but also give rise to different approaches to treatment and pre-vention. The biomedical model, with its focus on medical responses to biological alterations, has resulted in the development of drugs and vaccines that have contrib-uted to a dramatic decline in mortality rates in the twentieth century. For example, immunisation programmes have contributed to the eradication of smallpox and reductions in susceptibility to diseases such as polio, diphtheria, tetanus, whooping cough, Hib, meningitis C, measles, mumps, rubella and tuberculosis (Department of Health, 1996, 2006).

As Engel points out, though, this model does not tell the whole story since bio-chemical defects represent only one factor among many that may culminate in active disease or manifest as illness. The human experience of illness may occur in the absence of an identifiable organic cause, and 'rational treatment' directed only at the biochemical abnormality does not necessarily restore the patient to health.

The biopsychosocial model, therefore, proposes a 'holistic' approach to illness, in which the task of the physician is to understand the human experience of 'illness' (rather than the more limited construct of 'disease') from the perspective of the patient (Engel, 1977) and 'it is recognised that the mind must not be bypassed or underestimated in any effort to deal with breakdowns, whether from stress or patho-logical organisms' (Cousins, 1990: xvi).

Engel's (1977) paper sparked considerable discussion surrounding the role of the doctor–patient relationship and doctor–patient communication in medical practice, and patients are now recognised as active participants in the treatment process, rather than passive recipients of medical advice. Suchman (2005) points out that Engel's paper reinforced the importance of **patient-centred care** – a term introduced a few years earlier – but also that the term **relationship-centred care**, introduced some years later, reflects a more balanced focus on the roles of both patient and clinician.

Proponents of relationship-centred care argue that, since health is an evaluative notion, reality is not just interpreted by the physician, but created via the process of dialogue, so, for example, a physician may agree when a patient worries that a family argument caused a heart attack, although this interpretation is inadequate as a *complete* explanation of cause (Borrell-Carrio, Suchman & Epstein, 2004). Borrell-Carrio et al. (2004) write that the physician's task is to come to a shared understanding of the patient's narrative with the patient, communicating evidence in terms the patient can understand, at a rate at which it can be assimilated, avoiding either uncritical acceptance of what the patient believes or uncritical negation of the patient's perspective.

Research evidence has demonstrated that doctor–patient interactions influence a range of biological and behavioural outcomes, as well as patient satisfaction (Kaplan, Greenfield & Ware, 1989, for example). A systematic review of this literature concluded that eliciting patients' beliefs about their illnesses and empowering them to become active participants in the treatment process, 'may stimulate patients to develop their own plans to improve their health and positively affect patients' self-efficacy so that they feel motivated to implement these, and confident about doing so' (Michie, Miles & Weinman, 2003: 204).

1.1.3 THE CHALLENGE OF CHRONIC ILLNESS

The biopsychosocial model is particularly important for treatment of chronic illness since responsibility for day-to-day management of the condition tends to lie largely in the hands of the patient, rather than the medical professional (Assal, 1999). Chronic diseases have now replaced acute infectious diseases as the major cause of mortality, accounting for around 60 per cent of deaths worldwide (WHO, 2005). Effective treatment is challenging since chronic conditions are often difficult to diagnose, treatments may not always be available and, if they are available, the associated side-effects may put an additional strain on the patient (Devins & Binik, 1996). Further, Holman and Lorig (2000) point out that, with chronic conditions, neither the disease nor its consequences are static – both interact to create changing illness patterns that require constant management.

Chronic conditions also differ from acute infectious disease in that the main risk factors are often behavioural, rather than biological. According to the World Health Organisation (2005), common modifiable risk factors underlie the major chronic illnesses, including tobacco use, physical inactivity and unhealthy diet. Each year, 4.9 million people die as a result of tobacco use, 2.6 million die as a result of being overweight or obese, 4.4 million die as a result of raised total cholesterol and 7.1 million die as a result of raised blood pressure. These risk factors are becoming increasingly prevalent in many parts of the world. For example, in the UK, the prevalence of over-weight children aged 2 to 10 years increased from 23 per cent in 1995 to 32 per cent in 2005 (Health Survey for England, 2008). The World Health Organisation projects a 17 per cent increase in deaths due to chronic illness from 2005 to 2015 (WHO, 2005).

The World Health Organisation suggests that these figures indicate a global **obesity epidemic** (see Box 1.2). In this case, though, the epidemic calls not for development of vaccines, but for the promotion of healthy behaviours and population-based support for prevention, weight maintenance and management of comorbidities and weight loss (WHO, 2003). This focus is also reflected in government policies. For example, in the UK, 'The NHS Improvement Plan' (DOH, 2004) identified long-term conditions as one of the three top priorities for the National Health Service in the period up to 2008, and the White Paper 'Choosing Health' (DOH, 2005) set out key principles for supporting the public so that people would make healthier and more informed choices with regards to their health.

BOX 1.2

The obesity epidemic

The World Health Organisation reports that increased consumption of energy-dense, nutrient-poor foods with high levels of sugar and saturated fats, combined with physical inactivity, have led to at least a three-fold increase in obesity rates since 1980 in some areas of North America, the UK, Australasia and China.

The obesity epidemic is not restricted to developed countries. Obesity often coexists with undernutrition in developing countries, but the rate of increase in obesity is often faster in developing countries.

Obesity is a major risk factor for chronic diseases, including type 2 diabetes, cardiovascular disease, hypertension and stroke, and certain types of cancer.

Obesity is assessed using the body mass index (BMI), defined as weight (in kg) divided by the square of height (in metres). A BMI of over 25 kg/m^2 is defined as overweight, one of over 30 kg/m^2 as obese.

Source: World Health Organisation (2003)

The psychological consequences of chronic illness also highlight the importance of a biopsychosocial approach to its long-term management. For example, Devins and Binik (1996) write that ambiguity regarding diagnosis and treatment may leave individuals with a sense of uncertainty and fear for the future; the condition may also lead to pain and disability and may interfere with their lifestyles by preventing their involvement in valued activities; they may find it difficult to maintain hope, self-esteem and feelings of control; and they may also have to deal with negative social stereotypes and stigma. These challenges are likely to be of great significance to them, though they are largely ignored in the traditional biomedical approach.

Thus, the relationship between psychological and physiological processes can be conceptualised as bidirectional, with psychological factors influencing the risk of physical illness and physical illness influencing the risk of psychological morbidity. The biopsychosocial model, therefore, highlights the need for appropriately designed interventions targeted at both biological and psychosocial processes. Assumptions of the biopsychosocial model are summarised below.

Assumptions of the biopsychosocial model

- Psychological and physiological processes are closely interrelated.
- Any imbalance in these processes may lead to ill health.
- Relationships between psychological and biological variables are generally bidirectional.
- Health outcomes may be altered via appropriately designed interventions.

1.2 EMERGING DISCIPLINES

1.2.1 BEHAVIOURAL MEDICINE, HEALTH PSYCHOLOGY AND PSYCHONEUROIMMUNOLOGY

The introduction of the biopsychosocial model of health has resulted in the rapid development of new fields of enquiry, including the discipline of **health psychology** and the interdisciplinary field of **behavioural medicine** (Baum & Posluszny, 1999). While behavioural medicine draws on a range of behavioural sciences, such as anthropology, epidemiology, sociology and psychology (Schwarz & Weiss, 1977), health psychology is firmly grounded in psychological theory and can be defined as (Matarazzo, 1982: 4):

> the aggregate of the specific educational, scientific and professional contributions of the discipline of psychology to the promotion and maintenance of health, the prevention and treatment of illness, the identification of etiologic and diagnostic correlates of health, illness, and related dysfunction, and to the analysis and improvement of the health care system and health policy formation.

Therefore, health psychologists not only conduct research to identify associations between psychological, biological and social variables in the aetiology of illness but also use this knowledge to develop, apply and evaluate interventions to improve health. These interventions may be targeted at an individual level (such as psychological interventions to improve pain in patients undergoing surgery), interpersonal or organisational level (such as improvements in doctor–patient communication within a hospital) or societal level (public health campaigns to reduce levels of smoking, for example).

In acknowledging the role of psychological variables in health, the biopsychosocial model also shares common ground with the discipline of **psychosomatic medicine**. Lipowski (1984) writes that the term 'psychosomatic' has been in use since the 1800s and has been used in the research literature to refer to physical disorders caused or aggravated by psychological factors, mental disorders caused or aggravated by physical factors, the branch of medicine concerned with 'mind–body relations' and the field of study concerned with the relationships between mind and body. Lipowski (1984: 156) describes the introduction of the journal *Psychosomatic Medicine* in 1939 as 'an event of singular importance for the development of psychosocial conceptualisations and medicine', but also points out that this did little to dispel the ambiguity of the term 'psychosomatic' or explain how two words, 'psychosomatic' and 'medicine', with such different levels of abstraction and discourse, may be meaningfully connected. Lipowski (1984: 158) argues that 'medicine' is concerned with issues of health and disease, whereas 'psychosomatic' has 'a broader and more abstract connotation, one that touches on the problem of mind and body, and hence pertains to views on the nature of man.'

The term 'biopsychosocial' is clearer on this point, since Engel (1977, 1980) describes illness in terms of interrelated systems with different levels of organisation (such as molecules, cells, the person, the family or society), but linked together in a hierarchical relationship so that change in one system effects change in the others (see Figure 1.1).

Engel explains that, whether a cell or a person, each system is influenced by its environment. A cell is a component of tissues, organs and a person; a person and two-person systems are components of family systems and community systems. In scientific work, the investigator is generally obliged to select one level on which to concentrate, although neither the cell nor the person can be fully characterised as a dynamic system without characterising the environment of which it is part. In contrast to the reductionist biomedical model, the biopsychosocial model characterises the 'patient' as an individual within a wider social system. Experience and behaviour at the person level influence and are influenced by system levels both above the person and at the lower levels.

This 'systems approach' is also evident in the relatively new discipline of **psychoneuroimmunology (PNI)**, in which interactions between the brain and immune system are studied at a neural and biochemical level, together with the resulting implications for health. Kiecolt-Glaser et al. (2002) explain that PNI emerged within the context of broader psychosomatic investigations and that the term 'psychoimmunology' was introduced by Solomon and Moos in their (1964) paper 'Emotions, immunity and disease: a speculative theoretical integration', although the majority of PNI studies have been published since the 1980s.

Lutgendorf and Costanzo (2003) have proposed an integrative model of psychoneuroimmunology and health psychology in which psychosocial and biological factors influence the aetiology and progression of disease as how an individual interprets and responds to the environment influences responses to stress, health behaviours, neuroendocrine and immune responses, and, ultimately, health outcomes.

Health psychology interventions can be designed to alter psychosocial processes, improve health behaviours and influence neuroendocrine and immune factors. A wide range of approaches to intervention have been developed and evaluated, including

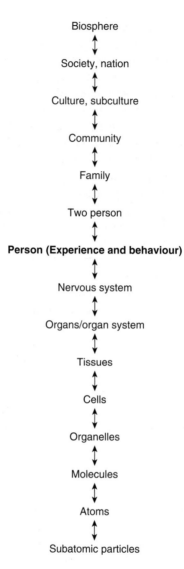

FIGURE 1.1 Hierarchy of natural systems
Source: Engel (1980)

cognitive behavioural stress management (CBSM), relaxation, hypnosis, meditation, emotional disclosure, adherence-based interventions, sleep hygiene (controlling poor sleep habits), exercise, social support groups, psychotherapy, imagery, distraction, behavioural pain management, yoga, massage, biofeedback, drug or alcohol prevention or rehabilitation, psychotherapy and behavioural conditioning (see Figure 1.2). These interventions are discussed further in Chapter 7.

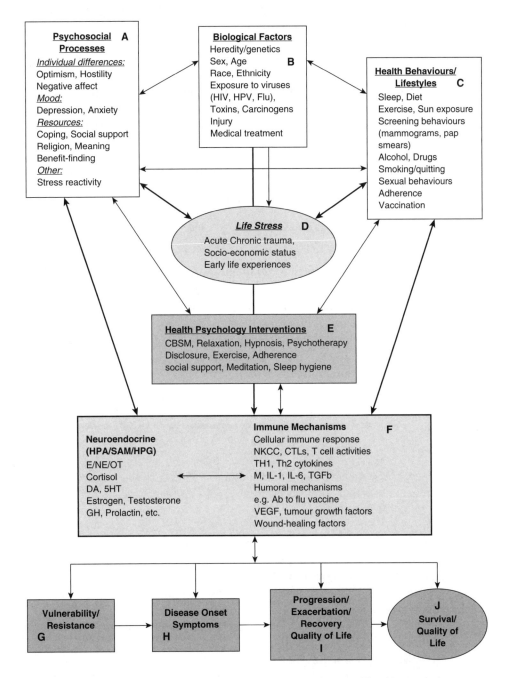

FIGURE 1.2   An integrative model of psychoneuroimmunology and health psychology

Source: Lutgendorf and Costanzo (2003)

1.2.2 PSYCHONEUROIMMUNOLOGY, PSYCHOENDOCRINOLOGY AND PSYCHOPHYSIOLOGY

Psychoneuroimmunology (PNI) shares similarities in terms of its approach with **psychoneuroendocrinology (PNE)** (the study of associations between psychological and endocrine (hormone) processes) and **psychophysiology (PP)** (the study of relations between psychological manipulations and physiological responses), although these fields differ with respect to their integration within the wider discipline of psychology. Ursin (1998: 556) writes that:

> The PP field is a respectable and well-developed part of psychology. Contemporary developments in brain mapping and brain imaging have increased the importance of this contribution. The PNI is still in its infancy as regards the serious contributions to psychological theory. The PNE has not received the interest it deserves. Too few psychologists understand endocrinology (and immunology), too few endocrinologists have any ideas about what psychology is all about.

These approaches also differ in scope. While PP research focuses on a wide range of physiological responses in relation to diverse activities such as sleep, problemsolving, reactions to stress, learning, memory, information processing and perception (Andreassi, 2000), PNI and PNE focus specifically on immune and endocrine responses respectively, with a particular emphasis on psychological disturbance, individual differences in responses to internal or external stimuli, and the immunological effects of **classical conditioning** (see Box 1.3).

BOX 1.3

Classical conditioning

Classical conditioning describes an associative learning process in which the subject (either human or animal) is presented with a stimulus (such as food) that reliably elicits a naturally occurring reaction (such as salivation).

This stimulus is referred to as an *unconditioned stimulus* (US) and the response is referred to as an *unconditioned response* (UR). This stimulus is repeatedly paired with a neutral stimulus (such as a light or bell), that would not normally elicit a specific response.

After repeated pairings, the previously neutral stimulus elicits the same response produced by the unconditioned one (salivation in response to a bell, for example). Once the previously neutral stimulus produces a reliable response in the participant, it is referred to as a **conditioned stimulus (CS)** and the response to this stimulus is referred to as a **conditioned response (CR)**.

Classical conditioning was first described by Ivan Pavlov, a physiologist studying digestion in dogs (1897, 1902, 1927). Cannon (1925) draws on these experiments in his description of the effect of emotions on digestion. Ader and Cohen (1975) later demonstrated that the immune system could be conditioned – a key discovery in the development of psychoneuroimmunology. **Conditioned immunomodulation** is discussed further in Chapter 2.

It is important to note that, although we can distinguish between endocrine and immune responses at a theoretical level, this distinction belies the complexity of inter-relations between these systems. For example, Brambilla (2000: 346) points out that:

> in the last two decades, numerous investigations have revealed that the immune and the neuro-endocrine functions amply interrelate in regulating the mechanisms of adaptation to internal and external stimuli.

The term psychoneuroimmunology may also be used to refer to both immune and endocrine responses. For example, Schedlowski and Tewes (1999: xi) write that:

> psychoneuroimmunology investigates the functional relationships among the nervous system, the neuroendocrine system, and the immune system. Although many of the communication pathways between these systems have yet to be elucidated, it is already well documented that the immune system is influenced and directed by neurochemical signals from both the nervous system and the endocrine system.

Brambilla (2000: 346) further points out that:

> more recently, the central nervous system (CNS) has been observed to be part of a triangle that includes the neuroendocrine and the immune system, each of which maintains a strict control of the function of the others.

1.2.3 PSYCHOLOGICAL RESEARCH METHODS

> The defining of a psychological construct and its measurement are complex tasks that take a long time to develop. Nevertheless, this process is crucial to psychological research, as hypothetical constructs such as emotions, personality traits, or cognitive abilities can never be directly observed. They can only be realised by the results of psychological tests.
>
> Tewes & Schedlowski, 1999: 114

The application of psychological methods to health-related research and practice represents an important advance since the discipline of psychology incorporates specialist knowledge in relation to the development and application of psychometric assessment methods and experimental manipulation of psychological processes (Tewes & Schedlowski, 1999).

The development of valid, reliable methods of assessing and manipulating psychological processes in relation to health is essential if psychological variables are to be incorporated into models of health and illness. For example, Roger (1998: 50) writes that:

> it is commonly assumed that stress causes illness, but there is little agreement over how either of these constructs should be defined … assuming that stress causes illness also raises questions about the mechanisms involved in 'translating' a cognitive process such as perceived threat into a diagnosable condition.

Roger points out, for example, that the **Type A personality** construct, characterised by impatience, competitiveness and hostility, was originally proposed as a

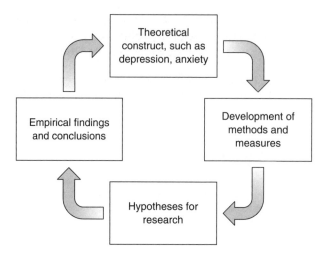

FIGURE 1.3   The process of defining and measuring psychological variables

contributory factor in heart disease, although different measures of a Type A personality are poorly correlated and vary in their association with coronary heart disease risk.

Tewes and Schedlowski (1999) explain that, although the function of variables such as molecules, cells or tissue can be described and analysed, psychological variables are not so readily defined and measured. The development of new methods and measures is therefore an ongoing process, involving continuous feedback between theory and empirical research. Thus, a specific construct, such as depression or anxiety, offers a theoretical background for the development of methods and measures; the results of these measurements allow us to form conclusions about theoretical constructs and develop hypotheses for further research, so that the theory and construct can be further evaluated and modified (see Figure 1.3).

Ongoing research has helped to clarify the aspects of personality most salient to an understanding of psychological processes in health and illness and identify the most valid methods for assessing psychological constructs. For example, Andreassi (2000) writes that the differences between Type As and Type Bs (relaxed, non-aggressive) are more reliable when structured interviews are used or there are extreme scores on the Jenkins activity survey (a self-report scale) than for other methods. Research evidence also suggests that links between a Type A personality and coronary artery disease (CAD) may be largely due to the effects of hostility (Miller et al., 1996, for example) and, specifically, that hostility may influence the risk of CAD risk via altered autonomic control (Sloan et al., 2001). The effects of psychological processes on the autonomic nervous system are discussed further in Chapter 2.

The measurement and conceptualisation of stress have also undergone significant development. For example, in early psychobiological research, stress was assessed using checklists of **stressful life events**, such as the social readjustment rating scale (SRRS) (Holmes & Rahe, 1967). According to the life events approach, events could be defined as stressful if they would normally demand readjustment of the average person's routine. The 'magnitude' of a particular event could be determined by the degree of adjustment this event would normally require. For example, in the SRRS, the death of a spouse is designated a magnitude of 100, while a change in living conditions is designated a magnitude of 25 (see Figure 1.4). Note that this checklist includes both positive events (such as a holiday) and negative events (such as bereavement). The checklist also includes items that may be a *symptom* of stress, rather than a cause of it (such as a change in sleeping or eating habits). Effects of stress on health-related behaviours are discussed in greater detail in Chapter 2.

More recent research, however, has indicated that people can respond in different ways to the same experience (in terms of emotion, cognition and behaviour and their physiological responses), so it is not possible to determine the magnitude of a particular event a priori. Rather, stress should be seen as a 'transaction' between the person and the environment (Cohen & Lazarus, 1979; Lazarus & Folkman, 1984, for example).

Key to this conceptualisation of stress is the notion that people evaluate (appraise) their environments and these appraisals influence the methods used to cope. Ursin (1998) suggests that **coping** and **appraisal** processes can be considered as 'filters', accounting for the individual differences in physiological responses observed in PNE research. Rather than view such individual variances as 'noise', we should seek to understand the nature of those filters. Increased understanding of them should allow researchers to move beyond a notion that the P part of PNE simply represents 'some sort of stress' and towards a more sophisticated model, linking the cognitive mechanisms that process the information available to the brain with endocrine, immune and psychophysiological phenomena (Ursin, 1998).

In order to tap such appraisals of stress, researchers have developed scales that allow individuals to indicate how they feel about recent experiences, rather than simply indicate the *number* of life events they have experienced (see Figure 1.5).

Alternatively, the *emotional* consequences of stressful events (the outcome of cognitive appraisal processes) may be assessed using measures of mood states, such as the profile of mood states (POMS; McNair et al., 1971) and positive affect–negative affect schedule (PANAS; Watson et al., 1988). Positive and negative affect are considered further in Chapter 3.

Measures have also been developed to tap individual differences in people's *responses* to stressful experiences. For example, the concept of **hardiness** was introduced to describe individuals who experience many stressful events without ill effects. Kobasa (1979) suggests that 'hardy' individuals have a greater sense of control over what occurs in their lives, feel committed to the various areas of their lives

Rank	Life event	Mean value
1	Death of spouse	100
2	Divorce	73
3	Marital separation	65
4	Jail term	63
5	Death of close family member	63
6	Personal injury or illness	53
7	Marriage	50
8	Fired at work	47
9	Marital reconciliation	45
10	Retirement	45
11	Change in health of family member	44
12	Pregnancy	40
13	Sex difficulties	39
14	Gain of new family member	39
15	Business readjustment	39
16	Change in financial state	38
17	Death of close friend	37
18	Change to different line of work	36
19	Change in number of arguments with spouse	35
20	Mortgage over $10,000	31
21	Foreclosure of mortgage or loan	30
22	Change in responsibilities at work	29
23	Son or daughter leaving home	29
24	Trouble with in-laws	29
25	Outstanding personal achievement	28
26	Wife begin or stop work	26
27	Begin or end school	26
28	Change in living conditions	25
29	Revision of personal habits	24
30	Trouble with boss	23
31	Change in work hours or conditions	20
32	Change in residence	20
33	Change in schools	20
34	Change in recreation	19
35	Change in church activities	19
36	Change in social activities	18
37	Mortgage or loan less than $10,000	17
38	Change in sleeping habits	16
39	Change in number of family get-togethers	15
40	Change in eating habits	15
41	Vacation	13
42	Christmas	12
43	Minor violations of the law	11

FIGURE 1.4 Social readjustment rating scale

Source: Holmes and Rahe (1967)

Items and Instructions for Perceived Stress Scale

The questions in this scale ask you about your feelings and thoughts during the last month. In each case, you will be asked to indicate *how often* you felt or thought a certain way. Although some of the questions are similar, there are differences between them and you should treat each one as a separate question. The best approach is to answer each question fairly quickly. That is, don't try to count up the number of times you felt a particular way, but rather indicate the alternative that seems like a reasonable estimate.

For each question choose from the following alternatives:

    0. never
    1. almost never
    2. sometimes
    3. fairly often
    4. very often

1. In the last month, how often have you been upset because of something that happened unexpectedly?
2. In the last month, how often have you felt that you were unable to control the important things in your life?
3. In the last month, how often have you felt nervous and 'stressed'?
4. [a] In the last month, how often have you dealt successfully with irritating life hassles?
5. [a] In the last month, how often have you felt that you were effectively coping with important changes that were occurring in your life?
6. [a] In the last month, how often have you felt confident about your ability to handle your personal problems?
7. [a] In the last month, how often have you felt that things were going your way?
8. In the last month, how often have you found that you could not cope with all the things that you had to do?
9. [a] In the last month, how often have you been able to control irritations in your life?
10. [a] In the last month, how often have you felt that you were on top of things?
11. In the last month, how often have you been angered because of things that happened that were outside of your control?
12. In the last month, how often have you found yourself thinking about things that you have to accomplish?
13. [a] In the last month, how often have you been able to control the way you spend your time?
14. In the last month, how often have you felt that difficulties were piling up so high that you could not overcome them?

---

[a] Scored in the reverse direction.

FIGURE 1.5   Perceived stress scale

Source: Cohen, Kamarck and Mermelstein (1983)

and view change as a challenge, rather than a threat. Other personality constructs corresponding to a sense of control have also been demonstrated to have important implications for health. These will be discussed further in Chapter 2.

In order to develop a sophisticated model of cognitive mechanisms treating the information available to the brain, it is also necessary to distinguish between related psychological constructs, since research has identified a wide range of psychological variables relevant to health. For example, 'appraisals', 'attributions' and 'illness representations' all involve cognitive processing and may explain why individuals can react in different ways to the same situation. These terms derive from different literatures, however.

The term 'appraisal' is most closely associated with emotion theory and is used to refer to the cognitive evaluation of ongoing stressful events (Cohen & Lazarus, 1979; Lazarus & Folkman, 1984), while the term 'attribution' derives from research focusing on individual differences in the ways people explain the causes of past events (Abramson, Seligman & Teasdale, 1978) and formulate outcome expectancies in relation to future events (Abramson, Metalsky & Alloy, 1989).

'Illness representations' is also used to refer to the process of cognitive evaluation (including causal explanations and outcome expectancies), but specifically in relation to illness (Leventhal, Meyer & Nerenz, 1980).

All of these concepts have been linked to coping and health outcomes. The distinctions between them and their contribution to our current understanding of relationships between psychological processes and physical health is discussed further in Chapters 2 and 3.

1.2.4 PSYCHOBIOLOGICAL INTERACTIONS

As we demonstrate throughout this book, psychological and biological processes are closely interrelated and these interrelationships have important implications for a wide range of health outcomes. Research evidence indicates that the way we feel influences the way we think about ourselves and the world around us. These thoughts and feelings can then influence what goes on inside our bodies and these physiological alterations, in turn, influence health – although the impact on health is, to some extent, dependent on individuals' abilities to maintain stability by adjusting their behaviour or cognition (see Figure 1.6).

Figure 1.6 provides an overview of some interrelationships between psychological and biological processes and their implications for health. The box to the right of the diagram lists a range of alternative terms or concepts that may be substituted for each of the elements in the model on the left. This list is not exhaustive, but serves to illustrate overlaps between a number of theories and concepts in health psychology. The arrows are bidirectional, since research indicates not only that psychological processes have implications for health but also that changes in health have implications for psychological processes and that psychological and biological processes may interact in determining the implications for health (this is explained further in the following chapters).

Although these processes are illustrated at the level of the individual, it is important to note that the entire system should be seen to operate within a social environment, in which the social and interpersonal contexts may shape biological and psychological

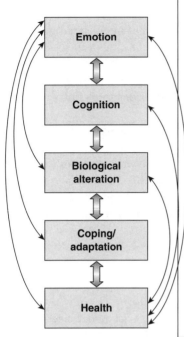

May be substituted for:

- a range of emotions – stress has been the most widely studied in this context, although there is a growing emphasis on positive, emotions and depression and anxiety may function as causes *and* consequences of physical illness

- appraisals, illness representations, beliefs, expectations, attributions

- alterations in neurochemistry, neurophysiology, all major physiological regulatory systems

- coping can refer to strategies selected and the expected results of these strategies (strategies include a range of behavioural/cognitive efforts to regain stability, which may involve engaging in health-damaging behaviours such as smoking, drugs, alcohol)

- multitude of health outcomes, such as anxiety disorders, depression, infectious illness, inflammatory/autoimmune conditions, cancer …

FIGURE 1.6   Psychobiological interactions and their implications for health

processes. As Engel (1980) highlights, the individual or person is best considered as a system, influenced by its (social) environment in much the same way that biological systems (such as organs and cells) are influenced by the environment in which they operate. Experience and behaviour at the person level provide the means by which social-level processes influence lower-level systems (see Figure 1.1).

SUMMARY

1.3

Changing conceptualisations of health and illness have important implications for the development of effective approaches to the treatment and prevention of illness, as well as the long-term management of chronic conditions.

It is now recognised that psychological processes play an important role in health, interacting with biological and social processes to influence a range of health outcomes. Further, it is evident that the psychological consequences of illness are not addressed by the traditional biomedical model of health. Research focusing on psy-chobiological processes will help to develop more effective patient interventions as they will address psychological as well as medical needs.

The biopsychosocial model can be considered as a model of interrelated processes influencing health and as a model of interrelated systems. At a theoretical level, we can postulate associations between biological, psychological and social systems, but, to study these interrelationships, we must develop valid, reliable methods of measur-ing psychological constructs and apply these methods in order to examine specific psychosocial and psychobiological processes.

Research demonstrating biological pathways underlying associations between cognitive and emotional processes and physiological functioning also provides an important contribution, indicating not only *if* psychological processes can influence physiological functioning but also *how* this can happen. These biological pathways are explored further in the following chapters, together with the implications of psy-chobiological processes for our understanding of susceptibility to chronic and acute illness, symptom severity and disease progression.

KEY TERMS

appraisal, behavioural medicine, biomedical model, biopsychosocial model, classical conditioning, conditioned immunomodulation, coping, disease, hardiness, health, health psychology, health psychology interventions, illness, normal distribution, obesity epidemic, patient-centred care, psychophysiology (PP), psychoneuro-endocrinology (PNE), psycho-neuroimmunology (PNI), psychosomatic medicine, relationship-centred care, statistical normality, stressful life events, type A personality

■Discussion questions

1 Which of the following factors do you think could influence your health and why?

• Your age
• Your gender
• Your level of income
• Your relationship with your spouse or partner
• Your relationship with friends and family
• Your personality.

2 How might the following behaviours *impact* person-, two-person, family- and community-level systems? How might these behaviours influence lower-level systems?

• Smoking cigarettes
• Drinking alcohol
• Taking prescribed medications
• Exercising.

3 Consider the opposite relationship. How might the behaviours *above* be *influenced by* person-, two-person, family- and community-level systems? How might these behaviours be influenced by lower-level systems?

4 Do you agree with the order of magnitude of the events listed in the social readjustment rating scale? Are all of the items relevant to you?

FURTHER READING

Baum, A. & Posluszny, M.D. (1999). Health psychology: mapping biobehavioral contributions to health and illness. *Annual Review of Psychology*, 50, 137–163.

Kiecolt-Glaser, J.K., McGuire, L., Robles, T. & Glaser, R. (2002). Psychoneuroimmunology: psychological influences on immune function and health. *Journal of Consulting and Clinical Psychology*, 70, 537–547.

Lutgendorf, S.K. & Costanzo, E. (2003). Psychoneuro-immunology and health psychology: an integrative model. *Brain, Behavior, and Immunity*, 17, 225–315.

Michie, S., Miles, J. & Weinman, J. (2003). Patient-centredness in chronic illness: what is it and does it matter? *Patient Education and Counselling*, 51, 197–206.

THE LINK BETWEEN STRESS AND ILLNESS

2

OVERVIEW

In Chapter 1 we considered theoretical associations between psychological variables (thoughts, feeling and behaviours) and biological variables. It is easy to see how behaviours such as drinking or smoking might influence biological processes, but how does something as (seemingly) innocuous as a thought or feeling influence what happens inside our bodies?

To begin to answer this question, it is useful to examine research focusing on stress. Stress is one of the most widely studied psychological predictors of physical health, and research has indicated that it is associated with a range of cognitive, emotional and physiological alterations.

Since the emergence of psychoneuroimmunology (PNI), the search for biological mediators of the stress–disease link has developed rapidly. In the interests of providing an accessible and coherent narrative, it is necessary to restrict the current discussion to a limited number of mediating mechanisms. A list of further reading is provided at the end of the chapter if you would like to delve further into this fascinating literature.

LEARNING OUTCOMES

By the end of this chapter you should be able to:

- explain how stress research has contributed to our understanding of psycho-biological processes in health and illness

- describe and contrast the transactional model of coping and cognitive activation theory
- explain the influence of perceived control on physiological and behavioural responses to stress
- describe the role of individual differences in interpreting and responding to stress
- describe the basic structure of the nervous, immune and endocrine systems
- explain how cells within these systems communicate
- describe the role of the SAM and HPA axes in responding to stress
- explain what is meant by 'classical conditioning' and 'conditioned immunomodulation'
- explain what is meant by the terms 'allostasis' and 'allostatic load' and differentiate between 'allostasis' and 'homeostasis'
- describe the 'sixth sense' concept and 'immune surveillance' hypothesis
- explain how stress might influence health outcomes, including susceptibility to the common cold, cardiovascular disease, type 2 diabetes and cancer.

2.1 THE HISTORY OF THE STRESS CONCEPT

In its medical sense, stress is essentially the rate of wear and tear in the body. Anyone who feels that whatever he is doing – or whatever is being done to him – is strenuous and wearing, knows vaguely what we mean by stress.

Selye, 1956: 3

Although we may know vaguely what we mean by 'stress', the precise definition of this construct has been widely debated. McEwen (2000) writes that the widespread use of this word in popular culture has made stress a very ambiguous word to describe in terms of the ways in which the body copes with psychosocial, environmental and physical challenges. It is also evident that the same term has been used in the research literature to refer to at least four distinct constructs:

- a stimulus ('stressor')
- subjective reports of an experience (in humans only)
- a general non-specific increase in arousal
- feedback to the brain from this response (Levine & Ursin, 1991; Ursin & Ericksen, 2004).

This ambiguity is perhaps not surprising when we consider the history of 'stress research'. Early discoveries that have shaped our current understanding of psychobiological responses to stress emerged not from deliberate manipulation or measurement of psychological variables but observations of the influence of environmental conditions on physiological processes in laboratory animals. Independently developed lines of enquiry in neuroscience and immunology have also contributed to our understanding of links between the brain and immune system, explaining how mental processes such as stress could influence health outcomes ranging from susceptibility to the common cold, to cardiovascular disease, type 2 diabetes and even some types of cancer. In this chapter, then, we will chart some of the key discoveries relevant to an understanding of links between stress and illness.

2.1.1 THE FIGHT OR FLIGHT RESPONSE

The study of psychobiological responses to stress can be traced back to the work of physiologist Walter Cannon (1871–1945). In *Bodily Changes in Pain, Hunger, Fear and Rage*, Cannon (1925) documented the findings of a number of laboratory studies examining the effects of strong emotional states in animals on digestion, nervous system activation, adrenal secretion and blood sugar and compared these responses to human case studies.

This work represented a significant advance in the understanding of physiological responses to negative emotions. In particular, Cannon highlighted the role of the **autonomic nervous system (ANS)** (see Box 2.1) in the expression of both fear and rage. Cannon (1925: 275) proposed that, although fear provokes an urge to run away and rage an urge to attack, both result from the same underlying impulse, with circumstances determining the dominant response, such that 'the cornering of an animal when in the headlong flight of fear may suddenly turn the fear to fury and the flight to a fighting in which all the strength of desperation is displayed.'

BOX 2.1

The autonomic nervous system

The nervous system is divided into the **central nervous system** (**CNS**, brain and spinal cord) and the **peripheral nervous system** (nerves that carry information to and from the central nervous system). Nerve cells (also called neurons, neurones) communicate using chemicals such as **neuropeptides** and **neurotransmitters**.

The **autonomic nervous system (ANS)** is the division of the peripheral nervous system responsible for controlling the functioning of a range of organs and glands. The autonomic nervous system has three divisions: the **enteric nervous system** (responsible for controlling intestinal functions), **parasympathetic nervous system** (also called the cranio-sacral division, responsible for rest and energy storage) and **sympathetic nervous system** (also called the thoracico-lumbar system, responsible for arousal and energy release).

The sympathetic and parasympathetic systems have contrasting actions on organs of the body. For example, the parasympathetic nervous system promotes digestion (such as stimulating salivary glands and dilating blood vessels supplying the gastrointestinal tract) and sexual function (by stimulating penile erection, for example), while the sympathetic nervous system directs blood flow away from the gastrointestinal tract and increases heart rate, enhancing blood supply to the lungs and skeletal muscles.

Source: Colman (2006)

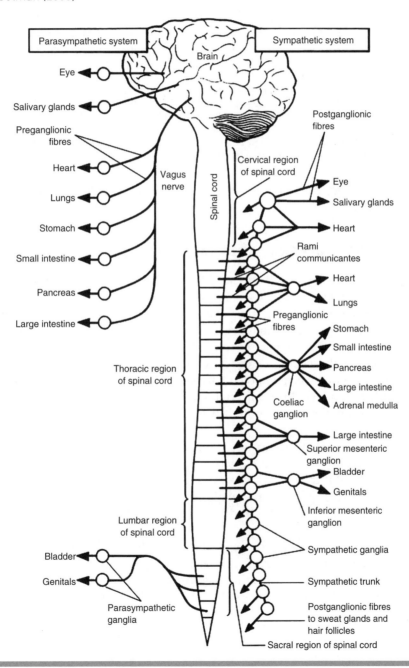

Cannon went on to conduct a number of studies investigating the role of the autonomic nervous system in maintaining stability, or **homeostasis**, in response to changes in the environment (examples of homeostasis include regulation of body temperature and blood sugar). These are summarised in another key publication – *The Wisdom of the Body* (Cannon, 1939). Here, Cannon (1939: 227) writes that the bodily changes associated with fear and rage (the **fight or flight response**) illustrate a natural defence of the body, since activation of the sympathetic nervous system associated with this response promotes a number of changes that prepare the organism to either escape or attack:

> respiration deepens, the heart beats more rapidly, the arterial pressure rises, the blood is shifted away from the stomach and intestines to the heart and central nervous system and the muscles, the processes in the alimentary canal cease, sugar is freed from the reserves in the liver, the spleen contracts and discharges its content of concentrated corpuscles, and adrenin is secreted from the adrenal medulla.

So, although stress may be perceived as aversive, according to Cannon, it should be considered adaptive and crucial for survival of the species.

2.1.2 THE GENERAL ADAPTATION SYNDROME

Hans Selye (1907–1982) extended Cannon's work by considering what happens if the fight or flight response to stress is prolonged.

Selye, an endocrinologist, conducted a series of experiments in which he injected rats with extracts of various organs in an attempt to uncover changes that could be attributed to an as yet undiscovered sex hormone.

Surprisingly, whatever extract he injected into the rats, the symptoms were the same – peptic ulcers, enlarged adrenal glands and atrophy of the thymus, spleen and lymph nodes. Even injecting the rats with formalin solution (a highly toxic fluid used in the preparation of tissues for microscopic study) produced the same effects.

This meant that the changes Selye observed could not result from the action of a sex hormone. To make matters even more complicated, the same effects could be observed if the rats were exposed to cold, heat, pain, forced exercise or other aversive experimental manipulations. To make sense of these rather baffling findings, Selye proposed that these rats were displaying a non-specific reaction to stress.

There was a major problem with Selye's theory, though, in that the world of medicine did not explain physiological changes in 'non-specific' terms. According to accepted wisdom, specific diagnoses must be made on the basis of specific physiological alterations. Selye, however, recalled that, as a young medical student, he had seen many patients for whom the characteristic signs of a specific disease were absent, although the patient was evidently 'ill'. These patients complained of feeling unwell and presented with aches and pains, intestinal disturbances with loss of appetite, fever, rash and other problems to which the physician attached very little significance. Selye proposed that these patients were displaying a 'syndrome of being sick' and suggested that this syndrome was every bit as important a topic of study as individual diseases.

Linking the failed animal experiments with his earlier observations of non-specifically sick patients, Selye proposed that the body responds in the same way to a broad range of stressors and that this **general adaptation syndrome (GAS)** comprises three stages:

- an alarm reaction on recognition of a stressor
- effort to resist, cope with or adapt to the stressor
- depletion of resources (resulting in exhaustion) if the stressor cannot be overcome.

Selye (1956: vii) suggested that it is through this general adaptation syndrome 'that our various internal organs – especially the endocrine glands and the nervous system – help to adjust us to the constant changes which occur in and around us.' Therefore, Selye argued that, although physiological responses to stress may be adaptive in the short term, prolonged activation of the body's stress response systems may be damaging to the organism, resulting in depletion of resources and ill health. Further, while Cannon's work highlighted the role of nervous system responses to stress, Selye's research also highlighted the role of the **endocrine system** (see Box 2.2).

BOX 2.2

The endocrine system

While the nervous system communicates via electrical and chemical messages, the endocrine system communicates via the release of molecules known as hormones. Hormones are carried via the bloodstream to distant organs to regulate organ functioning. The nervous and endocrine systems are linked via the **hypothalamic-pituitary-adrenal (HPA) axis**, comprising interactions between the hypothalamus (responsible for a range of functions, such as coordinating sleep–wake cycles, releasing hormones and the homeostatic regulation of temperature, hunger and thirst), the pituitary gland (responsible for controlling a range of bodily functions, such as growth and

(Cont'd)

sex organ function) and adrenal glands (responsible for regulating the stress response via the release of steroid hormones).

Source: Blakemore and Jennett (2001)

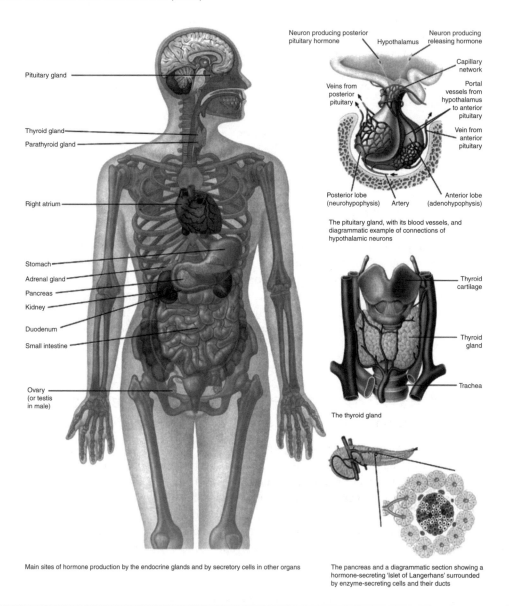

Neuron producing posterior pituitary hormone

Hypothalamus

Neuron producing releasing hormone

Capillary network

Veins from posterior pituitary

Portal vessels from hypothalamus to anterior pituitary

Vein from anterior pituitary

Posterior lobe (neurohypophysis)   Artery   Anterior lobe (adenohypophysis)

The pituitary gland, with its blood vessels, and diagrammatic example of connections of hypothalamic neurons

Pituitary gland

Thyroid gland
Parathyroid gland

Right atrium

Stomach
Adrenal gland
Pancreas
Kidney

Duodenum
Small intestine

Ovary
(or testis
in male)

Thyroid cartilage

Thyroid gland

Trachea

The thyroid gland

Main sites of hormone production by the endocrine glands and by secretory cells in other organs

The pancreas and a diagrammatic section showing a hormone-secreting 'Islet of Langerhans' surrounded by enzyme-secreting cells and their ducts

2.1.3 SUBSEQUENT RESEARCH

Research conducted in the decades following Cannon and Selye's discoveries has supported the role of both the nervous and endocrine systems in responding to stress. Links between the sympathetic nervous system and the adrenal medulla, highlighted by Cannon, are now referred to as the **sympathetic-adrenal-medullary (SAM) axis** (also called the sympathoadrenal medullary or sympatho-adrenal-medullary axis). The mechanism linking the nervous and endocrine systems in coordinating the physiological changes Selye described later became known as the **hypothalamic-pituitary-adrenal (HPA) axis.**

Although the SAM and HPA axes are often treated as separate systems, Evans and colleagues (2000: 40) suggest that they should be viewed as 'peripheral limbs of a single central "stress response system"'. This system is illustrated in Box 2.3.

BOX 2.3

The role of the HPA and SAM axes in responding to stress

The physiological alterations associated with the fight or flight response are triggered by the release of the neurotransmitter noradrenaline (NA) (also called norepinephrine (NE) from the locus coeruleus (LC) – also known as the locus caeruleus, locus ceruleus). When a potential threat is perceived, the LC releases NA into the hippocampus, cerebral cortex and hypothalamus. The hypothalamus sends nerve signals via the spinal cord to the adrenal medulla (the inner region of the adrenal gland, located on the kidneys), which releases neurotransmitters (such as adrenaline, also called epinephrine) into the bloodstream. Activation of the hypothalamus under stress triggers a chain of hormonal changes, starting with the release of a hormone called corticotropin-releasing hormone (CRH, also called corticotropin-releasing factor, or CRF). CRH stimulates the pituitary gland, which releases adrenocorticotropin hormone (ACTH, also called corticotrophin), which, in turn, stimulates the adrenal cortex (the outer region of the adrenal gland) to release steroid hormones called **corticosteroids** into the bloodstream (cortisol in humans, corticosterone in rats). Cortisol allows the organism to sustain resistance to the stressor, such as down-regulating certain inflammatory reactions and maintaining constant levels of blood sugar and blood pressure (see Evans, Hucklebridge & Clow, 2000; Maier & Watkins, 1998). A simplified diagram illustrating the role of the HPA and SAM axes in responding to stress is provided below.

(Cont'd)

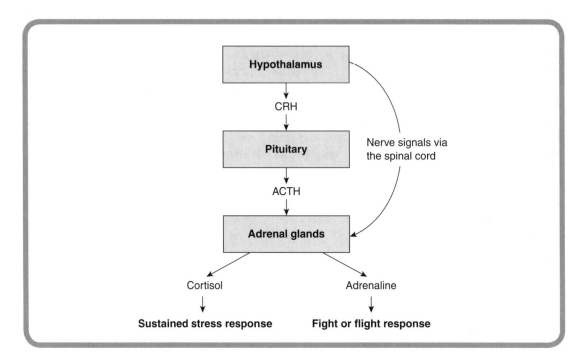

The link between stress and illness has also been supported by findings that the **immune system** – the body's defence against infectious illness – can be influenced by mental processes.

Until the 1970s, it was widely believed that the immune system operates autonomously, without direction from the brain, so mental processes could not influence susceptibility to infectious illness (Ader, 2003). A study by Ader and Cohen (1975), however, challenged this view, demonstrating that immune system functioning could be altered via classical conditioning (see Research in focus box 2.1). Although these findings were highly controversial, **conditioned immunomodulation** has now been demonstrated in a number of studies (see Ader (2003) for a review of this literature). The organs and cells that make up the immune system are illustrated in Box 2.4.

BOX 2.4

The immune system

The immune system defends the organism against attack by foreign invaders such as bacteria, fungi, parasites and viruses. This system has two main divisions: **innate** (natural) and **adaptive** (acquired/specific) immunity (illustrated below). Molecules or cells capable of generating an immune response are called antigen (from 'antibody generators'). The organs of the immune system (bone marrow, thymus, spleen and lymph nodes) are called **lymphoid organs**. Cells of the immune system (**leukocytes**) include granulocytes (neutrophils, eosinophils and basophils),

Among the most dangerous enemies we humans face are our own distant relatives, the microbes. No human being can long withstand their onslaught unprotected. We survive because the human body has a variety of effective defences against this constant attack.

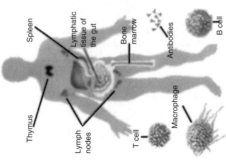

The mammalian immune system has two overarching divisions. The innate part [*left side*] acts near entry points into the body and is always at the ready. If it fails to contain a pathogen, the adaptive division [*right side*] kicks in, mounting a later but highly targeted attack against the specific invader.

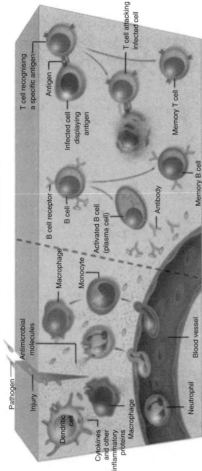

INNATE IMMUNE SYSTEM

This system includes, among other components, antimicrobial molecules and various phagocytes [cells that ingest and destroy pathogens]. These cells, such as dendritic cells and macrophages, also activate an inflammatory response, secreting proteins called cytokines that trigger an influx of defensive cells from the blood. Among the recruits are more phagocytes — notably monocytes [which can mature into macrophages] and neutrophils.

ADAPTIVE IMMUNE SYSTEM

This system 'stars' B cells and T cells. Activated B cells secrete antibody molecules that bind to antigens — specific components unique to a given invader — and destroy the invader directly or mark it for attack by others. T cells recognise antigens displayed on cells. Some T cells help to activate B cells and other T cells [*not shown*], other T cells directly attack infected cells. T and B cells spawn 'memory' cells that promptly eliminate invaders encountered before.

[*Cont'd*]

monocytes, which transform into macrophages, dendritic cells, natural killer (NK) cells and **lymphocytes** (B cells and T cells). T cells can be divided into two distinct subsets – killer T cells (which kill infected or cancerous cells) and helper T cells (which signal other cells using chemical messengers called **cytokines**). Cytokines secreted by lymphocytes and macrophages include lymphokines, interleukins (ILs), interferon (INF), tumour necrosis factor (TNF) and monokines (for a more detailed overview see Evans, Hucklebridge and Clow, 2000; Linnemeyer, 2008; see also Box 2.1).

Source: Kochar (2006)

RESEARCH IN FOCUS BOX 2.1

Ader and Cohen (1975) evaluated the impact of classical conditioning on immune processes in laboratory rats.

Methodology

Rats received repeated pairings of saccharine with an immunosuppressive agent. Three days after conditioning, the animals received the saccharine solution, immunosuppressive agent or neither.

Results

Ader and Cohen (1975) found that the rats presented with either the immunosuppressive agent or the saccharine three days after conditioning were significantly immunosuppressed. Evidence of immunosuppression was not present in non-conditioned animals nor in conditioned animals not exposed to saccharine after conditioning.

Conclusions and implications

Since conditioning is a mental process, Ader and Cohen's findings indicated that the immune system could be influenced by the brain. In response to these findings, the authors suggested that 'there may be an intimate and virtually unexplored relationship between the CNS and immunologic processes' (Ader & Cohen, 1975: 338).

Ader and Cohen (1982) later demonstrated that this conditioning paradigm could be used to induce immunosuppression in a strain of mice with overactive immune systems, resulting in significant reductions in rates of mortality in these mice. Conditioned immunomodulation may also have clinical implications for patients with autoimmune conditions. For example, Ader (2001) has reported a human case study in which a child with lupus was treated using conditioning to reduce the total amount of immunosuppressive drug prescribed. Conditioning has also been demonstrated to result in improved pulmonary function in asthmatic children (Castes, Palenque, Canelones, Hagel & Lynch, 1998) and decreased allergic symptoms in patients with a dust mite allergy (Goebel, Meykadeh, Kou, Schedlowski & Hengge, 2008).

The immune system is now recognised as being the third system in the psycho-neuroimmunology 'triangle' (Brambilla, 2000). Since these three systems – CNS, neuroendocrine and immune – each regulate the functioning of the others, the impact of stress on disease processes can only be understood by studying the complex interrelations between these systems.

2.1.4 LIMITATIONS OF THE GAS AND THE NEED FOR MORE COMPLEX MODELS

Not *all* of Selye's claims have been supported, however.

Although Selye proposed that individuals respond in the same way to a broad range of stressors, subsequent research has indicated that the stress response is not as 'general' as Selye suggested. Indeed, individual responses to stress appear to be influenced by a wide range of factors. For example, McDougall et al. (2005) reviewed a number of studies evaluating the physiological effects of stress in animals. These studies reveal variations in autonomic output dependent on the species or strain of animal exposed, previous experience and the stressor paradigm used. In humans, responses to stress are even more complex since SNS/HPA activation is less likely to be triggered by an objectively existing physical threat (such as an encounter with a dangerous predator) and more often triggered by a **psychosocial threat** involving 'the subjective perception and interpretation of often rather subtle and ambiguous changes of the outer world' (Huether, 1996: 298).

The GAS has therefore been replaced by more complex models describing the cognitive, behavioural and physiological processes via which psychosocial threat results in changes in physical functioning. These explanatory models are considered in the following sections.

COGNITIVE MODELS

2.2

Early research (discussed above) provided evidence that adverse environmental conditions could influence physiological processes. These models tell us little about the ways in which organisms determine that environmental conditions have potentially important implications for survival, however. For example, the ANS may be activated in response to a dangerous predator, but this system cannot by itself determine that a predator is present or that this predator poses a threat.

With modern stressors the situation is even more complex – how does one judge the level of threat posed by a stranger behaving erratically on a train or rumours of redundancies at work? How do we explain individual differences in response to these scenarios – why one individual may worry excessively while another is relatively complacent, for example?

The models discussed below offer useful conceptual frameworks for considering the cognitive processes involved in initiating, maintaining and terminating responses to threat, and help explain why individuals may differ in their responses to similar environmental conditions.

2.2.1 THE TRANSACTIONAL MODEL

According to the **transactional model (TM)** of coping (Cohen & Lazarus, 1979; Lazarus & Folkman, 1984, for example), individual responses to stress are shaped by two key processes – appraisal and coping.

The TM posits that stress is not simply an automatic response to an environmental threat, but results from a *transaction* between the environment and the individual that is 'appraised by the person as taxing or exceeding his or her resources and endangering his or her well-being' (Lazarus & Folkman, 1984: 19).

Appraisals involve both an evaluation of the situation in terms of its likely consequences (primary appraisal) and of the resources available to cope with the situation (secondary appraisal). Appraisals determine the methods an individual uses to cope, coping then determines the outcome of the encounter (favourable resolution, unfavourable resolution, no resolution), and emotion (both positive and negative) is generated in the process of appraisal, coping and outcome.

Three kinds of primary appraisal can be distinguished:

- irrelevant – no implications for the person's well-being
- benign–positive – the outcome is construed as positive
- stressful – the situation is associated with harm/loss, threat or challenge.

Methods of coping may involve efforts to manage or alter the problem causing the distress (problem-focused coping) and/or efforts to manage the emotional responses to the problem (emotion-focused coping). The relationship between appraisal and coping is not unidirectional. As Lazarus (1993: 16) has suggested, coping itself alters 'the person–environment relationship and how it is appraised'. The relationships between these variables can be seen in Figure 2.1.

Lazarus (1999: 75) explains that 'the premise of appraisal theory is that people (and non-human animals too) are constantly evaluating their relationships with the environment with respect to their implications for well-being.' By placing the individual in a dynamic interaction with an ever-changing environment, the TM provides a more complex account of cognitive and behavioural responses to stress than earlier models, acknowledging considerable potential variability between individuals and situations.

Although the TM has undoubtedly changed the way we conceptualise individual responses to stress, limitations have also been highlighted. For example, Bartlett (1998) points out that the model is more highly elaborated across the cognitive and behavioural domains than across the physiological domain, and that the physiological mechanisms linking stress and illness are not specified. The measurement of specific coping strategies associated with particular situational appraisals has also proved problematic, since the potential range of responses is vast and individual strategies may serve a number of functions (Bijttebier, Vertommen & Vander-Steene, 2001).

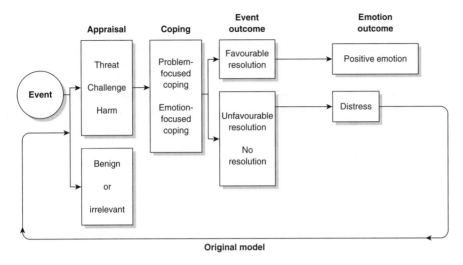

FIGURE 2.1 Theoretical model of the coping process

Source: Folkman (1997)

Despite these problems, the TM has helped to indicate how interventions may be targeted to reduce stress and improve health outcomes – by altering situational appraisals or by enhancing coping resources, for instance. Coping-based interventions are discussed further in Chapter 7.

2.2.2 COGNITIVE ACTIVATION THEORY

Individual variability in response to stress can also be explained within the framework of the **cognitive activation theory (CAT)** of stress (Ursin & Eriksen, 2004).

According to this theory, an alarm occurs when there is a discrepancy between what should be and what is – between the value a variable should have and the real value. The level of alarm is determined by the expectation of the outcome of the situation, together with specific responses available for coping. Response outcome expectancies are defined as positive, negative or none. Positive outcome expectancies are associated with coping, negative outcome expectancies are associated with hopelessness, and lack of expectancy outcome is associated with helplessness. The stress response can lead to both positive outcomes (training) and negative outcomes (straining), dependent on the type of activation, so phasic arousal is seen in individuals with positive expectancy, while sustained arousal may lead to pathology (see Figure 2.2).

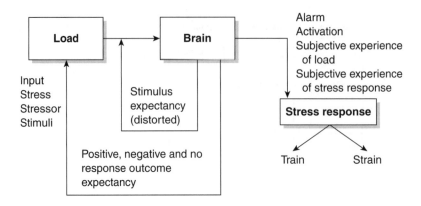

FIGURE 2.2   The cognitive activation theory of stress
Source: Ursin and Eriksen (2004)

Ursin and Ericksen (2004) write that the CAT offers formal definitions of coping, hopelessness and helplessness that are easy to operationalise in both humans and animals. So, for example, expectancy can be manipulated in animal studies by pairing a response (such as pressing a bar) with a negative (such as an electric shock) or positive outcome (food, for example) or exposing animals to non-escape situations (no relationship between response and reinforcement). Ursin and Ericksen (2004) point out that non-escape situations in animals result in a sense of helplessness that can become a generalised response expectancy, in much the same way that there is a general sense of helplessness when humans are exposed to repeated uncontrollable stressors (see Box 2.5). Previous experience of stress can therefore distort expectancies of future stressors.

Unlike the TM, the CAT does not attempt to describe the 'myriad coping thoughts and acts used for real-life harms, threats and challenges and the relational meanings on which they are based' (Lazarus, 1999: 110). Ursin (1998: 557), however, suggests that, since physiological changes associated with the states of helplessness and hopelessness have been studied extensively in humans and animals, the CAT conceptualisation of coping has 'predictive power for PNE, PNI, and PP, and, therefore, for health issues.' These physiological effects of prolonged, uncontrollable stress (in animal studies) include gastric ulcers, hypertension, cardiac failure, immune changes and changes in brain biochemistry similar to those occurring in depression and psychoses (Ericksen, Murison, Pensgaard & Ursin, 2005). Ericksen et al. (2005) write that these effects appear equivalent to the 'failed shutdown' in the allostatic load model (discussed in Section 2.3), although cognitive aspects are not included in the allostatic load model, as they are in CATS. For CATS, the important cognitive variable sustaining activation is the presence of persistent negative thoughts and expectancies.

Although the CAT is not as highly elaborated across the cognitive and behavioural domains as the TM, its concepts are easier to operationalise and the model does attempt (via the concept of 'straining') to explain the effects of stress on physiological functioning.

BOX 2.5

Helplessness, hopelessness and health

In the 1970s, Martin Seligman (1975) conducted a series of experiments with dogs in which the animals were exposed to a stressor (such as an electric shock) from which they could not escape. After repeated exposure to this situation, the dogs simply ceased trying to escape. Seligman referred to this state of passive acceptance of, and lack of attempt to escape from, stressors as 'learned helplessness' (Maier & Seligman, 1976, for example).

Although exposure to uncontrollable stressors can also produce learned helplessness in humans, Abramson and colleagues (1978) point out that humans differ from non-human animals in that mere exposure to uncontrollable stressors is not sufficient to produce helplessness – the individual must come to *expect* that outcomes will be uncontrollable.

Abramson et al. (1978) therefore proposed a cognitive reformulation of learned helplessness theory in which some individuals are more vulnerable to learned helplessness than others, and this vulnerability is related to the ways in which individuals explain the causes of events. According to this reformulation, people have characteristic 'explanatory styles' that vary along three main dimensions:

- *internality* – the extent to which the event is caused by the individual
- *globality* – the extent to which the cause may result in negative consequences in other areas of life
- *stability* – the extent to which the cause will be long-lasting.

These styles determine the extent to which expectations of future helplessness will be broad or narrow, short or long-lasting, and whether or not learned helplessness will lower self-esteem.

Abramson, Metalsky and Alloy (1989) later developed this model to explain a subset of depression referred to as 'hopelessness depression'. This model suggests that there are three vulnerability factors for the development of hopelessness:

- attributing negative events to stable and global causes – internality is de-emphasised in the hopelessness model
- a tendency to make negative inferences about the self as a result of the negative event – 'I am stupid', 'I am worthless' and so on
- a tendency to infer that negative events will result in dire consequences.

(Cont'd)

These factors not only increase vulnerability to depression but also physical health problems. For example, Peterson (1988) found that college students who believed that stable and global factors caused bad events experienced more days of illness in the following month and visited the doctor more frequently in the following year than students who explained bad events by reference to unstable and specific causes. Students who believed that stable and global factors caused bad events also reported more unhealthy habits, lower levels of success in changing those habits and more stressful occurrences than students who explained bad events as being due to unstable and specific causes.

2.2.3 PERCEIVED CONTROL

Inherent in both of the above models is the notion of **perceived control.**

In relation to the TM, a stressor is perceived to be controllable if the individual considers that his or her resources are sufficient to meet the perceived challenge or demand. In relation to the CAT, perceived control is associated with the expectation of a positive outcome.

A number of researchers have linked perceptions of control to physiological and behavioural responses in relation to threat. For example, Huether (1996) writes that the extent to which a stressor is perceived to be controllable determines not only the severity of the stress response but also the balance between the SAM and HPA response. If a stressor is perceived to be controllable, SAM activation will be channelled into specific activation of behavioural responses to the stressor, and the HPA-axis is not at all or only slightly activated. If the stressor is perceived to be uncontrollable, however, arousal will continue to rise, resulting in activation of the HPA axis. Holahan and Moos (1987) also consider that perceived control influences behavioural responses to threat, and propose that avoidance coping is a response to threatening situations when personal and contextual resources are scarce.

Perceived control may interact with other situational characteristics in determining cognitive, behavioural and physiological responses to threat. For example, activation of the endocrine system under threat is specifically associated with experiences of stressors that are perceived to be novel, unpredictable and uncontrollable, likely to result in negative consequences and have some element of ego-involvement (Mason, 1968). Frankenhaeuser (1982, 1986; Lundberg & Frankenhaeuser, 1980) proposes that cognitive behavioural processes in stressful situations have two components: effort and distress. Effort is a state of high personal control and active coping and is associated with adrenalin secretion. Distress is a state of low personal control with avoidant coping and is associated with cortisol excretion. Responses involving both effort and distress are associated with both cortisol *and* adrenalin secretion.

Although controllability can be considered a cognitive appraisal of a specific situation, the notion of perceived control is also relevant to research evaluating links between personality dispositions and responses to stress. Several personality constructs correspond to either belief in one's abilities to influence situational outcomes (such as 'self-efficacy' Bandura, 1977; 'locus of control', Rotter, 1966; 'hardiness', Kobasa, 1979) or generalised positive outcome expectancies ('dispositional optimism', Scheier & Carver, 1987).

Studies evaluating stress-related illness have suggested that these personality variables may either exert direct effects on health via health-related behaviours or act as buffers, reducing the impact of stress on health. This buffering effect may operate via behavioural or biological pathways. For example, optimists have been reported to demonstrate more adaptive coping with stress, more positive health habits and better immune function (Scheier & Carver, 1992; Segerstrom, Taylor, Kemeny & Fahey, 1998, for example).

Control expectancies also appear to be important for psychological health, since a lack of belief in one's abilities to influence situational outcomes and generalised expectations of negative outcomes are associated with a lack of motivation and depression, particularly in relation to events that are afforded a high degree of importance (Abramson, Metalsky & Alloy, 1989; Bandura, 1989, for example).

Control expectancies are also important determinants of health-related behaviours and are incorporated into most health behaviour models, such as the health belief model (HBM, Becker, 1974), theory of planned behaviour (TPB, Ajzen & Madden, 1986), trantheoretical model (TTM, Prochaska & DiClemente, 1983) and social cognitive theory (SCT, Bandura, 1986).

Social cognitive theory is the most relevant to a consideration of psychobiological processes in health and illness. This theory developed from social learning theory (Bandura, 1977), which states that expectations of personal efficacy determine whether or not coping is initiated, the degree of effort expended and how long coping is sustained in the face of obstacles and aversive experiences.

Expectations of personal efficacy are derived from four types of information:

- performance accomplishments – personal mastery experiences
- vicarious experience – observing others perform threatening activities without adverse consequences
- verbal persuasion – leading the individual to believe, through suggestion, that he or she can cope successfully
- physiological states – cognitive appraisal of emotional arousal in relation to feared stimuli/scenarios.

Dipositional optimism and self-efficacy are also linked to the concept of **self-regulation** – the process via which individuals maintain control over thoughts, feelings, cognitions and actions (Bandura, 1991; Carver & Scheier, 1981). This concept is discussed further in Chapter 7.

In general, then, perceived control (associated with SNS activation and adrenalin release in relation to threat) appears to be a prerequisite for behavioural responding. When the individual does not consider his or her resources sufficient to meet the perceived challenge or demand, or anticipates negative outcomes, avoidant coping is more likely to occur. For some individuals, negative outcome expectancies or low control beliefs may represent a relatively stable disposition and also generalise across situations, increasing the risk of both stress-related illness and depression in relation to life events.

BIOLOGICAL MODELS

2.3

The theories and constructs discussed above are useful for defining the psychological conditions associated with activation of the body's stress response systems – that is, the 'P' part of PNI. They do not explain, however, why activation of the SAM and HPA axes under stress may result in ill health. After all, both systems play an important role in mounting (and sustaining) an effective behavioural response to threat, and their roles can therefore be considered adaptive.

To explain why stress can result in ill health, it is also necessary to explain how adaptive physiological processes can result in damage. In this section, therefore, we will consider theoretical frameworks that help to explain the protective and damaging effects of stress. Biological explanations for individual differences in responses to stress are also considered.

2.3.1 ALLOSTATIC LOAD

The allostatic load model was introduced in order to explain why biological alterations that are designed to *protect* the organism can also be harmful.

The term **allostasis** was introduced to refer to systems that maintain stability during change (Sterling & Eyer, 1988), and **allostatic load** to refer to the biological 'cost' associated with these systems (McEwen & Stellar, 1993).

Allostasis is proposed to differ from homeostasis in that physiological parameters must be maintained outside the normal range in order to match chronic demands (either physical or psychological), essentially altering the normal homeostatic 'set point' for all physiological systems (Sterling & Eyer, 1988). While homeostatic alterations (such as an ANS response to acute threat) may be adaptive, maintaining an allostatic state in the long term results in physiological wear and tear, leading to pathology (see Table 2.1).

For example, Clow (2001) explains that, although the elevated heart rate and blood pressure associated with the fight or flight response are essential for ensuring sufficient oxygen and energy supply to the muscles and brain, repeated or prolonged episodes of elevated heart rate and blood pressure can result in damage to the heart

TABLE 2.1 From homeostasis to pathology

Homeostasis	Allostasis	Pathology
Normal set point	Changing set point	Breakdown
Physiological equilibrium	Compensated equilibrium	Outside equilibrium
No anticipation of demand	Anticipation of demand	No anticipation any more
No adjustment based on history	Adjustment based on history	No adjustment possible
Adjustment carries no price	Adjustment and accommodation carry a price	External interventions needed – treatments
No pathology	Leads to pathology	Disease

Source: LeMoal (2007)

and blood vessels. Similarly, although HPA activation under threat is important for maintaining resistance to the stressor, repeated or prolonged HPA activation can result in excess blood glucose and free fatty acids. Since the types of stressors humans typically encounter afford little opportunity for fighting or fleeing, this liberated energy is rarely utilised and, instead, clogs up the blood vessels, restricting blood flow and contributing to the risk of stroke and heart attack, as well as contributing to insulin resistance, abdominal obesity and development of type 2 diabetes (Clow, 2001; McEwen & Seeman, 1999). These effects are likely to be exacerbated by behavioural responses to stress. For example, overeating associated with chronic stress also contributes to development of abdominal obesity and reduced insulin sensitivity. Further, the combination of stress plus a high-fat diet results in greater abdominal fat storage than either stress or high-fat diet alone (Epel, 2009).

The impacts of stress mediators on immune function can also be both protective (allostatic) and damaging (allostatic load). McEwen and Seeman (1999) explain that adrenal steroids promote allostasis together with other catecholamines by promoting movement ('trafficking') of immune cells to organs and tissues where they are needed to fight infection or other challenge, but that chronic overactivity of these same mediators produces immunosuppressive effects.

Consistent with this model, experimental evidence has revealed that participants exposed to the common cold under controlled laboratory conditions were at a greater risk of disease if they had recently experienced episodes of chronic (but not acute) stress (Cohen et al., 1998). Other research has supported effects of stress on susceptibility to infectious illness (Cohen et al., 1998) and indicated that stress can influence immune response to vaccinations against flu, pneumonia or hepatitis B, or reactivate latent herpes viruses such as the Epstein-Barr virus (EBV) (Glaser, 2005). Increased susceptibility to infectious illness under conditions of chronic stress is likely to indicate a shift in the balance between 'cellular' and 'humoral' immunity (see Box 2.6).

BOX 2.6

The Th1/Th2 balance

Two subsets of helper T cell have been identified that differ in terms of their cytokine profile (Mosmann & Coffman, 1989). The function of cytokines secreted by these two subsets (Th1 and Th2 cells) is largely counter-regulatory. For example, the type 1 response activates macrophages and inhibits B cells, while the type 2 response helps B cells and deactivates macrophages (see Box 2.4).

The **Th1 response** (also referred to as **cellular** or **cell-mediated immunity**) involves the use of killer T cells and NK cells to destroy infected cells. This is beneficial for responding to a virus or allergy, but has detrimental effects in relation to arthritis and autoimmune disease. Characteristic cytokines are IL-2, INF-y and TNF-a.

The **Th2 response** (also referred to as **humoral** or **antibody-mediated immunity**) involves the use of molecules that bind with the antigen in order to clear it from the body. This response is beneficial in relation to arthritis and autoimmune disease (owing to down-regulation of Th1 response), but has detrimental effects in relation to viruses and allergies. Characteristic cytokines are IL-4, IL-5, IL-6, IL-10 and IL-13.

The balance between Th1 and Th2 immunity is regulated by neuroendocrine systems (including the HPA axis), which exhibit **circadian patterns** (a rhythmic 24-hour cycle in relation to sleep). This regulation results in nocturnal Th1 dominance and diurnal Th2 dominance. The Th1/Th2 balance is also influenced by psychological stress – acute stress tends to shift the balance towards Th1 immunity, while chronic stress shifts the balance towards Th2 immunity. Gender differences have also been reported – the immune system is biased towards Th1 dominance in females and this may explain the higher prevalence of arthritis and autoimmune disease in females.

Source: Carter & Dutton (1996); Evans, Hucklebridge & Clow (2000)

Allostatic load results from not only repeated and/or prolonged activation of the body's stress response systems but also inadequate activation of the same systems (see Figure 2.3). McEwen (1998) explains that an inadequate response is problematic since this may result in overactivity of other systems that are normally controlled by allostatic systems. For example, cortisol controls certain inflammatory processes, and an inadequate HPA response to stress has been noted in patients with inflammatory conditions such as rheumatoid arthritis (RA), systemic lupus erythematosus (SLE) and multiple sclerosis (MS) (Kemeny & Schedlowski, 2007). Unlike infectious illness, which results from failure of the immune system to identify and destroy invading micro-organisms, inflammatory autoimmune diseases are believed to result from an overactive (Th1) immune response in which the immune system attacks healthy cells that are normally present in the body (see also Box 2.5). Hence, illness is associated with both ends of the continuum.

Although the allostatic load model has been largely used to explain protective and damaging effects of biological stress mediators, it can also be used to explain adaptive

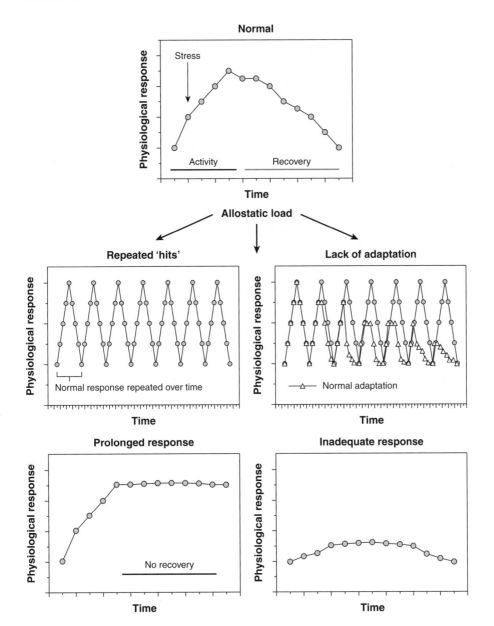

FIGURE 2.3 Four types of allostatic load

The top graph illustrates the normal allostatic response, in which a response is initiated by a stressor, sustained for an appropriate interval, then turned off. The remaining graphs illustrate four conditions that lead to allostatic load: repeated 'hits' from multiple novel stressors; lack of adaptation; prolonged response due to a delayed shutdown; and inadequate response that leads to compensatory hyperactivity of other mediators, such as inadequate secretion of glucocorticoids, resulting in increased levels of cytokines (normally counter-regulated by glucocorticoids)

Source: McEwen (1998)

(short-term) and damaging (long-term) effects of behaviours associated with stress. For example, behaviours such as drinking and smoking may act as behavioural analogues for the body's allostatic systems, providing short-term stress relief while contributing to long-term negative mood and health states (McEwen & Wingfield, 2003). Dietary factors are also relevant to the allostatic load model, since low blood glucose levels appear to prevent stress-induced activation of the HPA-axis, while glucose intake after a period of fasting may restore the HPA response (Gonzalez-Bono, Rohleder, Hellhammer, Salvador & Kirschbaum, 2002). Therefore, drinking, smoking and overeating during periods of stress may perform an immediate adaptive function, even if the long-term consequences of these behaviours are damaging.

Effects of stress on the development of depression, anxiety disorders, hostile and aggressive states and substance abuse may also be explained in relation to the allostatic load model, since the effects of stress on neuronal structures and neurotransmitter function may be both adaptive in the short term (contributing to memory and learning processes, for example) and maladaptive in the long-term (resulting in neuronal atrophy and chemical imbalance, for instance) – see Box 2.7. Further, hostility and depressive illness are associated with cardiovascular disease and other systemic disorders, suggesting that imbalances in brain function increase allostatic load, affecting the health of other systems in the body (McEwen, 2000).

BOX 2.7

Controversies: can stress shrink your brain?

Patients with post-traumatic stress disorder (PTSD) experience flashbacks, nightmares, sleep problems, emotional numbness, loss of pleasure, increased startle reflex and problems with memory and concentration. Brain-imaging studies have also revealed something quite startling – these patients appear to have lost part of their brain. The hippocampus (a brain region responsible for 'declarative memory' or memory for explicit knowledge) is smaller than average. So, is it possible that stress can shrink your brain?

Sapolsky (1999) explains that there are several possible explanations for this 'shrinking brain' phenomenon:

- high levels of stress hormones during exposure to trauma result in atrophy of neurons in the hippocampus
- the brain-imaging studies are really revealing a pre-existing vulnerability – that is, people with smaller hippocampi are more likely to develop PTSD following trauma than people with larger hippocampi
- a third hypothesis, proposed by Yehuda and colleagues, suggests that neuronal atrophy is caused not by excessive stress hormones during stress, but by increased sensitivity to stress hormones after stress.

In support of the first hypothesis, a wide body of research with animals and humans provides evidence that exposure to glucocorticoids results in atrophy of hippocampal neurons. The hippocampus has a high concentration of glucocorticoid receptors, and stress-level glucocorticoids can disrupt normal functioning of hippocampal neurons by, for example, starving them of glucose. In humans, there is evidence of hippocampal atrophy among patients with Cushing's syndrome, depression and Alzheimer's disease. Differences in glucocorticoid levels and cognitive impairment are also evident in these populations (McEwen & Sapolsky, 1995).

The second hypothesis is difficult to evaluate since most PTSD studies are retrospective. There is some evidence, however, that individual differences in personality and gender modulate the risk for PTSD following trauma; individual differences in stress response system responsivity may also be implicated (Stam, 2007).

In support of the third hypothesis, studies have revealed lower than-normal-cortisol levels in patients with PTSD, suggesting that increased sensitivity to stress hormones may result in lower cortisol secretion (Yehuda, 2002, for example). Other studies, however, have reported normal or higher-than-normal cortisol levels in patients with PTSD (Lindley et al., 2004, for instance).

Even more controversially, brain imaging research focusing on patients with chronic PTSD (15 years after exposure to trauma exposure) has failed to find any difference in hippocampal volume between PTSD patients and controls (Jatzko et al., 2006). Perhaps PTSD did not cause the previously described changes in hippocampal volume or perhaps the patients in the Jatzko et al. study had recovered their hippocampal volume over the years following the traumatic experience.

Others have pointed out that effects of stress on the brain are not all bad. While glucocorticoid secretion associated with prolonged stress may damage neuronal structures, secretion of catecholamines (adrenaline, noradrenaline) in response to acute stress can facilitate delivery of glucose to the brain and enhance memory formation. This may explain why we remember where we were when we heard that JFK had been shot, or Princess Diana had died (McEwen & Sapolsky, 1995).

The allostatic load model has important implications for the way in which health outcomes are assessed in research. Rather than relying purely on diagnosed disease, McEwen and Seeman (1999) suggest that measures of physiological functioning should be obtained across a number of regulatory systems, including the HPA-axis and SNS (cortisol, DHEA [a functional antagonist of cortisol], adrenaline, noradrenaline) as well as the cardiovascular system (such as diastolic and systolic blood pressure) and metabolic processes (such as waist–hip ratio, cholesterol). Changes in cardiovascular and metabolic processes can be seen as both outcomes of primary (chemical) mediators and contributors to disease processes.

2.3.2 BRAIN–IMMUNE COMMUNICATION AND THE 'SIXTH SENSE' CONCEPT

Research examining channels of communication between the brain and immune system has also helped to explain why physiological alterations designed to protect the organism can result in illness.

As discussed previously, the immune system was long believed to operate autono-mously, without direction from the brain. Research, however, has demonstrated that, while it is true that individual cells of the immune system are not connected to the nervous system, sympathetic noradrenergic nerve fibres innervate lymphoid organs, including the thymus, spleen and lymph nodes (Felten, Felten, Carlson, Olschowka & Livnat, 1985), so the brain appears to be 'hard-wired' to the immune system.

Other research has revealed chemical links between the nervous and immune sys-tems, since cells of both systems have receptors for neuropeptides, cytokines and neurotransmitters (Blalock & Smith, 2007; Elenkov & Chrousos, 1999, 1999a). Blalock (1984) suggests that these molecules are responsible for relaying chemical information between the brain and immune system. This signalling may alert the organism to the presence of both cognitive stimuli (such as stress) and non-cognitive stimuli (such as infections, tumours or allergens). In this way, Blalock suggests that the immune system should be considered as a *sixth sense*, capable of detecting stimuli that cannot normally be seen, touched, heard, smelled or tasted.

Maier and Watkins (1998, 2003) highlight the significance of pro-inflammatory cytokines in the sixth sense concept, drawing parallels between the sickness pattern (in response to infection and injury) and physiological alterations (in response to both stress and depression). Pro-inflammatory cytokines are key elements in the process that signals the brain that infection and injury occur, and they are implicated in triggering the sickness pattern and neural activation associated with bacterial products, resulting in alterations such as loss of appetite, reduced activity and sleep disturbances (Maier & Watkins, 2003). Maier and Watkins point out that these disturbances are also seen in patients with depression. They suggest, therefore, that brain-immune circuitry evolved to protect the organism against infection and injury and stressors (as well as cognitions resulting in depression) have essentially co-opted this circuitry, explaining why stres-sors 'make animals and humans sick' (Maier & Watkins, 1998: 94).

High levels of depression have also been reported in patients receiving recom-bitant cytokines for the treatment of cancer and viral infection (see Capuron & Dantzer, 2003 for a review). Dantzer (2005) therefore suggests that cytokines func-tion as a motivational signal that tells the brain to change the organism's priorities towards dealing with the threat presented by pathogens or other danger signals, and this results in changes at the subjective, physiological and behavioural levels, similar to the process that coordinates the subjective, physiological and behavioural responses to fear resulting from contact with a potential predator.

Blalock and Smith (2007) highlight the role of corticotropin-releasing hormone (CRH) in bidirectional brain-immune communication. CRH is one of the hormones of the HPA-axis (see Figure 2.3) and has been reported to have a variety of effects on the immune system. Conversely, CRH production by leukocytes appears to be impli-cated in immune-to-nervous system communication involved in localised analgesic responses to inflammatory pain (Blalock & Smith, 2007).

Rather than operating autonomously, therefore, it is evident that the immune sys-tem interacts with the CNS and neuroendocrine system in coordinating responses to threats, whether those threats come in the form of an invading micro-organism, a predator or even a perceived psychosocial threat.

2.3.3 THE 'IMMUNE SURVEILLANCE' HYPOTHESIS AND THE DEVELOPMENT OF CANCER

In addition to the health impacts discussed above, dysregulation of the body's stress response systems may influence the development of cancer. According to the **immune surveillance hypothesis**, cancer cells arise regularly, but are usually detected and removed by the immune system, which performs a constant surveillance function (Burnet, 1957; Thomas, 1959). When the immune system is suppressed, however, this surveillance system breaks down, increasing the chance for tumours to develop and grow. Immune surveillance may form part of a more general process of immunoediting – a process responsible for both eliminating tumours and sculpting tumours as they develop (Dunn, Bruce, Ikeda, Old & Shreiber, 2002).

Consistent with the immune surveillance theory, suppression of the immune system in HIV and organ transplant patients has been linked to increased risk of certain cancers – mainly virus-related ones, such as Kaposi's sarcoma (KS) and non-Hodgkin's lymphoma (NHL) (Busnach et al., 2006; Kinlen, 2004; Mueller, 1999).

With regard to the psychological modulation of immunity, a number of animal studies have demonstrated that exposure to stressors such as inescapable electric shocks, forced swimming, abdominal surgery and social stress are associated with an increased susceptibility to developing tumours, decreased survival time and impaired immune response to tumours, although stress-induced changes to the outcome of a disease are influenced by a number of interacting factors, including genetic background of the animal, its previous history, nature of the stressor and type of immune response generated (Vissoci, Nunes & Morimoto, 2004).

Evidence of stress-induced immunomodulation in the development of human cancer is more difficult to demonstrate since this necessitates studies focusing on large populations over a number of years and considering interactions between several psychological and biomedical risk factors (Garssen & Goodkin, 1999; Vissoci et al., 2004). There is some evidence to suggest, however, that stress can increase susceptibility to certain cancers in humans. For example, Levav et al. (2000) followed a cohort of 6284 Jewish Israelis who lost an adult son in the Yom Kippur War or in an accident between 1970 and 1977. Rates of cancer among bereaved parents were compared to non-bereaved controls. Results indicated an increased incidence of lymphatic and haematopoietic malignancies, as well as melanomas and respiratory cancer. Survival data indicated that the risk of death was increased by bereavement if cancer had been diagnosed before the loss, but not after.

Longitudinal studies have also provided evidence to support the role of the immune system in mediating the impact of psychological factors on how the cancer progresses. For example, in a series of studies, Levy et al. (1985, 1987, 1990, 1991) reported that breast cancer patients who demonstrated poor adjustment and lack of social support had lower natural killer (NK) cell activity and that NK cell activity was a predictor for how the disease progressed and if it recurred. Associations between depression and cancer have also been identified. A number of randomised controlled trials have indicated that psychotherapeutic approaches can not only reduce anxiety and depression but also increase survival time in cancer patients, although evidence is mixed, with some studies reporting no survival advantage associated with psycho-therapeutic support (Spiegel & Giese-Davis, 2003).

2.3.4 BIOLOGICAL EXPLANATIONS FOR VARIATION FROM INDIVIDUAL TO INDIVIDUAL

Biological explanations have been provided for not only the link between stress and illness but also individual variability in cognitive, behavioural and physiological responses to stress. For example, Korte et al. (2005) suggest that there may be evolutionary reasons for organisms adopting different behavioural strategies to cope with stress. In particular, they argue that natural selection maintains a balance between different behavioural traits and strategies, preserving genes for both high and low levels of aggression. Highly aggressive individuals (hawks) adopt the fight or flight response when defending territory, while non-aggressive individuals (doves) show a freeze or hide response. Hawks have lower HPA axis activity, higher sympathetic activity, and are bolder and less influenced by environmental changes than doves. The cost of low HPA axis and high sympathetic activation in hawks comes in the form of hypertension, cardiac arrhythmias and inflammation. The cost of high HPA axis activity for doves comes in the form of vulnerability to infection. Although doves are not characterised by high sympathetic activation, they also develop cardiovascular disease, since hypercorticolism influences pathogenic mechanisms contributing to cardiovascular risk (Korte et al., 2005).

Studies of gender differences in responses to stress also suggest HPA hyper-reactivity in men, associated with high rates of cardiovascular disease and diabetes, and HPA hypo-reactivity in women, associated with high rates of autoimmune disease (see Kudielka & Kirschbaum, 2005 for a review).

The effects of HPA activation may also differ according to developmental stage. For example, animal studies have demonstrated that the HPA axis can be 'programmed' via manipulations in early development, including prenatally (such as maternal stress, exposure to synthetic glucocorticoids and restriction of nutrients) and postnatally (neonatal handling, maternal deprivation, modified maternal behaviour and exposure to synthetic glucocorticoids, for example). This research suggests that exposure to glucocorticoids during sensitive periods in development may determine the 'set point' of the HPA axis and predispose the individual to development of cardiovascular, metabolic and neuroendocrine disorders in adulthood (Owen et al., 2005; Seckl, 2001; Seckl & Meaney, 2004). The HPA axis set point may also be partly determined by genetic factors (McEwen & Seeman, 1999).

SUMMARY

2.4 The research discussed in this chapter has provided evidence of inter-relationships between psychological and biological processes with respect to health and illness. Cognitive processes are necessary for the detection of environmental threats in much the same way that immune processes are necessary for the detection of physiological threats. Once a potential threat is detected, cognitive *and* physiological systems operate in synchrony. SNS activation facilitates behavioural responses, which may terminate the threat before the HPA axis is fully activated. If, however, the threat is sustained and uncontrollable (or perceived to be) or the coping responses are insufficient to terminate the threat, arousal will continue to rise, resulting in activation of the HPA axis.

Over the longer term, continued HPA activation, associated with persistent negative thoughts and expectancies, results in the development of an allostatic state in which all resources are directed towards the task of defending the organism from danger. This allostatic state, however, is achieved at a considerable cost, producing wear and tear across multiple systems of the body, increasing the risk of health outcomes ranging from the common cold to cardiovascular disease and even some types of cancer. Impacts on brain function also increase the risk of pathogenic psychological states and psychiatric disorders, which often overlap with physical morbidity. Further, individual experiences of stress may influence psychological and biological responses to future stressors by altering beliefs and expectations or changing HPA set points.

Throughout the stress process, therefore, psychological and biological processes are very closely intertwined. Further research will help to elucidate these psychobiological interactions and develop psychobiological approaches to prevention and treatment of illness.

KEY TERMS

adaptive immunity (also called acquired or specific immunity), allostasis, allostatic load, autonomic nervous system (ANS), cellular immunity (also called cell-mediated immunity, Th1 response) central nervous system (CNS), circadian patterns, cognitive activation theory (CAT), conditioned immunomodulation, corticosteroids, cytokines, endocrine system, enteric nervous system, fight or flight response, general adaptation syndrome (GAS), homeostasis, humoral immunity (also called antibody-mediated immunity, Th2 response) hypothalamic-pituitary-adrenal (HPA) axis, immune surveillance hypothesis, immune system, innate immunity (also called natural immunity), leukocytes, lymphocytes, lymphoid organs, neuropeptides, neurotransmitters, parasympathetic nervous system (PNS), peripheral nervous system, psychosocial threat, sympathetic-adrenal-medullary (SAM) axis, sympathetic nervous system (SNS), transactional model (TM) of coping

■Discussion questions

1 Why study associations between stress and illness?

2 If stress *does* increase the risk of illness, does it matter what the underlying mechanisms are?

3 Could the theoretical models discussed in this chapter inform the development of interventions to prevent or treat illness?

4 Can you think of particular groups at risk of allostatic load?

5 Should we consider health-related behaviours – drinking, smoking, overeating – as adaptive or maladaptive?

6 What would be the likely implications of attempting to refrain from these behaviours during stressful periods, such as during exams?

FURTHER READING

Evans, P., Hucklebridge, F. & Clow, A. (2000). *Mind, immunity and health: the science of psychoneuroimmunology*. London: Free Association Books.

Jones, F. & Bright, J. (2001). *Stress: myth, theory and research*. London: Pearson.

Sapolsky, R.M. (2002). *Why zebras don't get ulcers: guide to stress, stress-related disease and coping*. New York: Henry Holt & Company.

POSITIVE PROCESSES IN HEALTH AND ILLNESS

3

OVERVIEW

In Chapter 2 we discussed research that has demonstrated associations between psychological processes, biological processes and health outcomes. Although much of this research has focused on stress, recent research has suggested that positive states and traits are also pertinent to the discussion of psychobiological processes in health and illness.

Research focusing on positive states and traits helps us to move away from a disease model of human functioning, with interventions designed to alleviate existing pathology, and towards a broader 'positive psychology' model, with interventions aimed at the prevention of illness as well as the promotion of health and well-being.

In this chapter, then, we consider the role of positive processes in health and illness, including positive emotions, positive dispositions, and factors promoting health and well-being. We also consider what the emergence of a more 'positive psychology' means for established models of emotion and coping, as well as what it means to be psychologically 'well'.

LEARNING OUTCOMES

By the end of this chapter you should be able to:

- describe the role of positive emotions in human adaptation

- discuss the impacts of positive emotions on physiological functioning

- describe the processes by means of which patients find meaning in their experiences of illness

- discuss relationships between positive emotions, appraisals, coping and physical health

- describe trends in the research literature relating to emotions and health

- explain what it means to be psychologically 'well'

- compare and contrast the hedonic and eudaimonic approaches to well-being

- discuss social and environmental influences on well-being

- consider evidence for and against the notion that well-being is genetically determined

- describe the process via which positive emotions are created.

3.1 FROM STRESS TO EMOTION

> Although stress and coping are still important, social scientists have begun to realize that these concepts are part of a larger rubric – the emotions.
>
> Lazarus (1991)

The models discussed in the previous chapter help to explain how adverse environmental conditions impact physical health and why individuals differ in their responses to similar environmental conditions. These models have focused almost exclusively on negative emotions, however. It is not clear, therefore, to what extent positive emotions may be implicated in human adaptation. For example, if stress helps to alert us to potential danger and mobilise our resources to deal with real or appraised threat, what is the role of joy or contentment? Do *positive* emotions have any impact on physiological functioning? From an evolutionary perspective, is there any *reason* for us to experience positive emotions?

Traditional models of emotion have also focused mainly on the experience of acute emotions as opposed to stable dispositions. Lazarus (1991) writes that acute emotions (such as joy) come and go in relation to specific adaptational encounters, while stable dispositions or moods (such as happiness) are more related to the individual's general sense of well-being. Research focusing on the concept of well-being indicates that mood assessed over a period of years (rather than on a moment-to-moment basis) appears to bear little relationship to life circumstances (health, income, demographic factors and so on) and, while positive or negative life events may impact well-being in the short-term, these effects ameliorate over time. Such findings beg the question as to whether or not interventions aimed at enhancing positive emotions or coping in relation to specific life events have any lasting impact on well-being – perhaps some people are simply more resilient to stressful life conditions than others or genetically predestined to experience more positive moods.

In this chapter, therefore, we turn our attention to positive states and traits. In Section 3.2 we consider theoretical models relevant to an understanding of the role of positive and negative emotions in adaptation and interrelationships between emotion, coping and health. In Section 3.3 we examine the concept of well-being and consider to what extent positive emotion may be amenable to psychological intervention.

EMOTION, COPING AND HEALTH

3.2

In this section we consider three theoretical accounts of associations between emotions, coping and health.

The first theory considered – the **broaden and build theory** (Fredrickson, 1998) – is proposed as an alternative to purportedly generic models of emotion, which, Fredrickson argues, are really models of negative emotion and do not account for the form and function of positive emotions.

The second is a modified version of the transactional model of coping (Lazarus & Folkman, 1984), which previously considered positive emotions as relevant only to situations with favourable outcomes (see Chapter 2). Folkman (1997) now suggests that this model should be extended to include a role for positive emotions in coping with ongoing stressful situations.

The final theory – the **commonsense model of illness representations** (Leventhal, Meyer & Nerenz, 1980, for example) – helps us to consider how patients form cognitive and emotional representations of their experiences of illness. Research conducted within this framework suggests that emotional and cognitive representations of illness have implications for both physical health and psychological well-being.

3.2.1 THE BROADEN AND BUILD THEORY OF POSITIVE EMOTIONS

Fredrickson (1998) writes that most emotion theorists have built their models to fit the specifications of prototypical emotions such as fear and anger, and have assumed that these models also provide sufficient explanation for other emotions, including the positive emotions. For example, since fear and anger have been linked to urges to escape or fight, emotion theorists have argued that emotions must have evolved to get us out of life-and-death situations by narrowing our responses towards a specific set of behavioural options ('specific action tendencies') that have served our ancestors well in life-threatening circumstances. Emotions have also been linked to specific facial configurations, which are thought to function as important signals – for example, warning others of potential danger (Ekman, 1992). It is not evident that *all* emotions share these features, however. Fredrickson (1998; Fredrickson & Levenson, 1998) points out that actions associated with positive emotions are typically vague and non-specific, so joy, for example, is associated with aimless activation, interest with attending and contentment with inactivity (Frijda, 1986). Also, positive emotions are not associated with specific facial expressions but share a particular form of smiling – the 'Duchenne smile' (Ekman, 1992). Consequently, Fredrickson (1998; Fredrickson & Levenson, 1998) suggests that it is not reasonable to assume that the adaptive value of positive emotions is simply isomorphic to the adaptive value of negative emotions and, while traditional accounts may be retained for negative emotions, that an alternative theory is needed to account for the form and function of positive emotions.

Fredrickson (1998) argues that, since some positive emotions (interest, for example) appear to spark changes in primarily cognitive activity rather than physical action, it is more useful to speak of 'thought–action tendencies' rather than specific action tendencies and, instead of presuming that these thought–action tendencies are specific, it is more useful to discuss the relative breadth of the momentary thought–action repertoire.

Using this terminology to paraphrase traditional action-orientated models, Fredrickson (1998: 304) writes that *negative* emotions function to *narrow* an individual's thought–action repertoire, by 'calling to mind and body the time-tested ancestrally adaptive actions represented by specific action tendencies'. *Positive* emotions, however, *broaden* the individual's thought–action repertoire, prompting individuals to discard automatic behavioural scripts and pursue novel, creative thoughts and actions. So, *joy*, for example, inspires an urge to play and explore, *interest* is an instigator of creative endeavour and learning, *contentment* involves integration of new experiences into one's self-concept and worldview, and *love* encourages interaction with loved ones (Fredrickson, 1998). Positive emotions appear to share not only the feature of *broadening* the individual's thought–action repertoire but also the feature of *building* the individual's personal resources, ranging from intellectual resources, to physical resources, to social resources.

Fredrickson (1998) proposes that these resources can be drawn on in later contexts. By broadening thought–action repertoires, Fredrickson and Levenson (1998: 193) also propose that positive emotions 'loosen the hold that negative emotions gain on an individual's mind and body', effectively 'undoing' the physiological impacts of negative emotions and restoring homeostasis. This is referred to as the **undoing effect**.

Fredrickson and colleagues have presented a number of studies that support the broadening and building effects of positive emotions (reviewed in Cohn & Fredrickson, 2006). For example, people in positive emotion states have been demonstrated as taking a 'big picture' view, attending to the general outline of images rather than the details, increasing their use of adaptive reframing and perspective-taking coping skills, finding more varied and adaptive ways to use their social support network, broadening their sense of self to include close and potentially close others, and recognising people of different races in ways more similar to their own.

Fredrickson and Joiner (2002) and Burns et al. (2008) demonstrated reciprocal relationships between positive emotions and coping – with the experience of positive emotions and adaptive coping serially enhancing one another, resulting in upward spirals towards enhanced emotional well-being.

The 'undoing effect' has also gained empirical support. In two separate studies, cardiovascular activity returned to normal more quickly after cessation of a stressor if the participant watched a positive emotion film as opposed to a neutral or negative emotion film during the recovery period (Fredrickson & Levenson, 1998; Fredrickson, Mancuso, Branigan & Tugade, 2000: see Research in focus box 3.1).

RESEARCH IN FOCUS BOX 3.1

Fredrickson, Mancuso, Branigan and Tugade (2000) examined the 'undoing effect' of positive emotions experienced in the immediate aftermath of a stressful task.

Methodology

Participants (170) were told that they would be given 60 seconds to prepare a speech on a topic to be determined and that there was a 50 per cent chance that the computer would assign them to deliver this speech to a video camera (in reality, none of the participants was assigned to deliver the speech).

Following this stress-induction procedure, participants viewed a short film designed to elicit one of four emotions (amusement, contentment, no emotion or sadness). Cardiovascular reactivity was assessed throughout.

Results

Contentment-eliciting and amusing films produced a faster rate of cardiovascular recovery than neutral or sad films (see below).

Conclusions and implications

The findings suggest that positive emotions experienced in the immediate aftermath of a stressful task may help to reduce the duration of cardiovascular activation.

In other studies, Fredrickson et al. (2000) also demonstrated that the positive emotion film clips did not on their own elicit change in cardiovascular reactivity and did not buffer against the effects of a subsequent stressor. The impact of positive emotions on cardiovascular reactivity therefore appears to be specific to undoing the impact of anxiety-related arousal.

(Cont'd)

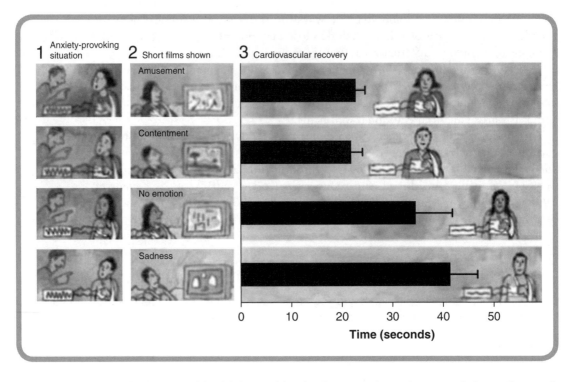

The broaden and build theory has also been used as a framework for understanding **psychological resilience** – the ability to bounce back from negative emotional experiences and flexibly adapting to the changing demands of stressful experiences. People who score highly on a self-reported measure of resilience experience more positive emotions in relation to both laboratory stressors and real-life stressors, report finding more positive meaning in relation to stressors in daily life, and show faster rates of cardiovascular recovery following laboratory stressors. Further, positive emotions at least partially mediate these beneficial effects of resilience (Tugade & Fredrickson, 2004).

Fredrickson, Tugade, Waugh and Larkin (2003) found that positive emotions experienced in the wake of the 11th September 2001 terrorist attacks fully accounted for relations between a precrisis resilience and the later development of depressive symptoms and a precrisis resilience and postcrisis growth in psychological resources.

According to the broaden and build theory, then, positive emotions, while not appearing to conform to 'generic' models of emotion, do nonetheless perform an important function, helping to undo the physiological effects of negative emotions and respond more adaptively to our environments.

Research conducted in relation to the 'broaden and build' theory has highlighted associations between positive emotions and coping, suggesting that positive emotions have important implications for coping with current stressors (such as facilitating coping by putting things into perspective), as well as situations that may be encountered in the future (building resources to draw on when needed), and they may explain individual differences in the ability to bounce back from negative emotional experiences. Associations between positive emotions and coping are considered in greater detail in the following section.

3.2.2 THE TRANSACTIONAL MODEL OF COPING

> The co-occurrence of positive and negative psychological states throughout enduring and profoundly stressful circumstances challenges us to consider a model of coping that takes positive states into account.
>
> Folkman (1997: 1207)

Like models of emotion, coping theory has traditionally paid little attention to positive emotion. For example, Folkman and Moskowitz (2000: 647) write that:

> historically, coping has most often been evaluated in relation to its effectiveness in regulating distress … What has been underrepresented in coping research is an approach that looks at the other side of the coin, an approach that examines positive affect in the stress process.

Positive emotion has not been entirely ignored by coping theorists. For example, Folkman and Moskowitz (2000) explain that positive emotions have been discussed in relation to situations appraised as challenging and the cessation or favourable resolution of stressful conditions. Evidence of positive emotion experienced in relation to enduring stressful conditions has, however, challenged coping theorists both to describe the kinds of coping processes that people use to generate or sustain positive emotion in such conditions, and to consider the adaptational significance of positive emotion in the stress process.

In fact, high levels of positive emotions have been reported in even the most distressing life circumstances. For example, Folkman (1997) reported participants' descriptions of their daily experiences of caring for a partner with AIDS. These descriptions often displayed a determination to look on the bright side or find a deeper meaning. With the exception of the period immediately surrounding the partner's death, the ability to achieve positive states of mind was not severely compromised.

In Folkman's (1997) study, four types of coping were associated with positive psychological states during caregiving and bereavement:

- positive reappraisal – reframing the situation in a more positive light
- goal-directed problem-focused coping – being engaged in personally meaningful goals
- spiritual beliefs and practices
- the infusion of ordinary events with positive meaning.

Folkman (1997) therefore suggests adding three pathways to the original transactional model of coping (see Figures 3.1 and 3.2):

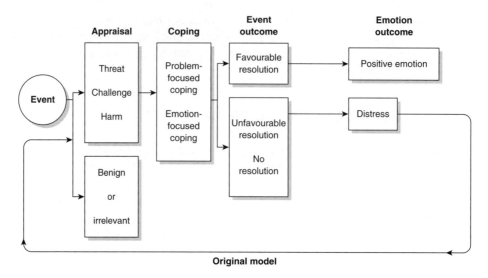

FIGURE 3.1   Theoretical model of the coping process
Source: Folkman (1997)

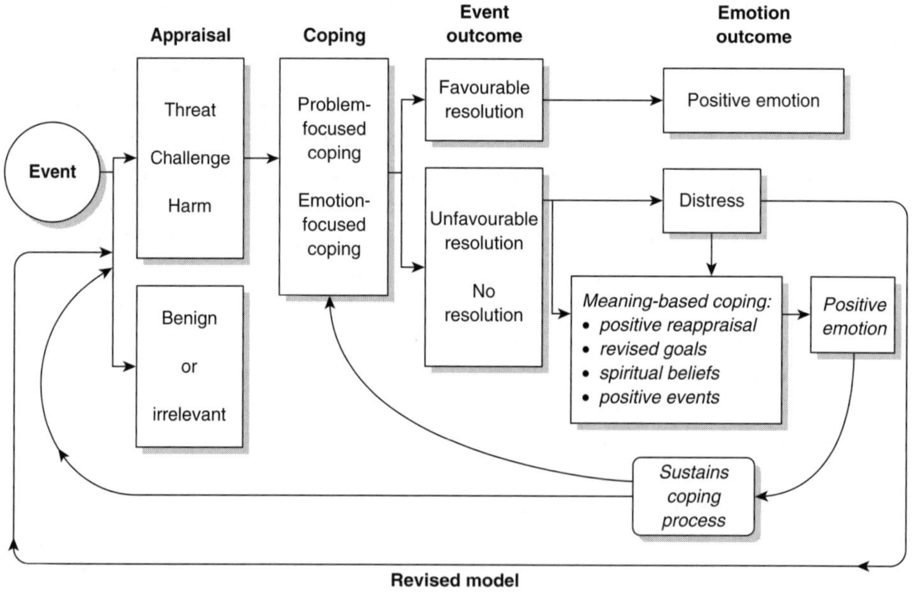

FIGURE 3.2   Revised theoretical model of the coping process
Source: Folkman (1997)

- positive psychological states that are the result of meaning-based processes individuals use to cope with the stressor itself (such as those discussed above)
- coping as a response to distress rather than the conditions that create distress
- a pathway leading from the positive psychological states back to appraisals and coping, helping to sustain renewed coping efforts.

According to Folkman's (1997) modified model, then, positive emotions may result not only from events with favourable resolutions but also from events with no resolution or an unfavourable resolution, provided the individual is able to find meaning or benefit arising from his or her experiences. Further, positive affect can co-occur with stress, and positive affect in the context of stress has important adaptational outcomes.

Other research supports the notion of positive emotions existing in the face of adversity, with reports of co-occurring positive and negative emotions in relation to experiences such as chronic illness, injury and bereavement (Folkman & Moskowitz, 2004). A number of studies have also reported positive reappraisal, positive meaning and **benefit-finding** in relation to stressful life experiences. Also, the ability to find benefits from one's experiences has been linked to reduced distress following experiences such as bereavement, heart attack and exposure to disasters involving extensive damage to property and loss of life (Tennen & Affleck, 1999).

Studies of the psychological aspects of major medical problems indicate not only that patients can find positive meaning in their experiences but also that such benefit-finding occurs in the *majority* of patients. Benefit-finding in patient populations has been linked to better physical health outcomes – for example, better cardiac health and lower probability of reinfarction in men who had survived a first heart attack, lower CD4 T lymphocyte decline among bereaved HIV-seropositive men and reduced impact of pain on activity limitation in rheumatoid arthritis patients (reviewed in Tennen & Affleck, 1999). In these studies, benefits cited included changes in lifestyle, increased understanding of self, personal growth, greater appreciation of loved ones and altered values and life philosophies. Studies with cancer patients have also presented evidence that positive coping may have implications for *survival*, although these findings have been subject to considerable debate (see Box 3.1).

Therefore, it seems that benefit-finding and positive appraisal of illness and medical threat may actually be quite common, and such meaning-based coping may be important not only for psychological well-being but also for physical health (and possibly even for survival). Therefore it is important to understand the process by which patients find meaning in their experience of illness. This process will be considered further in the following section.

BOX 3.1

Controversies: does coping influence chances of surviving cancer?

Tschuschke et al. (2001) investigated associations between coping and survival in a sample of 52 adult leukemia patients receiving bone marrow transplants (BMT).

Interviews were conducted with a random sample of patients receiving treatment in the BMT unit. These patients were then followed up over a five-year period to examine the effects of their coping styles (assessed at interview) on their survival. Coping style proved to be a predictor of survival independent of the stage of the disease at transplant. The most powerful predictor was a combination of low distraction coping and high levels of 'fighting spirit' – a coping style characterised by optimism, control and determination to fight the disease. These findings are consistent with previous studies reporting effects of coping on surviving cancer (Greer, Morris & Pettingale, 1979, for example).

Other studies, however, have failed to find such an association between coping style and surviving cancer. A systematic review published in 2002 identified 26 studies investigating the association between coping and surviving cancer. Ten of these investigated the impact of fighting spirit on survival, but positive findings were confined to the two small studies cited above. Evidence that other coping styles play a role was also weak. The reviewers therefore concluded that, 'people with cancer should not feel pressured into adopting particular coping styles to improve survival or reduce the risk of recurrence' (Petticrew, Bell & Hunter, 2002: 1066).

The authors of a number of the studies included in this review have challenged the conclusion that evidence for the significance of coping is lacking. For example, Watson (2002) points out that, although Watson, Haviland, Greer, Davidson and Bliss (1999) did not find evidence for the prognostic significance of fighting spirit, recurrence was predicted by helplessness/hopelessness. Also, Tschuschke (2002) points out that the larger studies investigating the impacts of fighting spirit used self-report measures of coping, which are unlikely to reveal an association with coping, while the two smaller studies used semi-structured interviews.

One point on which researchers and reviewers agree is that there is significant variability in the research methods employed to investigate associations between coping and the outcomes for people with cancer, and that greater methodological rigour is warranted. A recent review concluded that claims about the role of positive factors in extending the lives of people with cancer have been exaggerated and do not fit with the available evidence. The reviewers urge positive psychologists not to run ahead of what they know, and to 'rededicate themselves to a positive psychology based on scientific evidence rather than wishful thinking' (Coyne & Tennen, 2010: 16).

3.2.3 THE COMMONSENSE MODEL OF ILLNESS REPRESENTATIONS

As discussed above, individuals differ not only in their responses to stressful life events but also in their responses to illness and medical threats. Further, it is evident that the

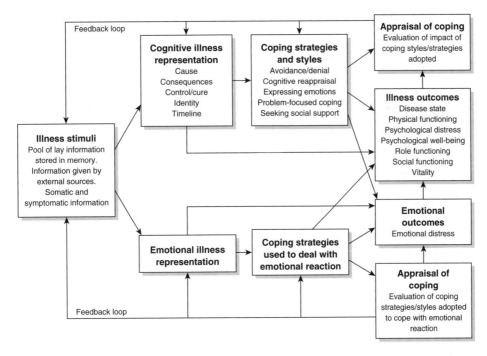

FIGURE 3.3 Schematic representation of Leventhal et al.'s (1980) commonsense model of illness representations

Source: Hagger and Orbell (2003)

meaning individuals construct in relation to ill health has important implications for health outcomes, but how do we construct meaning from illness experiences and how do patients' personal models of their illnesses influence their health and well-being? In order to answer these questions, it is necessary to turn to Leventhal's commonsense model (CSM) of illness representations (Leventhal, Meyer & Nerenz, 1980).

According to Leventhal's model, individuals form both cognitive and emotional representations of their illnesses on the basis of a broad range of information (doctor's diagnosis, information from friends, physical sensations, bodily changes and so on). Cognitive representations involve beliefs regarding the identity of the illness (disease label, diagnosis, symptoms), its cause and consequences, the timeline (that is, beliefs about the course of the illness) and its curability and controllability.

On the basis of these representations, patients form an understanding of the meaning of their illnesses, and this meaning guides subsequent attempts at coping. Similar to the transactional model (see previous section), the CSM proposes that individuals may attempt to cope with both the problem itself (the illness as it is cognitively represented) and the emotional impacts of the illness (emotional representations of the illness). Further, coping attempts are appraised by the individual and these appraisals feed back to modify the representations of the illness and subsequent coping behaviours (see Figure 3.3).

The CSM has been applied to a wide range of illnesses, including diabetes, hypertension, IBS, psoriasis, multiple sclerosis, asthma and arthritis. A meta-analysis of empirical studies adopting the CSM presented support for the validity of the illness cognition dimensions (Hagger & Orbell, 2003). Across the 45 studies reviewed, perceived *controllability* of the illness was associated with cognitive reappraisal, expression of emotions and problem-focused coping, perceptions of the illness as highly symptomatic (identity), having a chronic *timeline* and serious *consequences* were associated with avoidance coping and expressing emotions. Perceptions of the illness as curable or controllable were associated with better psychological, social and physical outcomes, while the consequences of illness, the timeline and identity demonstrated negative associations with these outcomes.

A number of studies have also compared representations of illness among patients and non-patients. For example, Anagnostopoulos and Spanea (2005) compared representations relating to breast cancer in patients with the disease, patients with benign breast conditions and healthy controls. The non-malignant women's representations of illness were characterised by weak beliefs regarding curability and controllability and an overestimation of the negative physical, social and economic consequences of breast cancer. These women also held strong beliefs about the role of environmental factors in causing breast cancer. The authors suggest that healthy women may perceive that environmental factors have a greater role to play than is the case, owing to a need to focus on causal factors that are potentially controllable, and that they may hold more negative perceptions of breast cancer owing to the inaccurate messages about the disease prevalent in the mass media (such as portraying it as a disease mainly affecting young women, causing both early death and children to be abandoned – see Burke et al., 2001).

Godoy-Izquierdo and colleagues (2007) examined the content of lay beliefs about three physical diseases (flu, cancer and hypertension) and two mental diseases (depression and schizophrenia) in healthy people without direct experience of these diseases, people suffering from these diseases and people who had coexisted with others who had suffered from these diseases. The results indicated that experience of a particular disease influenced the content of the lay models. In general, patients and relatives of patients perceived the diseases as less chronic, less serious with less impact on daily life and well-being, and more capable of being cured or controlled than those who had no experience of them.

According to the commonsense model, then, both emotional and cognitive processes are important to an understanding of the ways in which patients make sense of and cope with their illnesses. Emotional and cognitive processes also mediate between the experience of the illness and its outcomes, with implications for understanding interindividual variations in both physical health and psychological well-being. Research conducted within the CSM framework also indicates that, while healthy people may perceive the experience of major medical threat or chronic illness as wholly negative, patients themselves often hold more positive perceptions of their conditions. This may explain why the experience of ill health does not necessarily impair the individual's capacity to experience positive emotions.

WELL-BEING

3.3 Ryan and Deci (2001) write that, for much of the last century, psychology's focus on the amelioration of psychopathology overshadowed the promotion of personal growth and well-being. Researchers are now starting to recognise, however, that, just as positive emotion is not simply the absence of negative emotion, well-being is not the absence of mental illness. Indeed, positive states and traits have become an important topic of investigation in their own right and researchers have attempted to address fundamental questions of human existence ('What *constitutes a "good" life?*' for example) to consider why individuals differ in their capacity to experience positive psychological states and how best to develop interventions aimed at promoting positive psychological outcomes.

This burgeoning field of research has been termed the 'positive psychology movement' (Ryan & Deci, 2001; Seligman, 2002). As it has developed, two principal approaches to defining and measuring well-being have emerged:

- the hedonic approach, which considers well-being to be equivalent to pleasure or happiness
- the eudaimonic approach, which considers well-being to consist of fulfilling or realising one's true nature, or 'daimon' (Ryan & Deci, 2001).

These are considered further in the following sections.

3.3.1 SUBJECTIVE WELL-BEING: THE HEDONIC APPROACH

Ryan and Deci (2001) write that **subjective well-being (SWB)** has reigned as the primary index of well-being during the last decade and a half.

According to this conceptualisation of well-being, 'people react differently to the same circumstances and they evaluate conditions based on their unique expectations, values and previous experiences' (Diener, Suh, Lucas & Smith, 1999: 277). Thus, it is not possible to determine another individual's level of well-being simply by knowing about his or her life circumstances – well-being is essentially a *subjective* construct. Accordingly, SWB may be defined as a broad category of phenomena that includes people's emotional responses (positive and negative affect), satisfaction with

TABLE 3.1   Components of subjective well-being

Pleasant affect	Unpleasant affect	Life satisfaction	Domain satisfaction
Joy	Guilt and shame	Desire to change life	Work
Elation	Sadness	Satisfaction with current life	Family
Contentment	Anxiety and worry	Satisfaction with past	Leisure
Pride	Anger		Health
Affection	Stress	Satisfaction with future	Finances
Happiness	Depression	Significant others' views of one's life	Self
Ecstasy	Envy		One's group

Source: Diener et al. (1999: 277)

life domains (work, family, leisure, finances and so on) and global judgements of life satisfaction (Diener et al., 1999) – see Table 3.1.

A wide body of research evidence has supported the notion that life circumstances are poor predictors of SWB. For example, Brickman, Coates and Janoff-Bulman (1978) demonstrated that lottery winners were not significantly happier than a control group, and a group of individuals with spinal cord injuries were not as unhappy as might be expected. Diener, Wolsic and Fujita (1995) found only small associations between physical attractiveness and SWB. Further, correlations between subjective well-being and income within nations tend to be small, and economic growth in developed societies has been accompanied by little rise in SWB (reviewed in Diener & Biswas-Diener, 2002). Demographic factors (age, gender, race, education, marital status and so on) also appear to account for only a small proportion of the variance in well-being (Diener et al., 1999). Thus being healthy, wealthy and wise does not necessarily make for a happier life.

Equally, a number of studies have revealed strong and consistent associations between SWB and personality traits. Costa and McCrae (1980) reported that personality traits predict differences in happiness over a period of ten years, extraversion influencing positive affect or satisfaction, and neuroticism negative affect or dissatisfaction. A number of subsequent studies have provided evidence that well-being is associated with high extraversion and low neuroticism. Extraversion and neuroticism, however, appear to be more closely associated with affective aspects of well-being, while cognitive and evaluative aspects of well-being are more closely associated with neuroticism and conscientiousness – a trait characterised by responsibility, foresight and orderliness (DeNeve & Cooper, 1998; Hayes & Joseph, 2003).

Diener et al. (1999) write that a number of theories have been developed to explain why personality is related to SWB. One conceptual model proposes that people have a genetic predisposition to be happy or unhappy. Consistent with this theory, twin studies have reported that around 40–50 per cent of the variance in current SWB may be explained by genes, with higher heritability estimates (around 80 per cent) reported for SWB over a 10-year period (Lykken & Tellegen, 1996; Tellegen et al., 1988). Diener et al. (1999), however, also point out that a number of other studies have found lower heritability estimates and, since genes have an influence on life events (Plomin et al., 1990), genes might influence SWB by making certain behaviours more likely in certain contexts.

Thus, it appears that there *is* a genetic component to SWB, but estimates of the size of this influence vary widely, and heritability estimates do not necessarily point to unchangeable predispositions to experience emotions (Diener et al., 1999).

3.3.2 RELATEDNESS AND EUDAIMONIC WELL-BEING

Extraversion may also influence well-being via positive relations with others. Ryan and Deci (2001) point out that the quality of interactions with others and feelings of relatedness on a day-to-day basis have been linked to well-being indicators.

Relatedness is a key component of eudaimonic approaches to well-being, such as Ryan and Deci's (2000) **self-determination theory (SDT)** and Ryff's (1989) six-factor model of **psychological well-being (PWB)**. While the hedonic approach (SWB) focuses on happiness, the eudaimonic approach focuses on meaning and self-realisation in terms of the degree to which a person is fully functioning (Ryan & Deci, 2001).

Self-determination theory (SDT; Ryan & Deci, 2000) posits three basic psychological needs – *autonomy*, *competence* and *relatedness* – and suggests that fulfilment of these needs is essential for well-being. Consistent with this approach, fluctuations in the fulfilment of these needs have been demonstrated to predict positive emotions including happiness and vitality (Reis et al., 2000; Sheldon et al., 1996).

According to Ryff's (1989) six-factor model, the core dimensions of psychological well-being are *self-acceptance, positive relations with others, autonomy, environmental mastery, purpose in life* and *personal growth*. These dimensions have been linked to both personality traits and physiological functioning.

Schmutte and Ryff (1997) demonstrated that extraversion, conscientiousness and low neuroticism were linked to self-acceptance, environmental mastery and purpose in life, while openness to experience was associated with personal growth: extraversion and agreeableness were linked to positive relations with others, and low neuroticism was linked to autonomy.

Psychological well-being and positive relationships with others have been linked to lower allostatic load and enhanced vaccine-induced cytokine production (Hayney, Love, Buck, Ryff, Singer & Muller, 2003), as well as lower levels of daily salivary cortisol, pro-inflammatory cytokines, cardiovascular risk and longer REM (rapid eye movement) sleep (Ryff, Singer & Love, 2004). *Subjective* (hedonic) well-being, however, does not appear to be closely tied to biological functioning (Ryff et al., 2004).

Research evaluating relationships between well-being and biological functioning is important because a key hypothesis of positive psychology is that well-being will be associated with optimal functioning of multiple physiological systems and that this biopsychosocial interplay contributes to delaying the onset of morbidity, helping us to maintain functional capabilities and extend periods of quality living (Ryff, Singer & Love, 2004). Ryff and Singer (2000: 30) suggest that probing the physiological substrates of flourishing is important for:

> mapping how positive psychological or relational experience is instantiated in neural circuitry, downstream endocrinological and immunological systems, and ultimately culminates in vitality and longevity.

Ryan and Deci (2001) write that, despite divisions over definitional and philosophical issues, the hedonic and eudaimonic approaches have tended to ask different questions and, therefore, complement each other. They also point out that evidence from a number of investigators has indicated that well-being is probably best conceived as a multidimensional phenomenon including aspects of both the hedonic and eudaimonic conceptions of well-being.

3.3.3 PERSONAL GOALS AND ADAPTATION EFFECTS

Finally, although circumstances typically account for only a small proportion of the variance in well-being, this is not to say that well-being is completely unaffected by environmental factors or life events. For example, although only modest associations have been revealed between income and SWB within nations, those associations are stronger within poorer nations (Diener & Biswas-Diener, 2002). Diener, Diener and Diener (1995) discovered that the degree to which a nation could meet the basic needs of its people (clean water, shelter and healthcare) was a strong predictor of SWB.

Other research has revealed that associations between resources and well-being are stronger when goals are taken into account. For example, Diener and Fujita (1995) assessed the relationships between resources and SWB in 195 college students, and found that, although individual resources were not highly correlated with SWB, resources taken together are moderately strong predictors of SWB, and resources are more closely associated with SWB, when they are relevant to the individual's goals. A tendency was found for people to choose personal goals for which they have relevant resources, and the degree of congruence between individual goals and resources was predictive of SWB.

The importance of attaining goals to well-being might also explain the associations observed between SWB and personality. For example, Hayes and Joseph (2003) suggest that conscientiousness is an important predictor of satisfaction with life because people high in conscientiousness are more able to function effectively in society and achieve their goals. The construct of self-efficacy has also been linked to both well-being and goal motivation. According to Bandura (1986, 1997, 2001) people high in self-efficacy are likely to set more difficult goals for themselves, expend effort to achieve their goals and persevere in the face of obstacles.

Also, the modest impact of life events on SWB is partly due to adaptation processes. Although people may react strongly to life events, over time, well-being drifts back towards the individual's happiness 'set point' (Williams & Thompson, 1993). This adaptation, however, is not necessarily complete. For example, Diener et al. (1999) point out that, although accident victims in the study by Brickman et al. (1978) did not appear as unhappy as might be expected, they did rate themselves as significantly less happy than controls. Diener et al. (1999) also highlight other studies demonstrating an incomplete adaptation to life events. For example, Verbrugge et al. (1994) reported that, although patients with one chronic health problem improved significantly over the year following their discharge from hospital, those with five or more physical health problems worsened during this period. Stroebe, Stroebe, Abakoumkin and Schut (1996) reported that, even after two years, people who had been widowed showed higher levels of depression than those who had not been bereaved.

More recent research also highlights an incomplete adaptation to life events. Lucas and colleagues (2004) found that, although unemployed individuals adapted towards baseline levels of life satisfaction over time, on average, they did not return to their former levels of satisfaction even after they became employed.

Further, adaptation to life events appears to be subject to individual differences. Lucas et al. (2004) revealed that people's initial reaction to unemployment strongly predicted how they would react in the long run. If a person experienced a big drop in satisfaction during unemployment, it was very likely that he or she would remain at a low level of satisfaction after getting a job. Change in satisfaction during the reaction period was moderated by sex, with women reporting less negative reaction to unemployment than men.

Therefore, although people do appear to demonstrate a tremendous capacity to adapt to life events, the *degree* of that adaptation varies as a function of both the initial impact of the event and individual differences.

3.3.4 THE 'FLOW' CONCEPT

While the models discussed above describe the structure of well-being (what distinguishes happy from unhappy individuals), Seligman and Csikszentmihalyi (2000) point out that it is also possible to consider well-being in relation to the process via which moments of happiness arise. According to Csikszentmihalyi, people are happiest when engaged in *autotelic* activities – that is, activities so engrossing or enjoyable they become worth doing for their own sake even though the activity may have no consequence outside itself.

Csikszentmihalyi (1975, 2000) interviewed people who reported pursuing activities for the purpose of enjoyment (chess players, rock climbers, dancers, musicians and others). Some of the participants described their experience of engaging just-manageable challenges as being 'in flow'.

Nakamura and Csikszentmihalyi (2002) suggest that the conditions of **flow** include perceived challenges or opportunities for action that stretch existing skills (neither under- nor overutilising them), a sense that you are engaging challenges at an appropriate level approximate to your capacities, clear proximal goals (knowing clearly what to do next), immediate feedback about the progress that is being made, intense and focused concentration on what you are doing, merging of action and awareness, loss of reflective self-consciousness, a sense that you can control your actions and a sense that time has passed faster than normal. Under these conditions, the individual operates at full capacity and is encouraged to persist with and return to the activity, thereby fostering the growth of skills over time (Nakamura & Csikszentmihalyi, 2002).

Csikszentmihalyi (1999: 824–6) suggests that 'happiness depends on whether a person is able to derive flow from whatever he or she does' and consequently 'people are happy not because of what they do, but because of how they do it. Therefore, if people can experience flow when working on production lines, they are likely to be happy, but if they don't have flow while lounging in a luxury resort, they are unlikely to be happy.

This does not mean, however, that external factors have no impact on well-being. It is evidently easier to experience flow in some situations than in others. For example, Bakker (2005) demonstrated that music teachers working in schools with high levels of autonomy, social support, supervisory coaching and feedback were more likely to experience flow at work than those who did not benefit from such support. Salanova, Bakker and Llorens (2006) demonstrated that both personal resources (self-efficacy) and organisational resources (including social support climate and clear goals) facilitate work-related flow and that it has a positive influence on personal and organisational resources. This bidirectional association between resources and emotional well-being is consistent with the upward spirals described by Fredrickson and Joiner (2002).

SUMMARY AND CONCLUSIONS

3.4

The research discussed in this chapter indicates that both acute emotions and stable dispositions are important for explaining individual differences in psychological and physical functioning. In very general terms, it is evident that:

- positive emotions facilitate adaptive outcomes
- they do this by undoing the physiological effects of negative emotions, broadening the thought–action repertoire and building resources
- positive emotions also influence (and are influenced by) appraisals and coping and are closely tied to meaning-based processes
- the impacts life events have on well-being depends on the emotional impact of the event, time elapsed since the event and individual differences
- the significance of resources for well-being depends on how relevant they are in terms of meeting basic human needs or achieving valued goals.

Evidence of stable individual differences in well-being suggests that some people may find it harder than others to experience positive psychological states. This does not mean that well-being cannot be altered, however. For example, Somerfield and McCrae (2000) point out that, while personality traits themselves may be difficult to change, the behavioural and cognitive styles associated with personality traits are probably more malleable. Cognitive and/or behavioural interventions may also help both to enhance the likelihood of making positive appraisals and finding benefits and to facilitate adaptive coping. Intervention approaches are discussed further in Chapter 7.

KEY TERMS

benefit-finding, broaden and build theory, commonsense model of illness representations, flow, psychological resilience, psychological well-being (PWB), self-determination theory (SDT), subjective well-being (SWB), undoing effect

■Discussion questions ▬▬▬▬▬▬▬▬▬▬▬▬▬▬▬▬▬▬▬▬▬▬▬▬▬▬▬▬

1 If you won the Lottery, do you think it would change your life? Are there aspects of your life that would remain unchanged? How important would the changes be for your well-being?

2 Looking at Table 3.1, consider how chronic illness is likely to influence each component of subjective well-being. Are all the implications for well-being negative or is it possible that some components could change for the better?

3 How can patients be helped to find positive meaning in their experiences?

4 Is it insensitive to encourage positive thinking in patients with chronic or life-threatening conditions? How would you deal with a patient who does not want to find positive meaning in his or her experiences?

FURTHER READING

Csikszentmihalyi, M. (1999). If we are so rich, why aren't we happy? *American Psychologist, 54*, 821–827.

Diener, E., Suh, E.M., Lucas, R.E. & Smith, H.L. (1999). Subjective well-being: three decades of progress. *Psychological Bulletin, 125*, 276–302.

Folkman, S. (1997). Positive psychological states and coping with severe stress. *Social Science Medicine, 45*, 1207–1221.

Fredrickson, B.L. (1998). What good are positive emotions? *Review of general psychology, 2*, 300–319.

Hagger, M.S. & Orbell, S. (2003). A meta-analytic review of the common-sense model of illness representations. *Psychology & Health, 18*, 141–184.

A HEALTHY DISPOSITION

4

OVERVIEW

In the previous chapter we introduced the notion of dispositional processes in health and well-being. This chapter examines the role of dispositional factors in determining disease risk, and considers the following questions. Are some people biologically or psychologically predisposed to ill health? If so, can health outcomes be influenced by behaviour change or psychological interventions? Is the behaviour we try to modify via psychological interventions itself genetically determined?

Finally, we'll examine the issue of genetic testing – what is the impact on a patient of learning that he or she has a genetic vulnerability to a disease such as cancer or diabetes? Does genetic risk information allow patients to take protective action or does it increase risky behaviours (drinking, smoking)? Is it better to test or not to test?

LEARNING OUTCOMES

By the end of this chapter you should be able to:

- describe the structure of the human genome
- explain what is meant by 'genetic disease' and the difference between single-gene, chromosomal and complex or multifactorial disorders

- explain how diseases are inherited

- explain how researchers differentiate environmental from genetic contributions to disease, and discuss the advantages and disadvantages of different research strategies

- describe the implications of the Human Genome Project (HGP) for identifying disease genes, elucidating gene–environment interactions and developing gene-based diagnoses and treatments

- explain what is meant by 'endophenotype'

- describe Waddington's (1957) epigenetic landscape model

- explain the terms 'epigenetics', 'epigenomics' and 'behavioural genetics'

- discuss the psychological and ethical implications of predictive genetic testing.

INTRODUCTION

4.1

As discussed in Chapter 1, the biopsychosocial model of health (Engel, 1977) has implications for not only the way we think about illness and disease but also the development of interventions to prevent or treat ill health.

According to this model, disease cannot be fully explained by deviations from the norm of biological (somatic) variables, but must be understood in relation to complex interrelationships between biological, psychological and social variables. Health outcomes may therefore be altered not only via biological interventions but also psychological and social interventions.

In this chapter, however, we consider the relative importance of biological, psychological and social influences on health more critically, with reference to discoveries arising from the study of genetic processes in health and illness. We consider to what extent individual differences in the risk of disease are genetically predetermined and to what extent they may be shaped by environmental factors (including the psychosocial environment). We also consider the extent to which health-related behaviours, such as drinking and smoking, may be genetically determined. In doing so, we question the extent to which health outcomes (and behavioural predictors of health outcomes) may be amenable to psychological intervention.

Finally, we consider how advances in genetic research will change the way we diagnose and treat disease. The psychological implications of these advances are discussed with a particular focus on predictive genetic testing.

HOW DO GENES INFLUENCE HEALTH?

4.2

In order to understand how genes influence health, it is useful to begin with a basic overview of the structure of the human **genome** ('genome' = the total DNA content that defines an organism), define key terms (such as genetic disease) and consider how disease can be inherited.

4.2.1 WHAT IS A GENE?

Genes are units of genetic information that are made up from **deoxyribonucleic acid (DNA)** found in almost all cells of the human body.

Genes carry instructions for making **proteins** – the basic building blocks of life. Proteins perform all of the body's vital functions, including growth and repair, fighting infections and detoxifying toxins.

Each gene has a specific location on a **chromosome** (a large stretch of DNA). Humans have 23 pairs of chromosomes, with 22 pairs classified as **autosomes** (any chromosome other than a sex chromosome) and 1 pair classified as **sex chromosomes**. Females have two X chromosomes (XX) and males have an X and Y chromosome (XY). During conception, humans receive matched pairs of chromosomes – one chromosome in each pair from each parent. The two chromosomes may have the same form of each gene (homozygous) or different forms (heterozygous). Alternative forms of a gene at a specific chromosomal location are called **alleles** (Graff, 2007; Slagboom & Meulenbelt, 2002).

Apart from identical twins, every individual has a unique set of genes, or, **genotype**. This unique genotype, however, is due to variation in only around one in every thousand DNA letters. *Most* of the DNA letters are the same for *all* human chromosomes and many are the same for other primates, other mammals and even other insects (Plomin, 2002). Further, even identical twins are not identical in **phenotype** (observable characteristics or traits). This is because the phenotype is influenced by both the genotype and environmental factors. The basic structure of the human genome is illustrated in Figure 4.1 and some more information about the above terms is given in Box 4.1.

4.2.2 WHAT IS A GENETIC DISEASE?

Genetic diseases are caused by changes in the genetic material (DNA sequence changes), but not *all* changes in the DNA sequence can cause disease. Changes with no effect on gene function are called **polymorphisms**, while changes with a functional effect on gene function are called **mutations**. Mutations may be either inherited (hereditary mutations) or acquired during a person's lifetime (Graff, 2007; Slagboom & Meulenbelt, 2002). The three major categories for disorders that are caused to

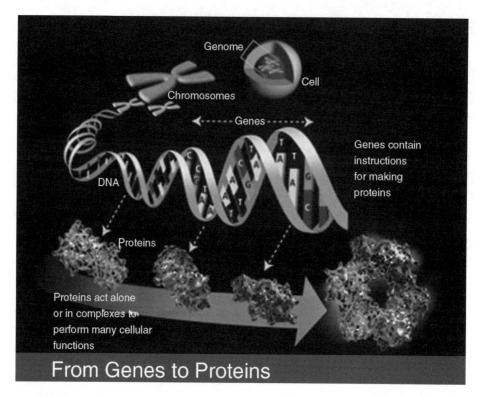

FIGURE 4.1 The structure of the human genome

Source: Human Genome Program, US Department of Energy (2003)

BOX 4.1

The human genome – the entire complement of the genetic material in a cell

DNA (deoxyribonucleic acid)

In most organisms, DNA is the primary material, containing the information for all the hereditary traits of the organism. DNA molecules are polymers consisting of two strands, made up of sequences of four nitrogenous bases (guanine, adenosine, thymine, cytosine), arranged like beads on a long string. The two strands are intertwined to form a double-stranded helix that resembles a spiral staircase. Bases pair together in a fixed order (cytosine (C) opposite guanine (G) and adenosine (A) opposite thymine (T)). The genetic information of a cell is processed from DNA by another polymer – ribonucleic acid (RNA) – into polypeptides that form the basic components of all proteins.

Chromosome

Large stretches of the DNA double helix, together with binding proteins, form a chromosome. In most cells of the human body, the genome contains 3000 million base pairs, arranged in 22 pairs of chromosomes (autosomes) and a pair of X chromosomes or X and Y chromosome (sex chromosomes). For all chromosome numbers (1–22) and the sex chromosomes, offspring obtain a chromosome from each parent, resulting in 22 pairs of autosomes and a pair of sex chromosomes. In contrast to somatic cells, human gametes (sperm and egg cells) have only one copy of each of the 22 autosomes and 1 sex chromosome.

Gene

The complete unit of DNA sequence that is transcribed and translated into a polypeptide, including the DNA sequences that regulate transcription. Together, transcription and trans- lation are known as gene expression. All somatic cells in an organism contain the same set of genes, yet different cell types show differences in cell function and responses to internal and external stimuli. This is entirely brought about by different patterns of expression for the same genes.

Proteins

The functional end points of the DNA template. The linear sequence of four bases contains the code for proteins, rather like the linear sequence of characters of the alphabet contains the words in written language.

Phenotype

The externally or internally detectable characteristics of an organism, including behaviour, that represent the influences of environmental and genetic information (genotype).

Source: Slagboom and Meulenbelt (2002)

some degree by genetic factors are **single-gene, chromosomal** and **complex** or **multifactorial disorders.**

Single-gene disorders (such as cystic fibrosis, sickle cell disease) are caused by a mutation in a single gene, and most follow Mendelian patterns of inheritance (see Box 4.2). Chromosomal disorders (such as Down's syndrome) result from an abnormal number of chromosomes or structural rearrangements of chromosomes; multifactorial disorders (such as schizophrenia and type 1 diabetes) result from complex interactions between genes and the environment. The pattern of inherit- ance for multifactorial disorders is complex and does not follow the Mendelian pattern (Graff, 2007). Damage to DNA during a person's lifetime (acquired mutations) can occur owing to endogenous causes (errors arising in normal cell replication, for example) or exogenous causes, including diet, alcohol, exercise and environmental toxins, including radiation and hazardous substances (Gidron, Russ, Tissarchondou & Warner, 2006).

BOX 4.2

Mendelian genetics

Gregor Mendel's laws of inheritance derived from the study of hybrid plants. Although many earlier biologists had noted the appearance of hybrid plants, it was not known how they arose. Mendel showed that there was a general rule for the appearance of these plants and an exact relationship between the traits displayed by hybrids and those displayed by their parents (Porteous, 2004). This relationship is shown below in the inheritance pattern for hybrid pea plants.

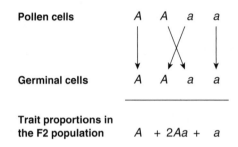

Mendel demonstrated that crossing parental plants with alternative trait forms – (A) and (a) – resulted in a population of plants that were all hybrids (Aa). Each of the hybrid plants in this generation displayed only one of the two alternative parental traits, defined as the dominating trait (A). When these hybrid plants were allowed to self-fertilise, the next generation displayed either the dominating trait (A) or the alternative form, defined as the recessive trait (a). The ratio of dominant to recessive traits was always close to 3:1. When a pollen cell bearing trait (A) or (a) fertilised a germinal cell bearing the same trait, all of their progeny displayed this trait. When a pollen cell bearing trait (A) fertilised a germinal cell bearing the alternative trait (a), or a pollen cell bearing trait (a) fertilised a germinal cell bearing the trait (A), the resulting plant was the hybrid (Aa). Trait proportions in the F2 (second filial progeny) population demonstrated an average distribution of 1:2:1 for the dominant, hybrid and alternative forms (A + 2Aa + a).

Source: Porteous (2004)

4.2.3 HOW ARE DISEASES INHERITED?

The pattern of inheritance in hereditary diseases is determined by both the type of chromosome the abnormal gene resides on (autosomal or sex chromosome) and whether the gene itself is dominant or recessive.

Dominant inheritance occurs when a mutant gene from one parent is sufficient to cause the disease, even if a normal copy is inherited from the other parent. In **autosomal**

dominant diseases, each individual has a 50 per cent chance of passing on the mutant allele to his or her children (since they may inherit either the mutant or normal allele) and if they inherit the mutant allele, they will inherit the disease.

In **autosomal recessive** diseases, each individual must inherit two copies of the mutant gene (one from each parent) to develop the disease. Since each individual has a 50 per cent chance of inheriting the mutant copy from each parent, children of two parents who both carry the gene have a 25 per cent chance of being born with two abnormal chromosomes (and therefore inherit the disease), a 25 per cent chance of being born with two normal chromosomes (healthy, no disease) and a 50 per cent chance of being born with one mutant chromosome and one normal chromosome (carrier, without disease).

Diseases may also be linked to the X chromosome. Since mothers have two X chromosomes and fathers have only one, fathers with an abnormal X chromosome can *only* pass on the mutant gene, whereas mothers have a 50 per cent chance of passing on the mutant gene to their children. Again, if the gene is *dominant*, individuals need only inherit one copy of the mutant gene to inherit the disease – this is referred to as **X-linked dominant inheritance**. If the father has the disease, he will pass on the mutant gene to all of his daughters, but none of his sons (since sons inherit the Y chromosome from their fathers). If the mother has the disease, she has a 50 per cent chance of passing on the mutant gene to each child.

If the gene is recessive, females must inherit two copies of the mutant gene to inherit the disease, but males will inherit the disease if only one mutant gene is inherited (since there is no matched X chromosome) – this is referred to as **X-linked recessive inheritance** (visit: www.nlm.nih.gov/medlineplus/ency/article/002048.htm). Patterns of X-linked inheritance are illustrated in Figure 4.2.

4.2.4 HOW CAN WE DIFFERENTIATE ENVIRONMENTAL FROM GENETIC CONTRIBUTIONS TO DISEASE?

Quantitative genetic strategies are used to determine if, and to what extent, a disease may be heritable. The most basic method involves studying relatives of patients with a particular disorder to determine if they are at greater risk of the disorder than would be expected by chance alone ('familial aggregation studies').

Risch (2001: 733), however, explains that, while family aggregation is a necessary condition to infer the importance of genetic susceptibility, it is not sufficient on its own, 'because environmental and cultural influences can also aggregate in families, leading to family clustering and excess familial risk'. For example, research has demonstrated that the probability of a child being obese is a direct function of the fatness level of remaining family members (Garn, Bailey, Solomon & Hopkins, 1981). Inheritance of obesity, however, can be due to social as well as genetic factors – for example, children inherit beliefs and attitudes towards eating and exercise as well as wealth and other determinants of socio-economic status (Sobal & Stunkard, 1989). Burgner, Jameison and Blackwell (2006) also point out that, in familial aggregation

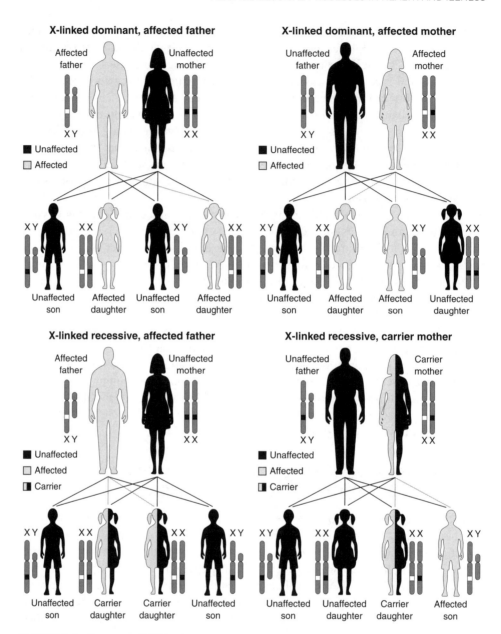

FIGURE 4.2 Patterns of X-linked inheritance

Source: US National Library of Medicine (2010)

studies of infectious diseases, transmission of pathogens between family members may increase the risk of disease and contribute to observed aggregation. Therefore, studies of familial aggregation can provide information about shared determinants (both environmental and genetic) in susceptibility to disease, but no supposition can be made about the causes of such aggregation.

Adoption studies provide a more powerful design for separating the effects of genes and environment because adoption creates a separation between an individual's biological and environmental influences. Since it is difficult to obtain access to information on biological relatives of adoptees, however, adoption studies typically focus only on common disease or trait outcomes (Risch, 2001). Hall, Madden and Lynskey (2002) also explain that it is increasingly difficult to conduct adoption studies since fewer children are available for adoption, except transnationally, and there are ethical concerns about such studies. Further, in some countries the practice is to match biological and adoptive parents on key demographic variables (such as religion or education), resulting in a correlation between genes and environment (Hall et al., 2002).

Alternatively, it is possible to examine genetic influences on health by determining whether identical (**monozygotic, MZ**) twins are more likely to share certain traits than non-identical (**dizygotic, DZ**) twins ('twin studies').

MZ twins derive from a single egg and therefore inherit identical genetic material, while DZ twins derive from two distinct fertilised eggs, so have the same genetic relationship as non-twin siblings, sharing around 50 per cent of their genes. Therefore, it is possible to estimate the heritability of a particular phenotype from twice the difference between MZ and DZ twins – that is, the proportion due to the shared family environment is the difference between the total twin correlation and the part explained by heritability (Boomsma, Busjahn & Peltonen, 2002). For example, for taking up smoking in adolescence, the typical MZ and DZ correlations are 0.9 and 0.7, leading to a heritability estimate of 40 per cent and a shared environment estimate of 50 per cent (0.9–0.4 for MZ or 0.7–0.2 for DZ twins) (Boomsma, Koopmans, van Doornen & Orlebeke, 1994, as cited in Boomsma et al., 2002). Some examples of heritability estimates from twin studies are shown in Figure 4.3.

Although the calculations above assume that environmental and genetic influences can be separated (and, therefore, contribute additive effects), twin data can also be used to study interactions of the genotype with environmental and demographic factors. For example, Heath, Eaves and Martin (1998) found that heritability for depression in married women was lower than in unmarried women, suggesting that environmental influences interact with the genotype to determine the risk of depression (as cited in Boomsma et al., 2002).

Twin studies have also been used to study co-morbidity between traits. For example, twin data suggest that genetic influences underlie the association between personality and alcohol use and abuse (Mustanski, Viken, Kaprio & Rose, 2003) and that most of the genetic vulnerability to abuse of different legal and illegal addictive substances is shared (True et al., 1999; Tsuang et al., 2001, both as cited in Uhl, 2006).

Twin studies are also useful for examining the prenatal programming of the risk of disease. Rose (2005) explains that evidence has accumulated that non-optimal

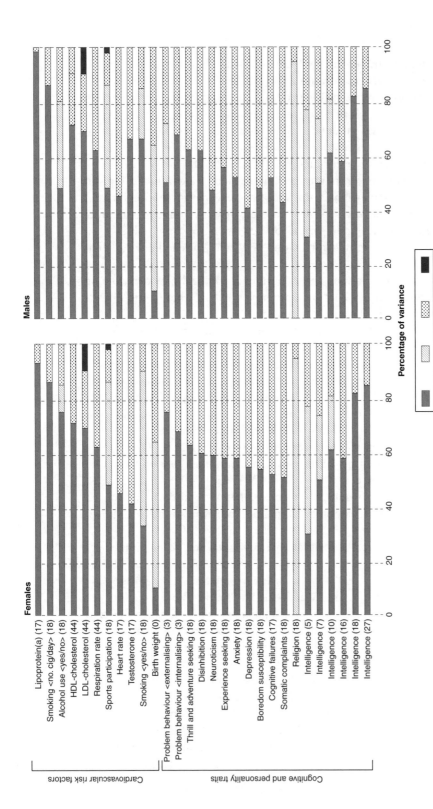

FIGURE 4.3 Examples of results from classical twin analysis. Percentage of variances explained by; genetic factors (dark grey), shared environmental factors (hatched bars), unique environmental influences (dotted bars) and differences in age (dark grey). The number in the brackets gives the modal age of the sample in years. Phenotypes were assessed in Dutch female and male twins (and in some cases also in their parents and siblings).

Source: Boomsma et al. (2002)

foetal growth, indexed by a low birth weight in full-term babies, is predictive of an increased risk of cardiovascular disease, non-insulin dependent diabetes, hypertension and metabolic syndrome, as well as an elevated risk of childhood behaviour problems.

Studies of birth-weight discordant MZ twins can be used to determine whether low birth weight is a causal risk factor or whether the association is due to third-variable confounds that might contribute to both low birth weight and the risk of disease or psychopathology.

Rose (2005) also reports that evidence of an association between low birth weight and disease among weight-discordant MZ twins is mixed, with some studies reporting the lighter twin to be at greater risk of disease, especially diabetes, but others failing to replicate these findings. The link, however, between birth weight and childhood behavioural problems has been confirmed in birth-weight discordant MZ twins. Such findings argue against a third variable cause (Rose, 2005).

Boomsma et al. (2002) write that, in general, for multifactorial traits (such as height and weight, neuroticism and blood lipid levels) and complex diseases (such as obesity, depression and cardiovascular disease), twin studies have shown that genetic factors contribute significantly to the variations seen at the population level. Although lifestyle risk factors, such as diet, smoking and lack of exercise, are often considered 'environmental', they might themselves be influenced by genes, so heritability for a particular disease might reflect the direct influence of disease genes, genes that are responsible for a variation in lifestyle factors or genes that modify the influence of lifestyle on disease risk (Boomsma et al., 2002).

4.3 GENETIC ADVANCES AND IDENTIFYING DISEASE GENES

The genomic DNA sequence of a number of key organisms, including that of Homo sapiens, has been completed. The field of biology has now entered a stage that is commonly referred to as 'post-genomic'.

Carter (2004: 37)

Completed on 14th April 2003, the Human Genome Project (HGP) was a 13-year project, initiated in order to identify all the genes in the human genome and determine the sequences of chemical base pairs that make up human DNA.

The annotated human genome sequence is publically available via the Ensembl database at www.ensembl.org, providing a valuable resource to scientific researchers (Carter, 2004). The sequencing of the human genome has been described as a 'landmark event' in the biomedical sciences (Carter, 2004) and a leap forward 'analogous to the changes brought by the microscope' (Patenaude, Guttmacher & Collins, 2002: 271).

In this section, we will explore the implications of the Human Genome Project (HGP) for identifying disease genes, elucidating gene–environment interactions and developing gene-based diagnoses and treatments.

4.3.1 IDENTIFYING 'DISEASE GENES'

Although quantitative genetic strategies (family studies, twin studies and so on) can help to determine whether or not a disease (or behavioural determinants of disease) might be genetically determined, what they cannot tell us is which gene specifically is responsible for the disease. To determine that, it is necessary to utilise molecular genetic strategies.

Plomin (2002) explains that, rather than studying naturally occurring genetic variation, the origins of molecular genetics lie in research that focused on the gene and how it works using an experimental approach that mutated genes, creating new genetic variation. This approach continues today in gene-targeting research using mice, in which a specific gene is mutated by inserting DNA that makes the gene malfunction.

Plomin (2002), however, points out that knocking out a gene and showing the induced mutation has an effect on the phenotype do *not* mean that naturally occurring DNA differences are responsible for hereditary influence on that phenotype. For example, although knocking out the gene 'leptin' (a gene involved in appetite suppression) makes mice obese, it turns out that naturally occurring DNA variation in this gene does *not* contribute to the substantial heritability of body weight.

The discoveries and techniques derived from the HGP make it easier for researchers to examine naturally occurring DNA differences in order to identify mutations associated with specific traits. Slagboom and Meulenbelt (2002) explain that the DNA sequence information produced as a result of the HGP provides a 'map' for navigating the genomic DNA of patients and families and has greatly facilitated the localisation of disease loci. Once disease genes are narrowed down to a small region of DNA, localised mutations must be demonstrated to be causal to the disease (since many DNA sequence variations in a region of positive linkage will carry DNA sequence variations that may be *neutral* to the disease). The process of localising and subsequently identifying a disease gene is called **positional cloning** (Slagboom & Meulenbelt, 2002).

Positional cloning has, so far, mainly been successful in identifying traits caused by a single locus (Slagboom & Meulenbelt, 2002). Plomin (2002) explains that, although there are thousands of single-gene disorders, these are rare disorders – usually one case in tens of thousands of individuals. In contrast, common disorders, such as obesity and hypertension, which show no signs of single-gene inheritance, are often as frequent as 5 per cent. For these common disorders, it is likely that individual genes contribute incrementally, analogous to probabilistic risk factors. Therefore, common disorders may be 'nothing more than the quantitative extreme of the same genetic and environmental factors that operate throughout the distribution' (Plomin, 2002: 913).

4.3.2 GENE EXPRESSION AND GENE–ENVIRONMENT INTERACTIONS

One of the most surprising findings of the HGP has been that humans only appear to have around 30,000 genes, which is similar to the estimate for mice and earthworms (Carter, 2004; Plomin, 2002). Therefore, the number of genes cannot be responsible for the greater complexity of the human species (Carter, 2004; Plomin, 2002). Rather, the complexity lies in the fine-tuned regulation of **gene expression** – how and when genes are 'switched on' (Slagboom & Meulenbelt, 2002).

Gene–environment and gene–behaviour interactions are thought to play an important role in gene expression. Slagboom and Meulenbelt (2002) write that, when studying the genetics of disease, it is possible to differentiate between mild (relatively symptomless) and severe manifestations. Whether carriers of the mild variant express the disease or trait or not may depend on environmental factors. For example, environment (stress) and behaviour (smoking, drinking, exercise) may influence serum hormone levels, the balance of endo/paracrine cell signals and/or the extracellular micro-environment, thereby revealing or amplifying the effects of existing genetic DNA sequence variations and inducing disease in carriers of disease gene variants (Slagboom & Meulenbelt, 2002).

Psychological factors (such as stress) may also induce disease in otherwise healthy individuals, via DNA damage resulting from unhealthy behaviours (such as smoking) or via biological routes (effects of chronically elevated norepinephrine or inflammatory cytokines) (Gidron, Russ, Tissarchondou & Warner, 2006). Gidron et al. (2006: 303) write that one important implication of such findings is that 'psychological factors may produce changes in the human genome beyond what was encoded by hereditary processes.'

When examining genetic determinants of behaviour, it is also important to acknowledge that individual genes may not be related to observed phenotypes, but, rather, to higher-order variables explaining individual variability in self-reported and observed behaviour (referred to as **endophenotypes**). For example, Lesch (2005) reports that a central serotonin (5-HT) deficit is thought to be involved in the pathogenesis of alcohol dependence by modulating motivational behaviour, neuroadaptive processes and resulting emotional disturbance. Consequently, many studies of the genetic basis of alcohol addiction have focused on the 5-HT transporter (5-HTT) gene. Lesch (2005) explains that, owing to its role in the fine-tuning serotonergic neurotransmission, a regulatory variant of the 5-HTT (which is associated with anxiety-related traits) is a key player in the neurobiological mechanism of gene–environment interaction in the aetiology of depression, and it contributes to the risk of developing alcohol dependence with antisocial behaviour and suicidality.

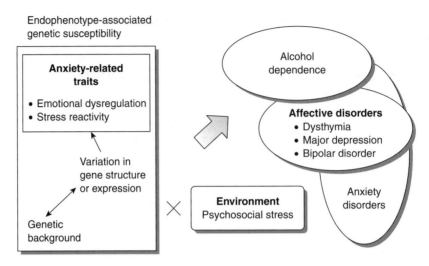

FIGURE 4.4 Causal model of emotional dysregulation as a candidate endophenotype of alcohol dependence

Source: Lesch (2005)

Figure 4.4 depicts a causal model of emotional dysregulation as a candidate endophenotype of alcohol dependence.

There has been considerable debate, however, regarding the role of the 5-HTT gene in depression, and some have argued that depression is purely a result of environmental factors rather than gene–environment interactions (see Box 4.3).

BOX 4.3

Controversies: depression – gene–environment interactions or simply environment?

Caspi et al. (2003) conducted a prospective longitudinal study to determine why stressful experiences result in depression in some individuals but not others. The serotonin system was selected for investigation since it is the target of selective serotonin reuptake inhibitor drugs (SSRIs) that are effective in treating depression. The findings, reported in *Science*, revealed that a functional polymophism in the promotor region of the serotonin transporter gene (5-HTTLPR) moderates the influence of stressful life events on the development of depression. Therefore, depression may be due to interactions between genes and the environment.

These findings, however, were recently called into question. Risch et al. (2009) conducted a meta-analysis of 14 studies that included data on stressful life events, the 5-HTTLPR genotype and depression. The findings indicated that the number of stressful life events was significantly associated with depression, but there was no association between the 5-HTTLPR genotype and depression, either in individual studies or averaged across studies. No interaction between the genotype and stressful life events could be identified. The authors therefore concluded that there is no evidence that the serotonin transporter genotype alone or in combination with stressful life events is associated with an increased risk of depression.

Others, however, have argued that the substantial variation in research methods in this area precludes the use of meta-analysis and that findings need to be considered in relation to methodological issues. A review of 34 studies (Uher & McGuffin, 2010) concluded that the 5-HTTLPR genotype *does* moderate the effect of environmental adversity in the development of depression, but this relationship is most clearly demonstrated when objective measures of adversity are used, as opposed to self-report measures. Findings were also influenced by the heterogeneity of participants, with no evidence of interaction between the 5-HTTLPR genotype and adversity in male adolescents. The authors therefore suggest that 'rather than reaching a premature yes-or-no verdict in a selective meta-analysis, appreciation of methodological heterogeneity and developmental context is needed to further our understanding of the etiology of mental illness' (Uher & McGuffin, 2010: 22).

4.3.3 GENE-BASED DIAGNOSES AND TREATMENT PROGRAMMES

Plomin (2002) suggests that DNA may eventually contribute to gene-based diagnoses and treatment programmes. For example, phenylketonuria (PKU) – a metabolic disorder that results in severe mental retardation – is caused by a single gene on chromosome 12 and can be largely prevented by a change in diet that prevents the mutant DNA from having its damaging effects.

Understanding genetic effects and gene–environment interactions in disease processes could also produce recommendations that certain subgroups avoid defined exposures, and identify the need for screening in order to facilitate early detection of disease in genetically susceptible people (Khoury et al., 2007). Patenaude et al. (2002: 272) suggest that:

> even greater hopes rest on the potential utility of **gene therapy** to fix problems in gene structure and function that lead to cancer and many other diseases. Although these steps are, in most cases, many years in the future, more immediate is the targeting of pharmaceuticals based on an individual's genetic characteristics.

This approach is referred to as **pharmacogenetics** or **pharmacogenomics**.

Carter (2004) writes that many common drug treatments are thought to be effective for only 50–70 per cent of patients and, for cancer, which by its nature exhibits extreme genetic heterogeneity, this may be as low as 25 per cent. Genes responsible for metabolising drugs display considerable genetic variation within populations, and so pharmacogenomic approaches may provide answers that will aid the selection of treatments for individuals with genetic deficiencies in metabolising drugs.

Nicotine replacement therapy (NRT) is also a strong candidate for pharmacogenetic approaches. At best, only one-quarter to one-third of smokers who use NRT to quit smoking will abstain for at least six months, and there is evidence for the role of genetic influences on the ability to quit smoking. Polymorphisms in nicotine metabolising enzymes and selected genes in the neurotransmitter pathways that mediate the effects of nicotine may have predictive validity for people's responses to NRT and so aid the development of tailored therapies (Ray, Schnoll & Lerman, 2007).

In general, then, knowledge of the human genome has the potential to bring improvements to the way in which we develop and implement drug treatments, and it may help to identify individuals who could benefit from preventative (behavioural or medical) interventions (Carter, 2004; Khoury et al., 2007; Plomin, 2002). As Khoury et al. (2007: 314) point out, however:

> the translation of genomic discoveries from the bench to the bedside is a long and arduous process that requires accumulation and synthesis of knowledge in many fields, including observational epidemiologic studies on gene–disease associations, gene–environment interactions, and clinical trials of efficacy of general and genotype-specific interventions.

Further, the possibility that psychological and environmental factors may produce changes in the human genome beyond that encoded by hereditary processes 'obscures the borders between heredity and environment, and complicates their relative etiological contribution to diseases' (Gidron et al., 2006: 303).

For the commonest diseases, therefore, the presence of a genetic mutation is neither necessary nor sufficient to cause the disease, and genetic discoveries do not rule out the need for interventions targeted at making changes to the environment or behaviour. Such interventions may be aided by advances in pharmacogenetics, such as tailored NRT for people attempting to quit smoking.

The relationship between genetics, environment and individual phenotype can be usefully explained with reference to Waddington's (1957) **epigenetic landscape** – shown in Figure 4.5. According to this explanation for variation in phenotypes, an organism, represented by a ball, rolls over an undulating landscape with valleys representing potential phenotypic end points. The shape of the landscape is determined by the individual's genotype, but environmental effects or small random variability at any number of developmental 'choice points' (such as random fluctuations in gene expression at early stages of embryogenesis) can push the organism into a particular phenotypic valley, from which it becomes difficult to emerge (Mitchell, 2007). Theoretically, then, applying environmental forces to the 'ball' via psychological interventions could also alter the developmental trajectory, resulting in different phenotypic end points – changing the individual from 'smoker' to 'non-smoker', for example (West, 2006).

4.3.4 EPIGENETICS, EPIGENOMICS AND BEHAVIOURAL GENETICS

While the term **epigenetics** (introduced in the 1940s) is used to refer to localised changes in gene expression that take place without a change in the DNA sequence, the genomics revolution resulted in the introduction of a new term – **epigenomics**. This term refers to changes in gene expression across many genes in a cell or organism (Jirtle & Skinner, 2007).

A

B

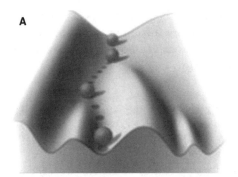
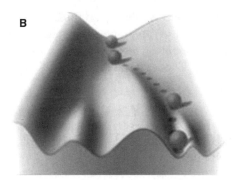

FIGURE 4.5 Waddington's epigenetic landscape

The diagrams illustrate the developmental process in two individuals (labelled A and B) with the same starting genotype (monozygotic twins, for example). Although these two individuals inherit the same probability of developing a certain phenotype, chance events and effects of the environment can result in different phenotype end points.

Source: Mitchell (2007)

The newly established field of **environmental epigenomics** aims to determine 'which human genes are likely to be involved in enhanced disease susceptibility when they are epigenetically deregulated by environmental factors' (Jirtle & Skinner, 2007: 259). The increasing recognition of the role of gene–environment and gene–behaviour interactions in determining gene expression has also contributed to the growth of **behavioural genetics**, defined (Plomin, 2000: 30) as:

> the genetic study of behaviour, which includes quantitative genetics (twin and adoption studies) as well as molecular genetics (DNA studies) of human and animal behaviour broadly defined to include responses of the organism from responses measured in the brain such as functional neuroimaging to self-report questionnaires.

PREDICTIVE GENETIC TESTING

4.4 As discussed above, advances in molecular genetics have important implications not only for conceptualising the relative contributions of genetic and environmental factors in the aetiology of disease but also for identifying and treating disease. Patenaude et al. (2002) write that genetic treatments and prevention strategies will become more fully integrated into clinical medicine as the translation of research findings becomes possible for a growing range of conditions. This revolution involves an important change, from treatments for diseases being based largely on what symptoms people present with, to prevention based on information available at birth in an individual's chromosomes, which means that individuals will have available to them much more specific prognostic information about their personal risks of having many common conditions.

Is this necessarily a good thing? Is it useful to know that one is at risk? (particularly if the disease cannot be prevented or cured)? What are the implications for the family of the person tested? What kinds of ethical issues are raised by **predictive genetic testing**? These questions are considered further below.

4.4.1 THE PSYCHOLOGICAL IMPLICATIONS OF GENETIC TESTING

Patenaude et al. (2002) highlight that, as tests are developed for a growing range of conditions, it will be important to consider the emotional impact of coping with our risk of having a number of illnesses years before their expected onset. Here, the task will be both determining how the notification of that risk affects attitudes and quality of life, and developing behavioural interventions to help people cope with their increased, but still incomplete, knowledge of what will happen. Psychologists will therefore play an increasingly important role.

The psychological impact of genetic risk information is complicated by the fact that a positive test result does not necessarily indicate that the individual *will* develop the disease in their lifetime or that anything can be done to prevent the illness. Shiloh, Ben-Sinai and Keinan (1999) write that, in some cases, such as predictive testing for Huntington's disease (HD), it is almost certain that carriers of the disease gene will eventually become sick and non-carriers will remain disease-free, but no measure can be taken to prevent, control or postpone the disease. In other cases, such as breast cancer, predictability can increase control of the disease (by extra surveillance to detect it early or by preventative mastectomy), but test results do not provide certainty that carriers *will* become sick or non-carriers will *not* develop the disease.

It is also important to determine how people respond to negative test results, since a negative test result for multifactorial diseases does not indicate that the individual will never develop the disease, and because for some diseases, such as breast cancer, it is important to remain vigilant and attend for screening. Alternatively, for some conditions, such as bowel cancer, the population risk is very low, and screening is not routinely recommended (Michie et al., 2002).

The individual must therefore be able to understand the implications of both positive and negative test results and utilise this information to make informed choices. The implications of positive and negative test results are discussed further below in relation to predictive genetic testing for Huntington's disease, breast cancer, ovarian cancer and colorectal cancer.

4.4.2 HUNTINGTON'S DISEASE

Even in the case of Huntington's disease, genetic testing may result in an uncertain prognosis. Van den Boer et al. (2001) explain that, for several years, Huntington's disease served as a paradigm for presymptomatic testing for hereditary diseases.

Huntington's disease is caused by a defective gene on chromosome four, in which the sequence CAG is repeated many times. It was thought that allele sizes of ≥ 40

CAG repeats lead to Huntington's disease while allele sizes < 40 do not, but, as Van den Boer et al. (2001) explain, allele sizes of 36–39 repeats are sometimes (but not always) associated with HD. There is also evidence that allele sizes sometimes show mutability, so an allele size of < 36 could change into an HD allele in the next generation. This means that patients with 36–39 repeats cannot have predictive certainty about their HD status from their test outcome and patients with < 36 repeats cannot be certain of the HD status of their offspring. It is not known what a safe margin is in the case of mutable CAG repeats and we do not know how or why an allele becomes unstable (Van den Boer et al., 2001).

Since nothing can be done to prevent HD, concerns have been raised that genetic testing may increase the risk of suicide. Meiser and Dunn (2000) report, however, that carriers and non-carriers do not differ significantly in terms of long-term psychological distress and that adjusting to the results is more dependent on psychological adjustment prior to testing than on the test result itself. They also highlight, however, that there is evidence that people who choose to be tested are psychologically selected for their likely favourable response to testing and the impact of testing on people in settings where less intensive counselling and eligibility protocols are used is unknown. They recommend, therefore, that genetic testing for HD is best offered as part of a comprehensive specialist counselling process.

The lack of a significant difference between carriers and non-carriers may also indicate coping by means of avoidance in carriers. For example, Decruyenaere et al. (2003) found that, although carriers did not differ from non-carriers in terms of distress five years after testing, they did report significantly less positive feelings and were more consciously avoiding HD-related situations and thoughts. Thus, Decruyenaere et al. (2003) suggest that post-test counselling should reinforce individuals' competence, raise their level of personal control over their lives and encourage them to actively cope with problems.

4.4.3 BREAST AND OVARIAN CANCER

Two disease-linked genes have been identified for breast cancer: the BRCA1 gene, located on chromosome 17, and the BRCA2 gene, on chromosome 13. The risk of breast cancer in women carrying a BRCA1/2 mutation is between 56 and 85 per cent. BRCA1/2 mutations also confer an increased risk of ovarian cancer – of between 20 and 60 per cent (Patenaude et al., 2002).

Most studies that have assessed the psychological impact of genetic testing for BRCA1/2 mutations indicate that non-carriers derive psychological benefits from testing, while no adverse effects are seen in carriers unaffected by cancer, but that women with a positive test result experience significant distress – even when they *anticipate* that the result will be positive (see Meiser, 2005, for a review). Studies of responses to BRCA1/2 testing also indicate that the uptake of prophylactic mastectomy and oophorectomy (surgical removal of breasts and ovaries) varies widely among unaffected BRCA1/2 mutation carriers. Also, among unaffected BRCA1/2 mutation carriers who do not opt for prophylactic surgery, studies show statistically significant increases in the uptake of annual mamographic screening following the genetic testing (Meiser, 2005).

4.4.4 COLORECTAL (BOWEL) CANCER

Genetic testing is also available for familial adenomatous polyposis (FAP) and hereditary nonpolyposis colorectal cancer (HNCC) – both risk factors for colorectal cancer (also called colon cancer or bowel cancer).

Studies evaluating the psychological and behavioural impacts of HNPCC testing indicate that unaffected non-carriers derive psychological benefits, and changes in levels of distress among carriers are only temporary. Further, the majority of carriers adopt appropriate screening behaviours after a positive test result, although a minority show hyper- or hypovigilant behaviour (reviewed by Meiser, 2005).

Patients' understanding of negative test results may be limited. Michie et al. (2002) found that, among individuals who had received a negative genetic test for FAP, about a third reported being likely to attend future bowel screening. This is despite a negative result meaning that they have a less than 1 per cent probability of having FAP and a population risk of 1:7500 of developing bowel cancer, and despite bowel screening being perceived as aversive. Those expecting to attend also perceived the genetic test to be less accurate and its results to be less certain and more threatening, and they attributed the causes of FAP more to behavioural factors than those who did not expect to attend.

These findings indicate that negative genetic test results may fail to reassure. Michie et al. (2002) suggest that, when testing is discussed, it may be helpful to elicit – and, if necessary, change – people's cognitions about the causes of the illness, accuracy of the test and certainty of the results (Michie et al., 2003). The emotional impact of testing is also influenced by the individual's level of psychological resources and so additional support and counselling may be necessary for those with low levels of such resources – see Research in focus box 4.1.

RESEARCH IN FOCUS BOX 4.1

Michie, Bobrow and Marteau (2001) evaluated the emotional impact of predictive genetic testing for familial adenomatous polyposis (FAP) in children and adults.

Methodology

A total of 208 unaffected subjects (148 adults and 60 children) at risk of developing FAP who had undergone genetic testing since 1990 completed measures of anxiety, depression, situational distress, perceived threat of test results and psychological resources (optimism, self-efficacy).

Results

In children who received negative results, levels of depression and anxiety were in the normal range and there was a trend for children receiving positive results to be more anxious and depressed than those receiving negative results. Children receiving positive or negative test results did not experience greater anxiety or depression than adults.

Adults receiving positive test results were highly anxious, with scores in the clinical range. The mean scores for depression and anxiety were in the normal range for adults receiving a negative test result. Regardless of the test results, adults were more likely to be clinically anxious if they were low in either optimism or self-esteem, and there were interactions between test result and psychological resources that were predictive of the frequency of clinical cases of anxiety.

Children and adults receiving positive results perceived their chance of getting FAP as higher, worried more about this and felt more threatened by their results than those receiving negative test results.

Conclusions and implications

The findings suggest that the children understood the significance of a positive test result and, in the short term at least, there were no adverse psychological consequences for children undergoing predictive testing for FAP.

The authors recommend that levels of care and support currently in place for children should be maintained, but adults with a positive test result would benefit from *more* support and counselling. Pre-test screening for psychological resources could be used as a basis for targeting this help at those most likely to experience high levels of anxiety.

4.4.5 IMPLICATIONS FOR RELATIVES

Armstrong, Michie and Marteau (1998) point out that genetic risk information is different from other types of risk information in that the identification of a problem in one person has implications for biologically related relatives. This link is important in the management of genetic problems as the 'illness' is not localised to the patient and, in the case of 'carrier' status, the patient may be unaffected by the genetic anomaly. Also, Patenaude et al. (2002) point out that, in families in which conditions such as breast and ovarian cancer occur with higher than expected frequency, family members may in the past have considered themselves to be at high risk. Now, however, genetic testing may divide the family into those at risk and those without the BRCA1/2 mutation, who are only at the population risk of approximately 10 per cent. Family members with the mutation must worry not only about themselves but also about passing on mutations to their children and grandchildren, while family members without the mutation are spared these fears.

It is not surprising, then, that uptake of genetic testing and the emotional consequences of it are influenced by both individual patient characteristics and family characteristics. For example, studies on the uptake of genetic testing for BRCA1/2 and HNPCC-related mutations show that disease status (affected v. unaffected with cancer), psychological factors (cancer-related anxiety or distress, perceived risk) and strength of family history (number of relatives diagnosed with cancer) are consistently related to the uptake of testing. Also, the risk factors for psychological distress following genetic testing include psychological factors (such as high levels of distress prior to testing, and past history of major or minor depression) and family factors (having lost a relative to hereditary cancer, those tested first in the family and those whose results differed from those of their siblings were most vulnerable, women with young children) (Meiser, 2005).

4.4.6 ETHICAL CONSIDERATIONS

Patenaude et al. (2002) also point out that genetic advances bring with them a number of ethical quandaries – whether it is ethical to offer genetic tests, what information people should be given about the limitations and risks of testing, who should be informed about genetic testing results and whether or not access to test results should be available to outside parties, such as employers and insurers.

Psychologists, working together with genetic counsellors, may provide a useful service in helping to find a resolution between the autonomy of relatives – who may not wish to take part in genetic testing – and the interests of the patient – for whom the test results of relatives may provide important information regarding the nature and location of familial mutation.

Patenaude et al. (2002) also suggest that psychological research may help to identify what characterises women who opt for prophylactic surgery following BRCA1/2 testing and those for whom this is undesirable, in order to develop interventions to aid women and professionals in the decisionmaking process.

SUMMARY

4.5

Advances in genetic research have implications for the way in which diseases are identified, treated and potentially prevented. The significance of such advances extend beyond the field of genetics – impacting all professions concerned with health-related research, disease prevention (at an individual or population level) and patient care.

For psychologists, genetic research has important implications in terms of both increasing understanding of the genetic determinants of personality traits and behaviours and delineating behavioural and biological routes via which traits and behaviours influence disease. Genetic research is also starting to uncover interactions between genes, behaviours and environments in determining disease onset and symptomatology. Research findings indicate that genetic factors contribute significantly to the variation seen at population level in relation to complex diseases. This does not rule out a role of psychological variables, however, since psychological factors can induce disease in both carriers of disease gene variants (by influencing gene expression) and non-carriers (via DNA damage resulting from unhealthy behaviours or the biological effects of stress).

At some point in the future, it may be possible to alter genetic susceptibility to disease via gene therapy. For many diseases, however, it is likely that fixing problems in gene structure and function will have a relatively small impact on susceptibility, since disease risk may be influenced by a number of genes, which may contribute additive and interactive effects, and the expression of these genes may depend in part on environmental influences. In the meantime, the major modifiable risk factors for chronic disease are behavioural, rather than biological. Therefore, it is important that psychological interventions keep pace with developments in genetic research (offering interventions that are tailored to individuals' genetic risk profiles) and taking into account each individual's personal model of the illness, which (with the rising profile of genetic research) may increasingly include genetic causal explanations.

Psychological approaches to preventing disease may also benefit from advances in pharmacogenetic research, such as supplementing psychological support for stopping smoking with individually tailored NRT. The application of psychology to the challenge of chronic illness will also become increasingly important as more individuals are able to obtain knowledge of their genetic risks before developing a disease. This means that individuals will need to cope with not only the experience of illness but also the emotional consequences of discovering that they are at increased risk of illness in the future, and even that they may have been spared the increased risk conferred by genetic mutations affecting other family members. The psychological and ethical implications of advances in genetic research and the increasing application of this research are likely to keep psychologists, medics and policymakers busy for many years to come.

KEY TERMS

alleles, autosome, autosomal dominant inheritance, autosomal recessive inheritance, behavioural genetics, chromosome, chromosomal disorders, complex or multifactorial disorders, deoxyribonucleic acid (DNA), dizygotic (DZ) twins, endophenotype, environmental epigenomics, epigenetic landscape, epigenetics, epigenomics, genes, genome, genotype, gene expression, gene therapy, monozygotic (MZ) twins, mutations, pharmacogenetics or pharmacogenomics, phenotype, polymorphisms, positional cloning, predictive genetic testing, proteins, sex chromosomes, single-gene disorders, X-linked dominant inheritance, X-linked recessive inheritance

■ **Discussion questions**

1 How could knowledge of the genetic basis of personality and behaviour influence the design of psychological interventions?

2 Would you want to know if you were at risk of a disease that could not be prevented? How might such information have a positive or negative impact on your quality of life?

3 What would be the implications for your family if you decided to be tested for a genetic disorder?

4 Should children be offered genetic testing for untreatable conditions?

FURTHER READING

Carter, N.M. (2004). Implications for medicine in the 'post-genomic era'. *Current Anaesthesia and Critical Care, 15*, 37–43.

Gidron, Y., Russ, K., Tissarchondou, H. & Warner, J. (2006). The relation between psychological factors and DNA damage: a critical review. *Biological Psychology, 72*, 291–304.

Meiser, B. (2005). Psychological impact of genetic testing for cancer susceptibility: an update of the literature. *Psycho-Oncology, 14*, 1060–1074.

Plomin, R. (2002). Individual differences research in a post-genomic era. *Personality and Individual Differences, 33*, 909–920.

Slagboom, P.E. & Meulenbelt, I. (2002). Organisation of the human genome and our tools for identifying disease genes. *Biological Psychology, 61*, 11–31.

PAIN

5

OVERVIEW

This chapter examines one aspect of experience where psychological and biological processes are particularly closely related – the experience of pain.

We begin by considering what the word 'pain' actually means. Is pain an emotional or a sensory experience? Does pain necessarily have to have a physical cause? How can we measure pain? How can individuals describe their pain to others in an objective manner? Is acute pain different from chronic pain?

We then go on to examine theories of pain and biopsychosocial aspects of pain and consider the implications of these theories for development of interventions.

LEARNING OUTCOMES

By the end of this chapter you should be able to:

- discuss the complexities involved in defining and measuring pain in both the research and clinical contexts

- describe commonly used measurement tools, their relative advantages and disadvantages and the contexts in which they may be used

- describe the difficulties faced by patients with pain and those caring for patients with pain, particularly in relation to communication and emotional support

- differentiate between acute and chronic pain

- differentiate between nociceptive and neuropathic pain

- describe common neuropathic pain syndromes

- explain the term 'referred pain' and describe the underlying mechanisms

- explain the importance of psychological variables for predicting long-term disability in patients with pain

- compare and contrast theories of pain and consider to what extent pain theories account for the influence of psychological and biological processes

- describe pharmacological and non-pharmacological therapies for pain, and discuss the relative advantages and disadvantages of different therapeutic approaches.

WHAT IS PAIN?

5.1 Imagine that you had to explain what the word 'pain' means to someone who had never experienced pain themselves. How would you describe it? How exactly does it feel? Is pain a sensory experience (like heat or cold) or an emotional experience (like distress or fear)? How does the pain of a headache differ from the pain of a physical injury, such as cut or burn? Does pain necessarily indicate damage to the body tissues? Would two people with the same tissue damage experience the same level of pain? How can we tell if another person's experience of pain is the same as our own?

These are questions that have troubled researchers for many years. In the following sections, we attempt to provide answers to these questions, first considering the defining features of pain, then examining different types of pain and theories put forward to explain the mechanisms underlying the experience of pain. We also consider how these theoretical models and the research evidence supporting them can help us to develop interventions to alleviate pain or improve how we cope with pain.

5.1.1 DEFINING PAIN

Researchers have struggled to arrive at a definition that adequately describes the complexity of the phenomenon we label 'pain'. For example, in a review of the literature, Summers (2000) identified several different definitions of pain. These are shown in Table 5.1. Summers (2000) writes that, in general, there is most consensus for the IASP (1979) definition, so, this is the definition we will use throughout this chapter.

TABLE 5.1 Definitions of pain

Reference	Definition of pain
Sternbeck (1968)	An abstract concept that refers to a personal, private sensation or hurt; a harmful stimulus that signifies current or impending tissue damage; and a pattern of impulses that operates to protect the organism from harm
International Association for the Study of Pain (IASP, 1979)	An unpleasant sensory and emotional experience associated with actual or potential tissue damage or described in terms of such damage
Fields (1987)	An unpleasant sensation that is perceived as arising from a specific region of the body and is commonly produced by processes which damage or are capable of damaging body tissues
McCaffery and Beebe (1989)	Subjective, and is whatever the experiencing person says it is, existing whenever the experiencing person says it does
Bonica (1990)	The subjective description of pain as well as when it is relieved

Source: Summers (2000)

According to this definition pain is:

• unpleasant
• both sensory and emotional
• potentially (but not necessarily) associated with tissue damage
• subjective.

Models describing the mechanisms underlying the experience of pain must therefore account for all of these features of pain.

5.1.2 RECOGNISING PAIN IN OTHERS

Since pain is subjective, only the person experiencing the pain can tell us how much pain he or she feels. Therefore, it is important that that person is believed. Despite this, Summers (2000) notes that the results of pain management reviews indicate that many patients are undermedicated and healthcare providers do not always believe patients have pain.

This problem is even more evident when we consider evidence relating to patients with cognitive impairment who may not be able to communicate their experience of pain in the same way as those without such difficulties. For example, the UK charity MENCAP recently highlighted the cases of six cognitively impaired adults who, they believe, died because healthcare professionals were unable to recognise their pain and distress and did not consult with or involve the families, who could have provided vital information to help doctors and nurses decide on appropriate treatment (MENCAP, 2007). This report highlights the crucial importance of listening to patients and their families and conducting thorough pain assessments in order to inform diagnosis and treatment.

Even for patients without cognitive impairment, it may be difficult to put the experience of pain into words. Schott (2004: 209) argues that 'pain is intrinsically impossible to convey to others and therefore language will always prove inadequate.' This difficulty with putting painful experiences into words is not something peculiar to pain, but, Schott argues, is similar to the difficulties with expressing other unpleasant sensory and emotional experiences, such as the schizophrenic who attempts to describe his auditory hallucinations or the epileptic his olfactory aura.

Pain is particularly difficult to convey to someone who has not had experience of it. For example, Schott points out that the pain of angina will be hard to convey to anyone who has not experienced myocardial ischaemia, and many women view the pains of childbirth as unimaginable to those who have not given birth. Schott also argues that when descriptors of pain are used, the meaning of these descriptors may vary for different patients and different experiences of pain. For example, a scald from boiling water might be described as 'burning', but this might be a very different burning sensation to that described by a patient with a different type of injury.

Since experiences of pain are difficult to communicate, caregivers' perceptions of patients' pain may differ considerably from patients' ratings of their own pain (Cano, Johansen & Geisser, 2004). Incongruence between patients' and caregivers' ratings of pain may have significant implications for both coping and health outcomes. In particular, a wide body of research has focused on the association between **catastrophising** (a coping strategy aimed at increasing attention or empathy from others (Sullivan, Trip & Santor, 2000)), caregiver support and health outcomes in pain patients.

Catastrophising has been associated with negative outcomes such as greater interference of pain in daily activities and increased use of pain medication (Sullivan et al., 2000). Boothby and Colleagues (2004) have also demonstrated that catastrophising is associated with negative responses to pain behaviours (such as expressing irritation or anger or ignoring the patient). Ciechanowski et al. (2003) further revealed associations between catastrophising, a fearful attachment style and depression in patients with chronic pain. It is possible, therefore, that an inability to communicate pain effectively may result in inadequate support from the caregivers, which leads to greater levels of catastrophising, increased distress and poorer health outcomes. Alternatively, catastrophising may lead to negative responses from caregivers, which then results in increased distress and poorer health outcomes.

Given the associations between social support, catastrophising and health outcomes, a number of researchers have suggested that chronic pain patients should receive skills training or therapy aimed at enhancing communication with caregivers and improving caregivers' responses to pain behaviours (Boothby et al., 2004; Thorn, Boothby & Sullivan, 2002, for example).

Researchers have also recommended that healthcare providers are trained to recognise non-verbal signs of pain (either chronic or acute) in patients. Non-verbal signs of pain, for example, movements or noises of women in labour, may be shaped by cultural norms and it is important that caregivers are aware of these influences so that culturally sensitive care can be provided (Trout, 2004).

How pain is communicated may also differ according to gender, socialisation and self-efficacy (Miller & Newton, 2006). Therefore, although it is important to remember that 'pain is whatever the experiencing person says it is' (McCaffery, 1968: 95), caregivers should also be sensitive to individual differences in communication styles.

5.1.3 MEASURING PAIN

The measurement of pain is complex and a number of measures have been developed and validated for use in different contexts with different populations.

Visual analogue scales (VAS) are commonly used to assess pain in clinical settings. These require patients to indicate their level of pain by placing a mark on a 10-cm line with anchors at either end ('no pain', 'worst possible pain' for example).

Alternatively, pain intensity can be rated using a numerical rating scale (NRS) (rating pain intensity from 0 to 10, for example) or using a verbal rating scale (VRS) with pain descriptors representing increasing intensity of pain (such as mild, discomforting, distressing, horrible, excruciating).

Alternative forms have also been developed for young children and patients with cognitive impairment, such as using visual depictions of faces to represent increasing levels of pain (Bieri et al., 1990; Herr, Mobily, Kohout & Wagenaar, 1998). Examples of these scales are shown in Figure 5.1.

Unidimensional scales have been criticised, however, because patients find it difficult to separate somatosensory and emotional aspects of pain and do not differentiate between the intensity of their pain and the distress caused by pain when asked to complete these measures. Therefore, although these scales are purported to measure the intensity of pain, scores more likely reflect a combination of sensory, emotional and other pain qualities (Knotkova, Clark, Mokrejs, Padour & Kuhl, 2004).

Thus, multidimensional measures have been developed to evaluate somatosensory and affective aspects of pain as separate constructs. For example, the McGill pain questionnaire (MPQ; Melzack, 1975) includes a pain drawing, a numerical intensity scale and a list of 20 pain descriptors. These descriptors tap the sensory, affective and evaluative dimensions of a person's pain. More recently, Melzack (1987) developed a short-form MPQ. This includes 15 pain descriptors, together with a visual analogue scale and a verbal rating scale, as shown in Figure 5.1.

Measures of pain in neonates tend to rely on identification of facial expressions and behaviours associated with pain. For example, the neonatal facial coding system (NFCS; Grunau & Craig, 1987; Grunau, Johnston & Kenneth, 1990) has been used

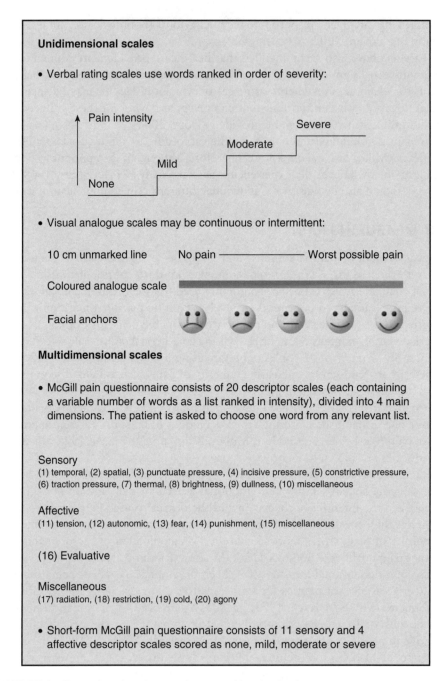

Unidimensional scales

- Verbal rating scales use words ranked in order of severity:

    Pain intensity

                                                    Severe

                                    Moderate

                    Mild

    None

- Visual analogue scales may be continuous or intermittent:

    10 cm unmarked line   No pain ————————— Worst possible pain

    Coloured analogue scale

    Facial anchors

Multidimensional scales

- McGill pain questionnaire consists of 20 descriptor scales (each containing
  a variable number of words as a list ranked in intensity), divided into 4 main
  dimensions. The patient is asked to choose one word from any relevant list.

Sensory
(1) temporal, (2) spatial, (3) punctuate pressure, (4) incisive pressure, (5) constrictive pressure,
(6) traction pressure, (7) thermal, (8) brightness, (9) dullness, (10) miscellaneous

Affective
(11) tension, (12) autonomic, (13) fear, (14) punishment, (15) miscellaneous

(16) Evaluative

Miscellaneous
(17) radiation, (18) restriction, (19) cold, (20) agony

- Short-form McGill pain questionnaire consists of 11 sensory and 4
  affective descriptor scales scored as none, mild, moderate or severe

FIGURE 5.1   Examples of scales used to record levels of pain

Source: Holdcroft and Power (2003)

to study pain behaviour of full-term, pre-term and older infants. Facial expressions coded using the NFCS have been demonstrated to be more specific to tissue damage than heart rate (Grunau, Oberlander, Holsti & Whitfield, 1998).

Also, the CRIES (Bildner & Krechel, 1996) instrument was developed to measure post-operative pain in infants up to six months of age, and provides a score for each of the following:

- Crying
- oxygen Requirement
- Increased vital signs
- Expression
- Sleeplessness

Assessment of pain in neonates is discussed further in Box 5.1.

King and McCool (2004) argue that, even in adults, *behavioural* responses to pain may be more critical indicators of pain than VAS scores, particularly in the case of acute, intense pain, where there may be no time to develop individualised responses. Where VAS scores *are* used to measure pain, they argue that it is impor-tant behavioural responses are not ignored. Pain behaviours may include grimacing, moaning, bracing, body stiffness and verbal complaints (Fordyce, 1976). These may be evaluated via unstructured observation of the patient or using formal scoring systems, such as the pain behaviour checklist (Kerns et al., 1991). As discussed in the previous section, an evaluation of pain behaviours should include a considera-tion of cultural and demographic differences influencing pain communication – a patient displaying few pain behaviours may still be experiencing pain.

BOX 5.1

Controversies: how should we assess and respond to pain in neonates?

Research focusing on pain in neonates has highlighted problems with the way pain is defined or conceptualised, assessed and treated. For example, Anand and Craig (1996) highlighted several problems in the widely accepted IASP definition of pain when applied to neonates and suggested that the reliance on self-reporting may have led to failure to acknowledge and treat pain in infants and young children.

In response to these concerns, the IASP has added a note to the definition of pain, stating that, 'The inability to communicate verbally does not negate the possibility that an individual is experiencing pain and is in need of appropriate pain-relieving treatment' (www.iasp-pain.org). Recent reports, however, acknowledge that pain-relieving treatments are still underused, par-ticularly in relation to the numerous minor procedures that are part of routine care for neonates (American Academy of Pediatrics, 2006).

(Cont'd)

In the absence of a verbal report, the assessment of pain in neonates relies on a combination of behavioural and physiological indicators. Ranger, Johnston and Anand (2007) point out that, although more than 40 pain assessment tools are available to measure pain in neonates, no single measure has demonstrated superiority over the others and no specific measure has been set as the 'gold standard' for pain assessment of infants in research or clinical practice. Further, although most assessment instruments incorporate both behavioural and physiological indicators, dissociation between these two classes of measures has been reported, with some interventions producing opposite effects on behavioural and physiological responses (such as reduced facial expression of pain, with increased heart rate). These effects can be difficult to interpret. The assessment of pain in neonates is also complicated by the fact that behavioural indicators of pain may be absent in some neonates, and responses to painful procedures are influenced by age, sleep/wake state and previous exposure to pain (Ranger et al., 2007).

In recognition of these challenges, the American Academy of Pediatrics (2006) has published recommendations for the prevention and management of pain in the neonate. These include recommendations for the assessment of pain and stress in the neonate and reducing pain from bedside care procedures, surgery and other major procedures.

Recommendations for reducing pain in relation to minor routine procedures include the use of both pharmacological and non-pharmacological treatments. Non-pharmacological treatments demonstrated to alleviate pain in neonates include the use of oral sucrose or glucose, non-nutritive sucking, kangaroo care (skin-to-skin contact), facilitated tuck (holding the arms and legs in a flexed position), swaddling and developmental care (which includes limiting environmental stimuli, lateral positioning, use of supportive bedding and attention to behavioural cues). See American Academy of Pediatrics (2006) for further discussion.

5.1.4 CATEGORISING PAIN

One reason it is so difficult to define and measure pain is that the word itself encompasses a wide range of diverse experiences. Russo and Brose (1998) write that the importance of defining pain as an experience rather than a sensation lies in recognising that *sensations*, neuroanatomically, have discrete pathways with specific receptors to allow for the detection and measurement of a stimulus. In contrast, an *experience* incorporates sensory components together with environmental and personality influences. The sensory component of pain is described as **nociception** – the physiological response to tissue injury.

Pain is commonly described as acute or chronic. Loeser and Melzack (1999) write that **acute pain** is elicited by substantial injury to body tissue and activation of **nociceptive transducers** (peripheral terminals of **nociceptors**) at the site of the tissue damage. The local injury does not overwhelm the body's reparative mechanisms, and healing can occur without medical intervention. Intervention may be useful, however, to speed healing or prevent or reduce pain.

Acute pain is seen after trauma, surgical interventions and some diseases. The term **chronic pain** refers to that which persists beyond the normal time of healing. Three months is the usual point of division between acute and chronic pain, although six months is normally used for research purposes (Merskey & Bogduk, 1994).

Loeser and Melzack (1999), however, suggest that it is not the *duration* of pain that distinguishes chronic from acute pain, but the inability of the body to restore its physiological functions to normal homeostatic levels. Similarly, Von Korff and Miglioretti (2005) point out that defining chronic pain by duration alone does not uniformly identify clinically significant pain problems. They suggest, therefore, that a prognostic approach to defining chronic pain might be more useful. This shifts the focus from the history of the pain to future outcomes, assessing patients in terms of both the severity of their pain and risk factors for unfavourable outcomes.

According to the prognostic approach, chronic pain should be considered as a dynamic state rather than a static trait, since outcomes are highly variable across patients and over time. A number of studies have highlighted the importance of psychological variables for predicting long-term disability in patients with pain (for example, see Research in focus box 5.1), and 'yellow flag' systems have been developed to identify patients at greatest risk (Hallner & Hasenbring, 2004; Linton & Hallden, 1997).

RESEARCH IN FOCUS BOX 5.1

Young Casey, Greenberg, Nicassio, Harpin and Hubbard (2008) evaluated a theoretically and empirically based model of the progression of acute neck and back pain to chronic pain and disability.

Methodology

Eighty-four patients attending an acute back pain clinic for new onset back or neck pain (of less than eight weeks' duration) completed questionnaires at baseline and three months later. The questionnaires assessed pain intensity, pain disability, cumulative trauma exposure (administered at baseline only), depression and beliefs about pain. The patients were also asked to report their utilisation of pain-related treatments and services, medications and complementary or alternative treatments. Hierarchical multiple regression analyses were used to predict pain and disability at three-month follow-up from the baseline measures.

Results

Cumulative exposure to trauma and depressive symptomatology at baseline independently and significantly predicted greater pain at follow-up, over and beyond the initial duration of the pain. Baseline depression, pain permanence beliefs and chronic pain intensity were significant and independent predictors of three-month disability. Depression mediated (accounted for) the effect of baseline disability on three-month disability.

(Cont'd)

Conclusions and implications

The findings suggest that cognitive, affective and trauma factors assessed at baseline can reliably predict the transition from acute to chronic pain and disability. Screening for these factors may therefore be important for preventing chronic pain. The authors suggest that exposure to trauma may be linked to chronic pain via the impacts of trauma on brain structures or anxiety on information processing. Further research is necessary to extend the current findings to diverse pain samples and evaluate mechanisms underlying associations between predictor and outcome variables.

Psychological variables can be considered as both input (contributing to the development of chronic pain and pain-related disability) and output (resulting from chronic pain and pain-related disability). Turk and Okifuji (2002) write that chronic pain will influence all aspects of a person's functioning – emotional, interpersonal, avocational and physical.

Psychological processes important for understanding the individual variability in pain-related disability include an interpretation of nociceptive input, the meaning attributed to pain and behavioural responses to it. For example, fear of pain is associated with avoidance of physical activities and may be more disabling than the pain itself (Turk & Okifuji, 2002). The perception of and adjustment to pain are likely to be influenced by the beliefs individuals acquire over their lifetime, and self-efficacy beliefs are likely to be particularly important in this (Turk & Okifuji, 2002). Assessment of patients with chronic pain may therefore include not only measures of the intensity of pain but also measures of fear avoidance beliefs (such as the fear avoidance beliefs questionnaire (FABQ; Waddell, Newton, Henderson, Somerville & Main, 1993), pain self-efficacy (such as the pain self-efficacy questionnaire (PSEQ; Nicholas, 2007) and coping (such as the coping strategies questionnaire (CSQ; Rosenstiel & Keefe, 1983). The concepts of coping and self-efficacy are discussed in greater detail in Chapters 2 and 3.

Not *all* pain is nociceptive, however. Some patients experience **neuropathic pain**, which is not fully understood but is thought to result from changes in the nervous system. Such pain is often experienced in parts of the body that otherwise appear normal; is generally chronic, severe and resistant to over-the-counter analgesics; and may result from various causes that affect the brain, spinal cord and peripheral nerves, including trigeminal neuralgia, diabetic neuropathy, cancer-related neuropathic pain, post-herpetic neuralgia, spinal cord injury, complex regional pain syndrome type II and post-surgical neuropathic pain (Gilron, Watson, Cahill & Moulin, 2006). For example, up to 80 per cent of amputees experience phantom limb pain – that is, pain referred to an amputated limb (Kooijman et al., 2000; Perkins & Kehlet, 2000; Sherman, 1994). Phantom breast pain may also be experienced following mastectomy and nerve damage contributes to the development of chronic post-operative pain, following breast surgery, thoracic surgery and hernia repair (Perkins & Kehlet, 2000).

Neuropathic pain can be divided into **stimulus-evoked pain** and stimulus-independent, or **spontaneous, pain.** The former involves a heightened reaction to a painful stimulus evoked by brushing or pressure (dynamic or static **hyperalgesia**) or tactile pain to an innocuous stimulus (**allodynia**), while the latter describes pain arising from spontaneous activity in the primary sensory neurons (Holdcroft & Power, 2003). Common neuropathic pain syndromes are described in Box 5.2.

BOX 5.2

Common neuropathic pain syndromes

Trigeminal neuralgia

Possibly the most excruciating of the neuropathic pain syndromes, it is most common in elderly people. A stabbing pain may be triggered by a light touch on the cheek, chewing or a cool breeze.

Diabetic neuropathy

A relatively common complication of diabetes. Clinical symptoms are progressive insensitivity to external painful stimuli, damage and deformity to the limb and development of chronic neuropathic pain.

Post-herpetic neuralgia

One of the commonest forms of neuropathic pain, it is defined as pain that persists for or recurs a month after the initial eruption of a herpes zoster infection. Patients describe severe aching and burning sensations. The area of pain can be associated with sensory deficit. Chronic symptoms are often associated with shooting, stabbing pains. The pain is constant and intense and often associated with unpleasant sensations and itching. Contact with clothing, changes in temperature, movement of the skin and emotional states are all likely to trigger allodynia.

Complex regional pain syndrome type II

Formerly known as causalgia, it refers to a condition where a nerve injury has occurred. The areas of the body most commonly affected are the hands and feet, although pain can spread to the entire limb. The pain may be described as intense burning, sometimes in combination with a stabbing pain.

Phantom pain

Pain referred to an amputated limb or body part. The pain may vary considerably in terms of its intensity, frequency and the nature of the sensation. Some patients describe a constant burning pain, while others report episodic, electric shock-type sensations.

Source: Strong, Unruh, Wright and Baxter (2002)

It is also useful to differentiate between cutaneous pain and pain arising from deep somatic structures. While the former is commonly described as a sharp or burning pain and is rarely referred to other body structures, the latter is often described as a diffuse, dull pain and is frequently referred to different sites. Pain felt at a site remote from the site of origin or stimulation is called **referred pain** (Arendt-Nielsen & Svensson, 2001). In the case of referred pain, musculoskeletal tissue in the referred area often becomes hypersensitive to painful stimuli and has a decreased pain threshold. This hyperalgesia is commonly accompanied by a state of sustained contraction of the muscle and, in long-lasting painful processes, a tendency to atrophy (Giamberalardino, Affaitati, Lerza & Vecchiet, 2004). The experience of myocardial infarction (heart attack) provides a typical example of referred pain. In the early stages, the pain has only a vague localisation and an oppressive and constrictive quality generally associated with pallor, sweating, nausea and vomiting. After ten minutes to several hours, the pain reaches the structures of the body wall and is commonly felt as a sharp pain in the left arm. Hyperalgesia often accompanies the symptom so that additional stimuli exerted on the area of referral increase the pain (Giamberalardino et al., 2004).

Simple referred pain (without hyperalgesia) can be explained by the convergence of inputs from deep and cutaneous tissues on common somatosensory spinal neurons – essentially, the brain 'misinterprets' the pain as originating in the muscle rather than the organs of the body. For example, Figure 5.2 illustrates referred pain in relation to a heart attack. The sensory inputs from the heart and arm converge on the same nerve pathways in the spinal cord.

Referred pain with hyperalgesia can be explained by a process of **central sensitisation** taking place in the central nervous system (CNS) (Giamberalardino et al., 2004). Central sensitisation is an increased excitability of neurons in the CNS triggered by a barrage of nociceptor activity, which increases the strength of synaptic connections between the nociceptor and the neurons of the spinal cord. Central sensitisation may account for the chronic widespread pain of fibromyalgia syndrome (FMS) and overlapping conditions such as irritable bowel syndrome, chronic fatigue syndrome, headaches and restless leg syndrome (Yunus, 2007).

5.2 THEORIES OF PAIN

5.2.1 SPECIFICITY AND PATTERN THEORY

Until the 1960s, there were two main theories of pain (Melzack & Wall, 1965):

- specificity theory
- pattern theory.

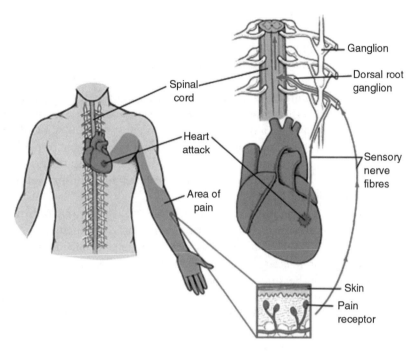

FIGURE 5.2   Referred pain

Source: Porter (2007)

Specificity theory holds that free nerve endings are pain receptors and generate nerve impulses carried by specific types of fibres in the spinal nerves to a pain centre in the thalamus. This theory proposes a direct invariable relationship between stimulus and sensation.

In contrast, pattern theory proposes that the intensity of the stimulus and central summation are the main determinants of pain – there are no specific fibres for pain and no specific nerve endings.

Both theories, however, fail to account for the diversity of the experience of pain discussed in the previous sections. For example, Melzack and Wall (1965) write that the existence of neuropathic pain states dramatically refutes the concept of a direct relationship between stimulus and sensation, and the psychological evidence also fails to support the assumption of a one-to-one relationship between the perception of pain and the intensity of the stimulus.

While overcoming some of the limitations of specificity theory, Melzack and Wall (1965) write that pattern theory also fails as a satisfactory theory of pain because it ignores the facts of physiological specialisation – that is, while pattern theory proposes that all fibre endings are alike, the physiological evidence indicates a high degree of fibre–receptor specialisation.

5.2.2 THE GATE CONTROL THEORY (GCT)

To account for the limitations of existing theories, therefore, Melzack and Wall (1965) proposed a new theory of pain: the **gate control theory (GCT)**.

The GCT incorporates both physiological and psychological dimensions and describes specific fibres and nerve endings as well as accounting for the patterning of inputs. According to this theory, stimulation of the skin evokes nerve impulses that travel to the dorsal horn in the spinal cord via afferent pathways consisting of **A-delta fibres** (fast, myelinated fibres carrying information about intense, sharp pain) and **C fibres** (slow, unmyelinated fibres carrying information about dull, throbbing pain). **A-beta fibres** (rapidly conducting non-nociceptive fibres) also transmit information relating to mild stimulation (such as gentle touch).

The substantia gelatinosa (SG) in the dorsal horn acts as a central control trigger that activates selective brain processes (attention, emotion, memories of prior experience and so on), which may open or close the gate for all inputs from any part of the body or for selective, localised gate activity. The gating mechanism is influenced by not only the stimulus-evoked activity but also the ongoing activity that preceded the stimulus and the relative amount of activity in A-beta and A-delta fibres. The inhibitory effect of the substantia gelatinosa is increased by activity in A-beta fibres (labelled 'L' for large in Figure 5.3) and decreased by activity in A-delta fibres (labelled 'S' for small in Figure 5.3).

Once the output of the spinal cord transmission exceeds a critical preset level, the action system triggers a sequence of responses. Sudden, unexpected damage to the skin is followed by:

- a startle response
- a flexion response
- postural readjustment
- vocalisation
- orientation of the head and eyes to examine the damaged area
- autonomic responses
- evocation of similar experiences in the past and prediction of the consequences of the stimulation
- other behaviours aimed at diminishing the affective and sensory aspects of the experience, such as rubbing the damaged area (resulting in activation of A-beta fibres).

Melzack and Wall (1965) write that there is no single 'pain centre' in the brain. Rather, the thalamus ('T' in Figure 5.3), limbic system, hypothalamus, brain-stem reticular formation, parietal cortex and frontal cortex are all involved in the perception of pain, and other brain areas are involved in the emotional and motor features of the behaviour sequence. The degree of central control exerted by cognitive and emotional processes depends in part on the temporal and spatial properties of the input patterns. Some pain, such as cardiac pain, rises so rapidly in intensity that the

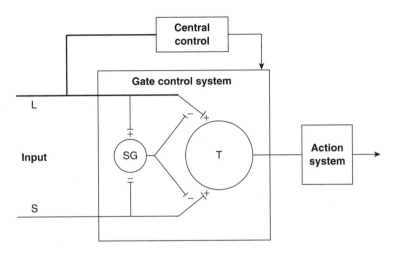

FIGURE 5.3   The gate control theory (GCT) of pain

Source: Melzack (1999: 125)

patient is unable to achieve control over it, while more slowly rising temporal patterns are susceptible to central control and the use of strategies such as distraction. The GCT is illustrated in Figure 5.3.

The GCT is important because it explains how the experience of pain may be influenced by both physiological and psychological factors and accounts for modulation of pain via non-noxious stimulation (such as rubbing the affected area, massage, bathing). Stimulation therapies are discussed further in Section 5.3.

Melzack (1999) also points out that a particularly important implication of the GCT is the emphasis on central neural mechanisms. The theory forced the medical and biological sciences to accept the brain as an active system that filters, selects and modulates inputs.

5.2.3 THE NEUROMATRIX THEORY OF PAIN

The GCT became one of the most widely known pain theories, and research has tested and validated the GCT mechanisms (Summers, 2000). It could not account fully for all pain phenomena, however – in particular, pain with no inputs from the body (such as phantom limb pain) is difficult to explain within this framework.

Melzack (1999) has therefore proposed a new theory to account for such phenomena – the **neuromatrix theory of pain**. According to this theory, a matrix of neurons in the CNS produces characteristic nerve impulse patterns for the body and the somatosensory qualities that we feel. This results in a perception of the body as a unity, identified as the 'self' and distinct from other people and the surrounding world. Although the synaptic architecture of this network is built in by genetic specification, the resulting **neurosignature** pattern of nerve impulses is modulated by sensory inputs as well as cognitive events such as psychological stress.

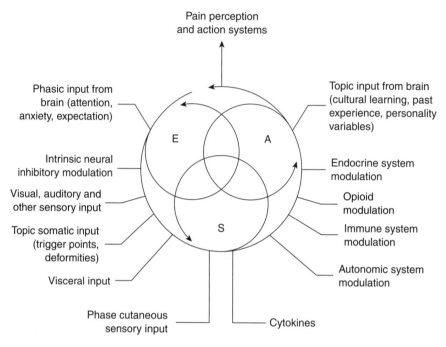

FIGURE 5.4 The body–self neuromatrix

Source: Melzack (1999: S125)

It may also occur because stressors (physical or psychological) act on stress-regulation systems, producing lesions of muscle, bone or nerve tissue, thereby contributing to the neurosignature patterns that give rise to chronic pain. Genetic influences on synaptic architecture may determine, or predispose towards, the development of chronic pain syndromes. The body–self neuromatrix and its modulatory inputs are illustrated in Figure 5.4. The circles within the neuromatrix represent smaller parallel networks that contribute to the sensory – discriminative (S), affective – motivational (A) and cognitive – evaluative (E) dimensions of pain.

The neuromatrix theory places genetic contributions and the neural hormonal mechanism of stress on a level of equal importance with the neural mechanisms of sensory transmission (Melzack, 2001). According to Melzack (1999) some forms of chronic pain occur due to the cumulative destructive effect of cortisol on muscle, bone and neural tissue (Chrousos & Gold, 1992) and this may explain both why many autoimmune diseases (Crohn's disease, multiple sclerosis, rheumatoid arthritis, scleroderma and lupus, for example) are also pain syndromes and why chronic pain becomes more common with increasing age. Melzack (1999) therefore argues an immediate recommendation arising from the neuromatrix theory is that interdisciplinary pain clinics should be expanded to include specialists in endocrinology and immunology. Such collaboration may help to reveal the underlying mechanisms of chronic pain and give rise to therapies to relieve unrelenting suffering.

Interactions between the brain and immune system may also help to explain responses to pain in the absence of subjective experience. For example, Neuman (2004) reports a case of a patient who was asked repeatedly by medical staff if he was experiencing pain during colonoscopy under deep sedation. Although the patient reported that he was not experiencing pain, the staff reported that his facial expressions signified pain. Neuman (2004) suggests that pain may be experienced unconsciously via the immune system and that the immune system communicates the experience of pain intersubjectively, in a similar way to that in which the immune system produces a 'sickness response' to infection and injury that may be interpreted by outsiders as indicating pathology without any assumption of intentionality or consciousness of the signalling system (see Chapter 2 for a discussion of the sickness response).

Neuman (2004) writes that Melzack's (1999) call for studying the neuromatrix of the pain experience may benefit from recent conceptualisations of the immune system as a complex cognitive system, and that studying pain by drawing an analogy with the immune system may deepen our understanding of the pain experience.

5.2.4 BIOCHEMICAL THEORY OF PAIN AND DRUG MECHANISMS

Summers (2000) writes that, in the 1970s, endorphins and opioid receptors were identified and a **biochemical theory of pain** was formulated (Millan, 1986).

Endorphins (classified as enkephalins and dynorphins) are endogenous, morphine-like substances that attach to pain receptors to modulate or decrease pain. It is predicted that, when acute pain is elicited, the endogenous opioids are released and associated with the stress response to modulate pain. Indeed, pain can also be controlled by administering exogenous, **opiate drugs** that bind to the **opioid receptors** in specified sites (Summers, 2000).

Opioid receptors occur at the level of the nociceptors, and opioid drugs, acting at peripheral opioid receptors on sensory nerves, can relieve inflammatory pain (Pleuvry, 2005). Large myelinated nociceptors, however, express low levels of opioid receptors, explaining the ability of opioids to suppress persistent pain, but not responses to new injury. High concentrations of opioid receptors are also found in the periaqueductal grey, nucleus raphe magnus and nucleus reticularis gigantocellularis, and systemic morphine induces analgesia at these sites. The limbic system also contains opioid receptors, and drugs acting at this point are thought to reduce the affective component of pain (Pleuvry, 2005). Opioid receptors are also found at other sites, including the thalamus and cortex (see Figure 5.5).

Since opiates affect the central nervous system, side-effects may include changes in cognition and psychomotor functioning, although there are no randomised controlled studies of cognition in chronic non-cancer patients taking opioids, and studies of psychomotor functioning do not indicate significant interference (Gallagher & Rosenthal, 2008). Opiates are also associated with other, potentially serious side-effects and, in some patients, may result in addiction or abuse. Gallagher and Rosenthal (2008) suggest that some patients (and some physicians) inappropriately rely on opioids to relieve suffering and emotional discomfort associated with pain

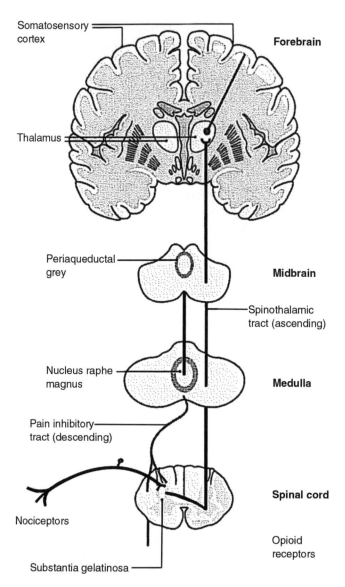

FIGURE 5.5   Site of endogenous opioid receptors
Source: Pleuvry (2005: 31)

when these problems may be more appropriately addressed by using psychological therapies or psychotropic medications.

The effects of pharmacological therapies for pain can also be explained in relation to the GCT. According to this theory, activation of peripheral nociceptors leads to transmission of the nociceptive signal to the brain via a gating mechanism in the dorsal horn (see above). Therefore, pain can be modulated using drugs that target the inflammatory mediators triggering peripheral nociceptors, act on the dorsal horn or on supraspinal sites (Wright, Benson & Callaghan, 2002).

As noted above, opioids may reduce inflammatory pain since opioid receptors occur at the level of nociceptors. Opiates also act at the level of the dorsal horn and at supraspinal sites and may be used in combination with other drugs to produce analgesia at these sites. For example, opioids may be administered in combination with other drugs in an **epidural block** (injection of anaesthetic into the epidural space near the spinal cord) and used in combination with anaesthetics to manage post-operative pain (Wright et al., 2002).

The peripheral inflammatory response may be modulated using **steroids, non-steroidal anti-inflammatory drugs (NSAIDs)** or topically applied **local anaesthetics**. Wright et al. (2002) explain that steroids (corticosteroids or glucocorticoids) are potent anti-inflammatory agents, although they are of limited value in the treatment of chronic pain owing to their severe side-effects. NSAIDs (aspirin, paracetamol, ibuprofen and so on) are usually effective against low- to moderate-intensity pain with clear inflammatory cause and are used as anti-inflammatory or analgesic agents in the management of rheumatoid arthritis, osteoarthritis, ankylosing spondyltis and soft tissue disorders. These drugs are also associated with side-effects, however, and long-term regular use of oral NSAIDs is not recommended, due to their toxic effects on the gastrointestinal tract and kidneys (Wright et al., 2002). Topically applied local anaesthetics can be used to reduce pain during procedures such as venepuncture, venous cannulation and the harvesting and placement of skin, although long-term use is limited owing to the development of skin reactions (Wright et al., 2002).

Tricyclic antidepressants can be used to treat pain in chronic pain states since these drugs inhibit the reuptake of neurotransmitters involved in the descending pain inhibitory pathways from the midbrain to the spinal cord, although these drugs do not produce an immediate improvement and are associated with a number of side-effects. Tricyclic antidepressants in conjunction with anticonvulsant drugs are used as frontline therapies for neuropathic pain states, which tend to be only partially opioid receptive (Wright et al., 2002).

NON-PHARMACOLOGICAL TREATMENTS FOR PAIN

5.3 Consistent with the GCT, pain may be alleviated via non-noxious stimulation of either peripheral nerves or the spinal cord – **spinal cord stimulation (SCS)**. Peripheral nerve stimulation may involve a range of techniques, such as rubbing or massaging the effected area, bathing in warm water, applying electrical stimulation, pressure or needling. Kotze and Simpson (2008) write that, although the GCT provides a convenient explanation for **stimulation-produced analgesia (SPA)** produced via these techniques, relieving pain by stimulation of nerves is not a new concept and stimulation methods were used long before the publication of the GCT. For example, the first book on acupuncture by the Yellow Emperor was written before 100BC and electrical analgesia was documented even earlier by Aristotle, who described the use of electric fish as a treatment for the pain of gout (Kotze & Simpson, 2008). Massage therapy also has a long history, predating modern theories of pain control. For example, Immamura and colleagues (2008) write that the most ancient references to the use of massage come from Babylonia (around 900BC), China (around 2700BC), India (around 1500–120BC), Greece (Hippocrates, 460–377BC, Asclepiades, Galen) and Rome (Plato, 427–347BC and Socrates, 470–399BC).

Clinical use of SPA techniques, however, differs from traditional approaches. For example, electrical analgesia these days is more likely to involve the use of **transcutaneous electrical nerve stimulation (TENS)** – a non-invasive method of applying electrical stimulation to the skin for pain control. Clinically, TENS is applied at varying frequencies, intensities and durations of pulsed stimulation. Sluka and Walsh (2003) explain that, with sensory-level TENS, the voltage is increased until the patient feels a comfortable tingling or tapping sensation without motor contraction – this is referred to as low intensity. With motor-level TENS, the intensity is increased to produce a motor contraction – this is referred to as high intensity TENS. Usually, high-frequency TENS is produced at low intensities – referred to as conventional TENS. Low-frequency TENS is typically produced at high intensities – referred to as strong, low-rate or acupuncture-like TENS. Sluka and Walsh (2003) write that these stimulation parameters are not commonly specified, nor kept constant among patients within a given study, and that other methodological problems in published trials make it difficult to determine the true clinical efficacy of TENS. Systematic reviews have supported the effects of high-frequency TENS for primary dysmenorrhoea and use of conventional TENS and acupuncture-like TENS for knee osteoarthritis. Other reviews, however, have failed to support the effects of TENS for chronic pain, chronic low back pain, labour pain, post-operative pain and post-stroke shoulder pain (reviewed in Sluka & Walsh, 2003).

Alternatively, electrodes may be implanted subcutaneously to stimulate peripheral nerves (**peripheral nerve stimulation**) or into the brain (**deep brain stimulation or motor cortex stimulation**) to treat refractory neuropathic pain states (such as after stroke). **Acupuncture** involves the insertion of solid needles into acupuncture points that may be close to the painful structure ('local needling') or distant but innervated by the same spinal cord segment ('segmental needling'). Needles may be left in place for a short period of time or manipulated or heated to increase the 'dose'. A weak, pulsed electrical current may also be passed through acupuncture needles (**electroacupuncture**), and acupuncture points can also be stimulated without piercing the skin by applying pressure (**acupressure**), laser or TENS machine (Kotze & Simpson, 2008).

Systematic reviews have supported the use of acupuncture for myofacial pain, knee osteoarthritis, dysmenorrhoea, mechanical back and neck pain and idiopathic headache, as well as evidence for the use of SCS in complex regional pain syndrome, failed back surgery with radicular pain and some other neuropathic pain states (Kotze & Simpson, 2008). These forms of SPA probably operate via different mechanisms from those involved with TENS. Kotze and Simpson (2008) write that high-frequency TENS stimulation selectively activates A-beta fibres and the predominant analgesic effect is probably spinal gating. For acupuncture, however, gate control seems to be less important than the production of endogenous opioids at the spinal cord and in the limbic system. Opioid production is central to the action of electro-acupuncture. SCS analgesia is probably not mediated by endogenous opioids. In animal models, SCS is associated with the selective inhibition of abnormally hypersensitive neurons in the dorsal horn and the increased release of the inhibitory neurotransmitter **gamma-aminobutyric acid (GABA)** in spinal neurons (Kotze & Simpson, 2008; Meyerson & Linderoth, 2006).

Cassileth and Vickers (2004) write that massage is included in treatment guidelines such as those of the National Cancer Network, which recommends considering massage for refractory cancer pain. These guidelines are supported by empirical evidence. For example, Cassileth and Vickers (2004) evaluated the effects of massage therapy in a sample of 1290 patients with cancer. Pain scores improved by 40 per cent following massage therapy and significant improvement was seen in other scores for symptoms – most notably anxiety.

A recent review of massage for chronic lower back pain (CLBP) concluded that there is strong evidence for massage being effective for non-specific CLBP and the effects are improved if it is combined with exercise and education and delivered by a registered therapist. Further, the benefits of massage for patients with CLBP are long-lasting (at least a year after the last session; Immamura et al., 2008). The review also concluded, however, that there is uncertainty about the mechanisms of action of massage therapy – if they are related to the release of endorphins, relaxation or both. Further research is needed to determine the type of massage that is indicated for different presentations, such as patients with higher baseline pain scores, muscle spasms, sleep disturbance, stress and anxiety symptoms.

Other manual therapies for pain include manipulation and mobilisation. Manipulation techniques involve the use of thrusts to the vertebrae or parts of a patient's body that act as a lever, resulting in movement of the components of a joint or group of joints beyond their normal physiological range (Maigne & Vautravers, 2003). High-velocity manipulations are associated with joint noises (cracks, clicks or pops) and are done at such a speed that the patient cannot control the technique. Mobilisations, however, do not involve a joint noise and allow the client to exert some control over the technique. They may involve sustaining positions to stretch or compress structures (Vicenzino & Wright, 2002).

A number of randomised controlled trials of manual therapies have been conducted and systematic reviews have yielded mixed results. For example, Hettinga and colleagues (2008) conducted a systematic review of mobilisation and manipulation for lower back pain of at least six weeks' duration. Although few high-quality randomised controlled trials (RCTs) could be identified, those included in the review revealed that a mobilisation or manipulation package is an effective intervention compared with general practitioner care, while manipulation used in isolation showed no real benefits over sham manipulation or an alternative intervention.

Vernon, Humphreys and Hagino (2007) revealed moderate to high-quality evidence that patients with chronic neck pain, not due to whiplash and without arm pain and headaches, show clinically important improvements from a course of spinal manipulation or mobilisation, while the evidence reviewed did not support a similar level of benefit from massage.

Gross et al. (2002) reviewed randomised controlled trials of manual therapy for mechanical neck disorders and revealed that manipulation alone, mobilisations alone, manipulation and mobilisation, and treatments including massage consistently showed similar effects to placebo or control conditions. Manual therapies combined with exercise, however, did improve pain and patient satisfaction.

Mullis, Hay and Lewis (2005) compared physiotherapy incorporating manual therapy with a brief psychosocial and exercise-based pain management programme (not including manual therapy). The clinical outcomes were the same for both groups at 3-month and 12-month follow-ups.

Although a number of RCTs have been conducted, evaluating the effects of manual therapy for patients with pain, little research has been directed at understanding the underlying mechanisms. Maigne and Vautravers (2003) suggest that, by stretching the ligaments, discs, joint capsules or muscles, spinal manipulation therapy may activate the diffuse descending pain inhibitory system, the neurons of which are isolated in the periaqueductal grey matter, and that forceful muscle stretching induces presynaptic inhibition of afferents from the skin. Placebo effects are also likely to play a role in the effects of spinal manipulation. Maigne and Vautravers (2003) write that a feeling of the vertebra having been returned to its normal position, a perception that the cracking sound indicates the therapy's effectiveness, and the manual contact preceding the manipulation all contribute to the placebo effect. The mechanisms underlying intervention effects and methods available for evaluating interventions (including randomised controlled trials and systematic reviews) are discussed in greater detail in Chapters 7 and 8.

SUMMARY

5.4 The research reviewed in this chapter indicates that pain is a complex phenomenon influenced by both psychological and biological processes. It cannot be assumed that two patients with the same degree of physical injury or the same medical condition experience the same intensity of pain and, indeed, patients may experience pain without any evident underlying pathology. The subjective nature of pain makes it difficult for patients to communicate their experiences in a way that will be understood by others and presents a challenge for the assessment of pain in clinical settings. Although a number of measures exist, it is likely that the assessment of an individual's pain will necessitate the use of more than one pain measure – for example, combining self-report measures with behavioural assessment and, in the case of chronic pain, assessment of psychological variables such as pain self-efficacy and coping. For children and people with cognitive impairment, it will also be necessary to consult with their families, who may be able to recognise more subtle individual signs of pain and distress.

Theoretical models such as the GCT and neuromatrix theories of pain help to elucidate the complex interrelationships between psychological and biological processes in the experience of pain and provide a guide for the development of interventions for patients experiencing either acute or chronic pain.

According to the GCT, pain is influenced by both noxious and non-noxious stimulation and central control exerted by cognitive and emotional processes. Therefore, pain may be alleviated via psychological, stimulation-based or pharmacological therapies. The neuromatrix theory adds the elements of genetic contributions and neural hormonal mechanisms of stress and underlines the importance of multidisciplinary approaches to the management of pain.

The biochemical theory of pain is used to explain both why certain drugs are administered and the biological processes underlying their analgesic effects. It is evident, however, that drugs used for pain relief may have a range of properties other than analgesia and the side-effects may limit their use for the long term. For patients with chronic pain, therefore, drug treatments alone are unlikely to provide adequate pain management, and psychological therapies may be necessary to address the impacts of pain on physical and psychosocial functioning. Psychological therapies for pain are considered further in Chapter 7.

KEY TERMS

A-beta fibres, acupressure, acupuncture, acute pain, A-delta fibres, allodynia, biochemical theory of pain, C fibres, catastrophising, central sensitisation, chronic pain, deep brain or motor cortex stimulation, electroacupuncture, endorphins, epidural block, gamma-aminobutyric acid (GABA), gate control theory (GCT), hyperalgesia, local anaesthetic, neuromatrix theory of pain, neuropathic pain, neurosignature, nociception, nociceptive transducers, nociceptors, non-steroidal anti-inflammatory drugs (NSAIDs), opiate drugs, opioid receptors, pattern theory, peripheral nerve stimulation, referred pain, specificity theory, spinal cord stimulation (SCS), spontaneous pain, steroids, stimulation-produced analgesia (SPA), stimulus-evoked pain, transcutaneous electrical nerve stimulation (TENS), tricyclic antidepressants

■Discussion questions ▬▬▬▬▬▬▬▬▬▬▬▬▬▬▬▬▬▬▬▬▬

1 Think of a time when you experienced pain. How did this affect your thoughts, feelings and behaviour? What would be the impact on your life if this pain persisted for weeks, months or years?

2 How might pain behaviours (such as grimacing, moaning and body stiffness) be interpreted in social situations? How do you think people would respond to someone displaying these behaviours?

3 How might previous experience of stress or trauma influence outcomes in patients with (a) acute or (b) chronic pain?

4 Has the gate control theory changed the way we treat pain?

5 Why does TENS appear to be effective for some patients or medical conditions, but not others?

FURTHER READING

Holdcroft, A. & Power, I. (2003). Recent developments: management of pain. *British Medical Journal, 326*, 635–639.

Kotze, A. & Simpson, K.H. (2008). Stimulation-produced analgesia: acupuncture, TENS and related techniques. *Anaesthesia & Intensive Care Medicine, 9*, 29–32.

Melzack, R. (1999). From the gate to the neuromatrix. *Pain, S6*, S121–S126.

Neuman, Y. (2004). What does pain signify? A hypothesis concerning pain, the immune system and unconscious pain experience under general anaesthesia. *Medical Hypotheses, 63*, 1051–1053.

AT RISK POPULATIONS

6

OVERVIEW

In the previous chapters we have highlighted the impacts of psychobiological processes on health outcomes. A wide body of research indicates that psychobiological processes can influence health, but how important is this link? For example, do we see higher rates of infectious illness or coronary heart disease in people with psychiatric illness or groups exposed to chronic stress over a number of years and, if so, could this be explained by psychobiological processes (such as allostatic load)? Could psychobiological processes act as mediators in the relationship between environmental stressors (economic hardship or stressful working conditions, for example) and ill health? Could the cumulative effects of psychological stressors account for age-related functional decline and morbidity?

In this chapter we consider to what extent psychobiological processes may explain variations in the risk of disease at the group level. Implications for the prevention of disease in at risk populations are also considered.

LEARNING OUTCOMES

By the end of this chapter you should be able to:

- discuss social gradients in health and the factors contributing to these gradients
- describe the processes contributing to coronary atherosclerosis

- discuss associations between socio-economic status and allostatic load and be aware of methodological issues inherent in this research

- discuss associations between psychiatric illness and chronic medical conditions and describe the mechanisms underlying these associations

- discuss the phenomenon of population ageing and the physical and mental health problems associated with ageing

- describe age-related changes in immune function

- describe pathways through which psychological variables may influence age-related illness

- discuss the 'altered homeostatic theory' and the 'telomere hypothesis'

- describe the major forces that may induce telomere dysfunction

- discuss associations between caregiving and health and describe the underlying mechanisms.

INTRODUCTION

6.1 In previous chapters we have mainly considered psychobiological processes in health and illness at the individual level. For example, we have considered why some people may be more likely than others to develop colds and flu (even when exposure to the pathogen is controlled) and why some people are more at risk of type 2 diabetes, coronary heart disease or chronic pain than others. As we will discuss in this chapter, differences in health and mortality also exist at the group level, such that being a member of a particular group can result in a shorter life expectancy and greater risk of disease. Furthermore, being a member of an 'at risk' group appears to impact health in a non-specific manner. For example, being a member of a low socio-economic status group increases the risk of death from all major causes, and people with psychiatric illness, long-term caregivers and older people are also at risk of a wide range of diseases, involving multiple physiological systems.

In the following sections we will look at each of these at risk groups in turn and consider:

- to what extent psychological processes (such as stress, depression) may contribute to the high risk of disease in these groups
- whether psychological processes impact health via behavioural or biological pathways.

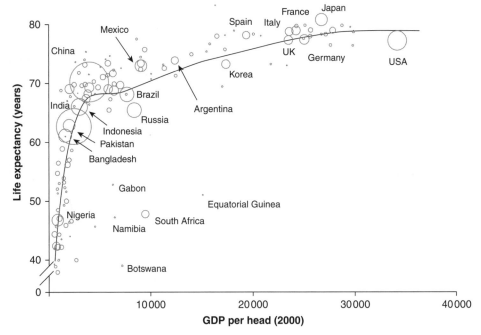

FIGURE 6.1   Life expectancy plotted against GDP per head. Circles have diameter proportional to population size

Source: Marmot (2006: 2086)

6.2 SOCIO-ECONOMIC STATUS AND HEALTH

> As physicians we are trained that the patient comes first and last. Searching out individual causes of disease, however, does not negate the importance of environmental causes.
>
> Marmot (2006: 2082)

Social gradients in health have been demonstrated both between and within countries. At a between-country level, it is clear that significant differences exist in life expectancy between the poorest and richest nations. For example, Marmot (2006) points out that the life expectancy in Swaziland is only 32.5 years, while the life expectancy in Japan is more than double that, at 82.2 years, and, in general, life expectancy increases in line with the income of a country (see Figure 6.1).

What is perhaps more surprising is that such gradients also exist within richer nations, such that being in a lower socio-economic status group can detrimentally impact health and mortality even where the members of that group are not poor in the usual sense of the word (Marmot, 2006).

For example, Marmot and colleagues (Marmot, Shipley & Rose, 1984; Marmot & Shipley, 1996) studied mortality in British civil servants – the Whitehall study. Marmot (2006) reports that, among these civil servants, none of whom was destitute, men second from the top of the occupational hierarchy had a higher death rate at 25-year follow-up than men at the top of the occupational hierarchy, and men third from the top had a higher rate of death than those second from the top.

The Whitehall II study (Marmot et al., 1991) extended these findings to women and revealed employment grade differences in the prevalence of ischaemia (lack of blood supply to the heart), angina (chest pain associated with ischaemia), symptoms of chronic bronchitis, self-perceived health status and health-risk behaviours, including smoking, poor diet and lack of exercise. Further analyses of the Whitehall data sets revealed links between employment grade and a number of health outcomes, including risk of coronary heart disease (Marmot, Bosma, Hemingway, Brunner & Stansfeld, 1997), metabolic syndrome (DeVogli, Brunner & Marmot, 2007) and rate of change in mental and physical functioning over a three-year period (Martikainen, Stansfeld, Hemingway & Marmot, 1999). Links between socio-economic status and rates of illness or mortality have also been confirmed in studies utilising panel data sets from the USA and Sweden (Adams, Hurd, Merrill & Rebeiro, 2002; Adda, Chandola & Marmot, 2003).

6.2.1 ACCOUNTING FOR SOCIAL GRADIENTS IN HEALTH

So, how do we account for such social gradients in health? Marmot (2006) explains that, in both poor and rich countries, poverty is more than the lack of money. In rich countries and poor, poverty means not participating fully in society and having limits on the way people lead their lives. These two factors – control and social engagement – can be used to explain the links between socio-economic status and health. For example, explanatory models of work stress have highlighted the importance of control relative to demands at work (Karasek & Theorell, 1990) and the balance between efforts and rewards (Siegrist & Marmot, 2006) as determinants of chronic stress. Marmot (2006) suggests that the expectation of reward in relation to effort expended is a key feature of social engagement, since part of living in a society is the expectation of reciprocal rewards. Marmot et al. (1997) revealed evidence that psychosocial work conditions (and control at work in particular) form part of the psychosocial mechanism underlying social inequalities in health among men, although control at home seems to be more important for explaining social gradients in health among women (Chandola, Kuper, Singh-Manoux, Bartley & Marmot, 2004). An effort–reward imbalance is linked to sick days in both men and women (Head et al., 2007).

The stress associated with lack of control and low social engagement might influence disease via health-related behaviours, such as smoking, alcohol consumption or dietary factors, or direct neuroendocrine pathways. Most work examining mechanisms underlying social gradients in health has focused on coronary heart disease (CHD, also called coronary artery disease – CAD), since there has been a large body of research on the biological pathways involved in CHD (Marmot, 2006).

Steptoe and colleagues (2002) explain that health-risk behaviours have been demonstrated to contribute to the higher incidence of premature cardiovascular disease in low socio-economic status groups, but that the gradient in health is not eliminated after taking health behaviour into account, indicating that other pathways are also involved. One of these pathways may involve impacts of low socio-economic status on allostatic processes, with chronic or repeated exposure to adversity and lack of protective factors (such as social support and effective coping) contributing to wear and tear on biological regulatory systems, such that they no longer operate within normal ranges (Steptoe & Marmot, 2004). Rather than contributing to acute cardiac events in people with advanced disease, it is likely that these processes contribute to the development of **coronary atherosclerosis** – the problem underlying CHD (see Box 6.1).

6.2.2 EVIDENCE FOR ALLOSTATIC MECHANISMS

BOX 6.1

Coronary atherosclerosis

Coronary atherosclerosis is a progressive disease involving a gradual thickening of the walls of the coronary arteries.

Steptoe and Marmot (2004) explain that the disease involves chronic vascular inflammation, beginning in the cells lining the vessel wall and leading to progressive accumulation of lipid, smooth muscle cells and white blood cells, such as macrophages, lymphocytes and platelets. This process is regulated in part by inflammatory cytokines such as interleukin (IL)-6 and tumour necrosis factor (TNF), as well as C-reactive protein (CRP) (white blood cells and cytokines are described in greater detail in Chapter 2).

At later stages, plaques (hard structures composed of fat, cholesterol and other substances) form on the internal vessel walls (see below) and the disease typically comes to light when the coronary arteries become blocked and the muscle of the heart fails to be supplied with blood. The person may then experience angina pectoris, myocardial infarction or death (Steptoe & Marmot, 2004).

(Cont'd)

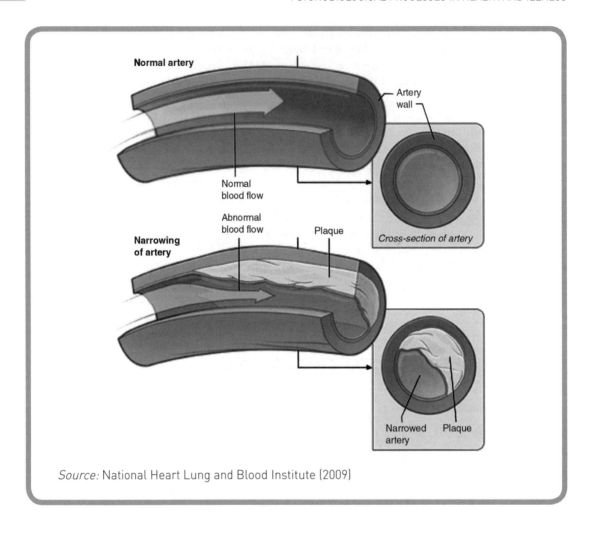

Source: National Heart Lung and Blood Institute (2009)

Consistent with a role for allostatic mechanisms in CHD, studies have revealed increases in blood pressure, CRP and pro-inflammatory cytokines (IL-1, IL-6, TNF) in response to stress, and socio-economic status differences have been observed in post-stress recovery in relation to a number of these measures (reviewed in Steptoe & Marmot, 2004). Recovery after stress is particularly relevant to the allostatic load model since chronic or repeated activation of biological regulatory systems is considered to result in an impaired ability to adapt over time (McEwen & Wingfield, 2003). Naturalistic monitoring of cortisol has also revealed links between socio-economic status and the cortisol awakening response, which is thought to indicate an anticipatory response associated with a realisation of the demands of the day ahead (Steptoe & Marmot, 2004).

Steptoe and Marmot (2004) point out that the differences observed across the social gradient, in both laboratory studies and naturalistic monitoring, are small, but the importance is that they are repeated on a regular basis for months or years of adult life and so are likely to have a cumulative effect on health in a similar way to the cumulative effects of repeated cigarette smoking.

Other research suggests that associations between socio-economic status and allostatic load may be more evident when measures are taken across multiple parameters. For example, Seeman et al. (2004) evaluated associations between socio-economic status, allostatic load and all-cause mortality in high-functioning older men and women, using a summary index of allostatic load composed of 16 biological measures. Findings indicated that higher allostatic load accounted for 35 per cent of the difference in mortality risk between those with lower socio-economic status and those with higher status – see Research in focus box 6.1.

RESEARCH IN FOCUS BOX 6.1

Seeman et al. (2004) examined seven-year mortality data (1988–1995) from the MacArthur studies of successful ageing, to test the hypothesis that a cumulative measure of allostatic load reflecting multiple physiological systems would serve as a mediator of socio-economic status differences in mortality.

Methodology

This study examined data from the MacArthur studies of successful ageing – a longitudinal investigation of high-functioning men and women, aged 70–79 (Berkman et al., 1993). Years of education completed was used as the primary measure of socio-economic status. Their allostatic load was measured using a cumulative index, composed of the measures below. Complete data were available for 657 participants.

Measures of allostatic load

- Systolic and diastolic blood pressure.
- Waist–hip ratio (an index of chronic levels of metabolism and adipose tissue deposition, thought to be influenced by increased glucocorticoid activity).
- Ratio of total to HDL serum cholesterol.
- Blood plasma levels of glycosylated haemoglobin (HbA1c – a measure of glucose metabolism over the past 30–90 days).
- Serum dehydroepinandrosterone sulphate (DHEA-S – a functional HPA axis antagonist).

(Cont'd)

- 12-h urinary cortisol excretion.
- 12-h urinary norepinephrine (NE) and epinephrine (EPI) excretion levels.
- Measures of inflammation (fibrinogen, interleukin-6 (IL-6), C-reactive protein (CRP) and low albumin).
- Creatinine clearance (a measure of renal function).
- Peak flow (a measure of lung function).

Results

Socio-economic status was a significant predictor of mortality (less education associated with greater mortality). Individual measures of allostatic load did not generally confer significantly increased risk of mortality. The cumulative index, however, was significantly associated with mortality and explained 35.4 per cent of the difference in the risk of mortality between those with higher versus lower socio-economic status. The cumulative index also provided independent explanatory power over and above baseline morbidity (as measured by doctor-diagnosed conditions).

Conclusions and implications

Findings suggest that a cumulative measure of biological dysregulation (allostatic load) can provide information on socio-economic-status-related differentials in risk of mortality beyond the explanatory power provided by traditional measures of health status based on doctor-diagnosed disease.

Seeman et al. (2004) suggest that, given the likely cumulative nature of the observed biological dysregulations, a life history perspective may offer important insights into socio-economic status-related differentials in life experiences that result in differential accumulations of biological wear and tear. They (Seeman et al., 2004: 1995) further conclude:

> an approach that takes a more comprehensive, multi-systems view of biological functioning – as contrasted with our historical bent toward focusing on the individual effects of specific biological parameters – may be more useful and appropriate as we seek to understand the multiple and cumulative pathways through which differences in socio-economic status result in disparities in health and longevity.

6.2.3 METHODOLOGICAL ISSUES

Other studies have supported associations between allostatic load and socio-economic status, although measures of both variables have varied across studies (Szanton, Gill & Allen, 2005). Szanton et al. (2005) write that the allostatic load literature is evolving and justification of the variables assessed would facilitate this evolution.

Measures of socio-economic status also warrant closer consideration since measures such as education, occupation and income are interrelated but represent different dimensions of status, with education relating more to social status in early life than present occupational status, and income relating to both levels of material resources and prestige (Kristenson, Eriksen, Sluiter, Starke & Ursin, 2004). As such, these variables can be expected to show different associations with environmental demands and coping resources across the lifespan.

Measures of socio-economic status are also likely to interact with race and ethnicity, as well as neighbourhood factors. For example, Szanton et al. (2005) point out that an African-American woman who graduated from a high school in North Carolina in the 1940s is unlikely to accrue the same economic advantage as a white man who graduated from a high school in North Carolina in the 1940s. Szanton et al. (2005) therefore suggest that analysis of these race, ethnicity and neighbourhood factors in conjunction with measures of socio-economic status may help both to explain associations between allostatic load and socio-economic health disparities and to aid the design of effective interventions (Szanton et al., 2005).

PEOPLE WITH PSYCHIATRIC ILLNESS

6.3

A substantial body of literature supports clinically important associations between psychiatric illness and chronic medical conditions (Roy-Byrne et al., 2008). Most research focuses on depression, but there is also strong evidence in support of the increased risk of medical illness, complications and mortality in patients with anxiety disorders.

Roy-Byrne et al. (2008) reviewed evidence in relation to five medical conditions – irritable bowel syndrome (IBS), asthma, cardiovascular disease (CVD), cancer and chronic pain. The evidence reviewed supports an increased risk of these diseases in patients with depression or anxiety disorders, although knowledge of underlying pathophysiological mechanisms is more advanced for some disorders (such as IBS, CVD) than for others (cancer, for example).

In the case of IBS, rates of psychiatric diagnoses in treatment-seeking patients range from 54 to 94 per cent, and IBS commonly overlaps with disorders such as fibromyalgia, chronic fatigue, anxiety disorders (including PTSD) and mood disorders. Roy-Byrne et al. (2008) point out that psychosocial stress is increasingly recognised as playing an important role in the onset, persistence and severity of IBS, regardless of presumed aetiology (such as infections, stress-related, inherited risk), and that the neural pathways which produce visceral pain signals also regulate the stress response, anxiety, mood and gastrointestinal function. Corticotropin-releasing factor (CRF) is a key mediator of these pathways and it is possible that CRF dysregulation, resulting from exposure to prolonged or severe stress, may be one potential neurobiological link between IBS and overlapping disorders (Roy-Byrne et al., 2008).

Note that the term 'patients' is used here, although alternative terms are commonly used in the mental health field (clients, consumers, service users and so on). The appropriateness of these terms has been hotly debated (Livingston & Cooper, 2004; Sluzki, 2000).

In the case of CVD, Roy-Byrne et al. (2008) report that depression is strongly associated with increased rates of serious cardiac events, all-causes mortality and cardiac mortality following myocardial infarction (MI), unstable angina and coronary artery bypass surgery, and emerging evidence suggests anxiety is also an important risk factor for both the incidence and progression of CVD. Underlying mechanisms linking CVD with depression and anxiety may include excess activation of the HPA-axis and SNS (resulting in increased inflammation, release of fatty acids above the levels needed for metabolic requirements and damage to the vascular endothelium) as well as poor health behaviours (such as smoking and excess alcohol consumption) among people with psychiatric illness.

Cognitive–evaluative factors (fear of heart attack, asthma attack, pain, catastrophic misinterpretation of symptoms and so on) and emotional reactions to diagnosis and treatment may also account for high rates of depression and anxiety in patients with chronic medical illnesses. Also, some medical treatments may impact mood directly. For example, Roy-Byrne et al. (2008) explain that medications used commonly in the treatment of cancer are associated with both anxiety (glucocorticoids, for example) and depression (such as interferon, glucocorticoids).

6.3.1 SCHIZOPHRENIA AND PHYSICAL ILLNESS

People with schizophrenia are also at increased risk of physical illness and early mortality, with cardiovascular illness-related deaths forming the largest contribution to the high death-rates observed in the disorder (Thomas, 2008). Again, it is likely that both biological and psychological processes play a role. Thomas (2008) explains that some antipsychotic treatments have effects that play a prominent role in weight gain and lipid dysregulation, and that the risk of mortality and morbidity is further compounded by the unhealthy lifestyle (lack of exercise and poor diet) adopted by many patients. Further, weight gain can impair quality of life as a result of decreased functioning, social stigmatisation and discrimination.

As well as weight gain, Thomas (2008) points out that treatments for schizophrenia have other side-effects with adverse psychosocial consequences, including sexual dysfunction and movement disorders (involuntary movements, muscle spasms, inability to initiate movement and so on). Adverse treatment experiences can also lead to patients not taking their medication, which is in itself a major risk factor for relapse and rehospitalisation and is likely to result in adverse effects on psychosocial functioning.

6.3.2 GENETIC AND SOCIODEMOGRAPHIC FACTORS

In addition to the mechanisms discussed above, links between psychiatric disorders and medical illness may also indicate common genetic vulnerability. For example,

McCaffery et al. (2006) reviewed evidence for common genetic contributions to depression and coronary artery disease (CAD).

The twin studies reviewed revealed evidence for heritability of both depression and CAD, and the only study to consider depression and CAD jointly suggested that almost 20 per cent of the variability in depressive symptoms and CAD was attributable to common genetic factors.

Considering underlying mechanisms, McCaffery et al. (2006) suggest that it is plausible that genetic variation related to inflammation and **serotonin** may be associated with both depression and CAD, although genetic variation related to *inflammation* has been primarily studied in relation to CAD, whereas genetic variation related to *serotonin* has been primarily studied in relation to depression (links between serotonin and depression are also discussed in Chapter 4).

Laboratory studies support a role of both serotonin *and* inflammatory mechanisms in depression and CAD. For example, McCaffery et al. (2006) explain that the interaction of low levels of serotonin in the brain with other neurotransmitter systems is thought to be important in the pathophysiology of depression. Serotonin may also contribute to CAD via both central mechanisms (such as mediating the effects of sympathetic activity on cardiovascular function) and peripheral mechanisms (inducing platelet aggregation, for example).

Inflammatory processes are implicated in all stages of atherosclerosis, and several of the inflammatory markers that increase the risk for CAD have also been associated with depression. Therefore, it is possible that genetic variations related to serotonin and inflammation could influence vulnerability to both CAD and depression, although further research is needed.

Sociodemographic factors may also account for links between psychiatric illness and medical conditions. For example, low socio-economic status is a risk factor for both psychological and medical morbidity (see previous section).

In general, then, it is likely that a wide range of biological, cognitive–evaluative, behavioural and social–environmental factors underlie associations between psychiatric illness and chronic medical conditions. These factors are summarised below.

- **Biological**
  - Genetic predisposition
  - Dysregulation of stress response systems (resulting in allostatic load)
  - Effects of medication on mood and psychosocial outcomes.

- **Cognitive–evaluative**
  - Fear of symptoms
  - Low self-esteem
  - Catastrophising
  - Hypervigilance.

- **Behavioural**
  - Poor adherence to treatment plans
  - Poor health behaviours
  - Reduced social functioning.

- **Social–environmental**
  - Sociodemographic risk factors
  - Social stigmatisation and discrimination.

6.4 OLDER PEOPLE

As a biosocial issue, ageing is the underlying basis of almost all major human diseases.

Clark (2008: 14)

According to the United Nations, **population ageing** – the process by which older individuals become a proportionally larger share of the population – was one of the most distinctive demographic trends of the twentieth century. Increases in the proportion of older people (60 years and older) are being accompanied by declines in the proportion of young people (younger than 15 years), and it is estimated that, by 2050, the number of older people will exceed the number of young for the first time (United Nations, 2002).

This demographic trend has important implications for public health since ageing is associated with functional decline and an increased risk of morbidity (see Box 6.2).

Ageing may also have implications for psychological well-being, even in the absence of disease. For example, researchers have noted that, compared to young people, healthy older people experience higher levels of depression, anxiety and stress, as well as sleep disturbances, difficulty concentrating and progressive cognitive decline (Collaziol, Luz, Dornelles, Cruz & Bauer, 2004; Luz et al., 2003; Salzman & Shader, 1978).

BOX 6.2

Patterns of morbidity with age

Vellas, Albarede and Garry (1992) write that patterns of morbidity with age can be divided into three situations:

- a progressive illness, such as Alzheimer's disease (AD), leading to rapid functional decline (A)
- a catastrophic event, such as stroke or a hip fracture, leading to a decline in function, with improvement after rehabilitation (B)
- normal ageing with gradual progressive functional decline (C).

These patterns (A, B and C) are illustrated below.

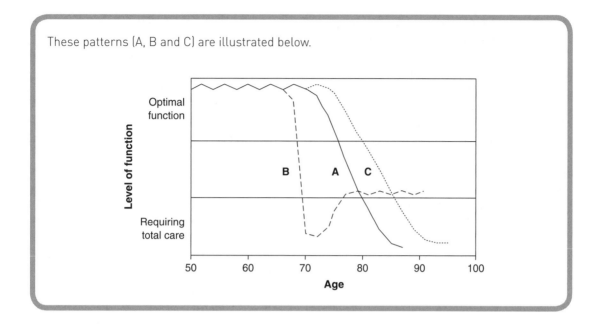

The ageing population represents a challenge to healthcare systems, and many governments are responding by developing and implementing policies to promote healthy ageing (Peel, McClure & Bartlett, 2005). In order to develop interventions to prevent or reverse age-related changes and maintain functional integrity of ageing, however, it is first necessary to understand the mechanisms underlying age-related morbidity.

Clark (2008) writes that, over the past 50 years, researchers have proposed a number of hypotheses that attempt to explain how age-related changes in macromolecules, cells, tissues, organs and systems may occur. This research has revealed that the progression and rate of ageing is highly variable and influenced by complex interactions between biological and environmental (psychological and social) factors (Clark, 2008).

6.4.1 AGE-RELATED CHANGES IN IMMUNE FUNCTION

For example, research evidence suggests that age-related illness is at least partly attributable to changes in immune function. The most reliable finding is altered T cell function with increasing age, which results partly from age-related degeneration of the thymus (**thymic involution**) and partly from **replicative senescence** – the characteristic of all normal somatic cells to undergo a limited number of cell divisions (the 'Hayflick limit').

While thymic involution is a consequence of ageing, replicative senescence is a consequence of cell division, not chronological time, and is therefore more related to exposure to antigens (Castle, 2000; Effros & Pawelec, 1997).

The humoral response is also impaired in older people, although innate immunity remains intact (Pawelec et al., 2002). Researchers have also noted an increased inflammatory immune response with advancing age, which is referred to as **inflamma-ageing** (Franceschi et al., 2000).

These age-related changes in immune function appear to operate in close concert with changes in endocrine function (referred to as **endocrinosenescence**). For example, consistent with documented increases in stress and anxiety with increasing age, researchers have noted elevated stress hormone levels in older people, suggestive of significant HPA activation. Increased glucocorticoid levels may account for age-associated changes such as thymic involution and lymphocyte decline, since similar changes have been observed in patients following glucocorticoid treatment (Collaziol et al., 2004). Other hormones (testosterone, oestrogen, progesterone, growth hormone and others), however, decline significantly with age (Straub Miller, Scholmerich & Zietz, 2000). Ershler and Keller (2000) point out that these changes may be implicated in inflamma-ageing since oestrogen and testosterone play a role in regulating interleukin-6 (IL-6), a potent mediator of inflammatory processes. In younger people, IL-6 is normally expressed at low levels, except during infection, trauma or other stress. After menopause or andropause, however, IL-6 levels are elevated even in the absence of infection, trauma or stress (Ershler & Keller, 2000).

Castle (2000) writes that the impact of these changes on disease processes is difficult to determine, since most studies in recent years have included only very healthy adults in order to separate age-related changes in immune function from the effects of disease on immune function, and that it is likely that changes in T cell function are compensated to some extent by up-regulation of other components of immune function.

Targonski, Jacobson and Poland (2007) point out that functional changes in immunosenescence tend to relate to inefficiencies and ineffectiveness of the immune response rather than complete immuno-incompetence. Ineffectiveness of the immune response may be manifested in poorer immune surveillance against cancer cells, contributing towards the increased incidence of malignant disease among older people (Targonski et al., 2007). Inflamma-ageing may also be a contributory factor since chronic inflammation is strongly associated with processes that contribute to the onset and progression of cancer (Spolentini et al., 2008).

Immunosenescence also has important implications in relation to infectious illness. For example, Castle (2000) reports that older people are more susceptible to the influenza (flu) virus and that the risk of infection is dramatically increased in the presence of one or more chronic illnesses. Older people also show an impaired response to vaccination compared to younger people, although the vaccination of people aged over 65 has been effective in reducing adverse events and mortality (Castle, 2000). Age-associated increases in IL-6 have been linked to diseases such as multiple myeloma, osteoporosis and Alzheimer's disease (Ershler & Keller, 2000).

6.4.2 THE ROLE OF PSYCHOLOGICAL FACTORS

A number of researchers have noted links between psychological factors (such as depression and stress) and age-related changes in immune and endocrine function.

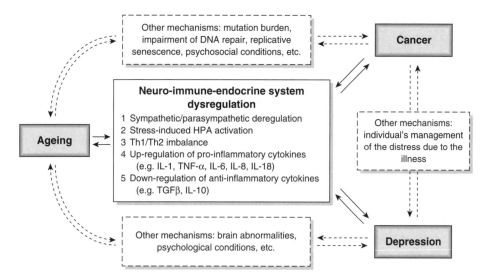

FIGURE 6.2 Biological and psychological interactions between cancer, depression and ageing

Source: Spolentini et al. (2008)

For example, Bauer et al. (2000) demonstrated that healthy older people experiencing chronic stress (long-term caregiving) had a blunted T cell proliferation in association with increased cortisol levels.

Spolentini et al. (2008) point out that depression is associated with disturbances in cellular immunity and up-regulation of inflammatory cytokine activation, and that depression is prevalent in both older people and cancer patients. Therefore, age-related changes in immune function may contribute to the increased risk of cancer and of depression and represent one of the factors explaining the link between depression and cancer (see Figure 6.2).

A review of studies evaluating the impacts of stress on immunity in older people concluded that stress processes 'mimic, exacerbate and sometimes accelerate the effects of ageing on immunity' (Hawkley & Cacioppo, 2004: 118). The authors of this review also suggested that restorative processes (such as sleep) may reduce some of the adverse effects of stress on the ageing immune system.

6.4.3 THE ALTERED HOMEOSTATIC THEORY AND TELOMERE LOSS

As indicated in Figure 6.2, neuro-immune endocrine system dysregulation is not the only pathway via which psychological variables may influence age-related illness.

Other pathways include a shift from parasympathetic to sympathetic regulation and loss of maintenance and repair functions. For example, Hellstrom (2006) reports that IHD, hypertension and diabetes share the same basic set of risk factors (endothelial dysfunction, dyslipidemia, inflammation and insulin resistance) and are treated by the same basic set of pharmaceutical and lifestyle factors (such as statins, aspirin, oestrogen or progesterone, exercise, weight loss and dietary modifications).

Risk factors for these disorders express sympathetic activation, while preventative factors exhibit parasympathetic activation. Hellstrom (2006) therefore suggests that these three disorders share a common basic pathogenic mechanism, which includes sympathetic activation, presumably as part of a homeostatic shift.

The **altered homeostatic theory** bases prevention on the principle of overbalancing the risk factors with preventative factors, producing a shift away from sympathetic activation and towards parasympathetic activation. Hellstrom (2006) therefore suggests that, since ageing is associated with increased risk of IHD, hypertension and diabetes, as well as a shift towards sympathetic activation, age should be considered as a modifiable risk factor in the same way as other risk factors. Further, it is possible that other age-associated diseases (such as Alzheimer's disease and cancer) may share a similar pathogenic mechanism since these diseases are also prevented by pharmaceutical and lifestyle agents that express parasympathetic activation and treat IHD, hypertension and diabetes (Hellstrom, 2006).

Several lines of evidence indicate that natural survival and longevity of a species is a function of its maintenance and repair capacities (such as the ability to repair DNA, react to stress and proliferate and facilitate the turnover of cells), while, there is a negative correlation between longevity and the rate of damage accumulation (Clark, 2008).

Research evidence suggests that maintenance and repair functions are influenced by interactions between genetic and psychosocial factors. For example, as noted above, all normal somatic cells undergo replicative senescence. This is thought to provide a barrier against the development of cancer by preventing cells from dividing enough to accumulate the many mutations required to become malignant (Zou, Sfeir, Gryaznov, Shay & Wright, 2004).

According to the **telomere hypothesis**, the counting mechanism for replicative senescence is provided by progressive shortening of **telomeres** – specialised DNA and protein structures at the end of chromosomes that act to protect chromosome caps (Gilley, Herbert, Huda, Tanaka & Reed, 2008; Zou et al., 2004). Each round of DNA replication results in shorter and shorter telomeres until the length reaches a critical level at which the cell can no longer reproduce. Gilley et al. (2008) point out, however, that the tumour-suppressing benefit of replicative senescence caused by shortening telomeres represents a 'double-edged sword' as shortened telomeres result in genomic instability, which is in itself related to several age-related disorders, including several cancers.

6.4.4 PATHWAYS TO TELOMERE DYSFUNCTION

Gilley et al. (2008) explain that several pathways lead to telomere dysfunction, including the effects of ageing, genetic factors and environmental factors. For

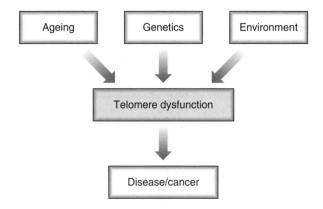

FIGURE 6.3 The main forces that may induce telomere dysfunction during development potentially leading to disease

Source: Gilley et al. (2008)

example, twin studies indicate that telomere length is at least partly genetic, although heritability estimates vary widely, and the findings also suggest there may be an effect of common environment on telomere length (Gilley et al., 2008).

Environmental influences on telomere length may include physical stressors (such as chronic environmental strain as a result of HIV infection or chemotherapy) and psychological ones, plus the effects of health-related behaviours. For example, Epel et al. (2004) found that women experiencing high levels of perceived stress had telomere lengths equivalent to low-perceived-stress women who were ten years older (cited in Gilley et al., 2008).

Gilley et al. (2008) report that smoking can significantly decrease telomere length, increasing the chances of telomere dysfunction. The inverse association between smoking and telomere length may explain some of the telomere dysfunction associated with cancer.

Overeating also contributes to telomere dyfsunction, and restricting calorie intake is one of the most reliable ways to increase lifespan. This, however, appears to increase cortisol, despite the widespread benefits for health, and it is not known if it actually increases telomere length (Epel, 2009).

Dispositional factors may also influence telomere length. For example, O'Donovan et al. (2009) demonstrated that dispositional pessimism (characterised by generalised negative expectations for the future) was associated with shorter telomere length and higher IL-6 concentrations in post-menopausal women.

The major forces that may induce telomere dysfunction are illustrated in Figure 6.3.

6.4.5 SUMMARY

In general, then, it seems that age-related diseases may share common pathogenic mechanisms, including neuro-immune-endocrine dysregulation, a shift from para-sympathetic to sympathetic activation and the loss of maintenance and repair capacities, culminating in damage accumulation, loss of homeostasis and an impaired ability to respond to environmental stress. The rate of progression of damage accumulation and loss of homeostasis, however, varies from one individual to the next and even between components of lower-level systems (organs, cells, macromolecules) within an individual (Clark, 2008). Research is only beginning to uncover the complex biopsychosocial interactions underlying this variability.

LONG-TERM CAREGIVERS

6.5
Another impact of the ageing population is the increased number of people acting as caregivers for relatives who are ill or require assistance with the personal activities of daily living. For example, in 2007, there were estimated to be around 476,000 people providing unpaid care for people with dementia in the UK alone, and the number of people with dementia is projected to increase by almost 40 per cent in the next 15 years (Alzheimer's Society, 2007; National Audit Office, 2007).

The impact of caregiving on health and well-being has been the subject of extensive research, and it is acknowledged that it can represent a 'health hazard', with most studies reporting high levels of anxiety, depression and other forms of psychological morbidity associated with the duration and intensity of the caregiving role (O'Reilly, Connolly, Rosato & Patterson, 2008). This research is also plagued by methodological issues, however, and conflicting findings have been reported (see Box 6.3).

BOX 6.3

Controversies: is caregiving a health hazard?

A number of studies and meta-analyses support a higher risk of physical health problems in caregivers compared to non-caregivers. O'Reilly et al. (2008), however, report that most studies have acknowledged considerable methodological difficulties in determining if caregiving per se causes ill health, as cross-sectional studies can only show an association and many studies either rely on subgroups of caregivers or fail to control adequately for potential confounds (such as level of income, education and health – all of which have been demonstrated to differ between caregivers and non-caregivers).

Conversely, some studies have revealed caregivers having better physical health compared to non-caregivers, which is likely to be due in part to a 'healthy caregiver effect' – individuals who are healthier are more likely to become caregivers and remain in the caregiver role (McCann et al., 2004; O'Reilly et al., 2008). This effect, however, cannot fully account for the reported positive impacts of caregiving. For example, McCann et al. (2004) found a significant mortality advantage for caregivers compared to non-caregivers (over a four-year period), even when adjusting for physical health at baseline. Further, a number of studies have revealed that the majority of caregivers report rewards associated with the caregiving role, including companionship, fulfilment, increased meaning in life and closer relationships with loved ones (see O'Reilly et al., 2008 for a review).

A number of studies have examined correlates of caregiver health. These studies have revealed several factors associated with both poorer physical health and poorer mental health (these include care recipient behaviour problems, cognitive impairment and functional disabilities, as well as the duration and amount of caregiving required). Additionally, poorer physical health has been linked to high vigilance demands (having to constantly monitor the care recipient), living with the care recipient and feelings of distress and depression, while poorer mental health has been linked to a higher-age, female gender and spousal relationship with the care recipient (Schulz & Sherwood, 2008).

Studies have also indicated that dementia-related caregiving is more challenging than caring for a person with physical disabilities alone. Also, caring for a person with dementia is associated with higher levels of distress and depression, as well as poorer physical health (Pinquart & Sorensen, 2007; Schulz & Sherwood, 2008).

6.5.1 PSYCHOBIOLOGICAL MECHANISMS

In many psychobiological investigations, caregiving is used as a model for evaluating the impacts of chronic stress on immune function. For example, in a meta-analysis of 13 studies examining the influence of psychological stress on antibody responses following flu vaccinations, Pedersen-Fischer and colleagues (2009) found that five studies compared the increased antibody levels of caregivers following vaccination to non-caregivers. The remaining studies focused on associations between self-reported stressful life events/perceived stress and increased presence of antibodies following vaccination. This meta-analysis revealed a similar association between psychological stress and responses to vaccination across all stress indicators. Caregivers have also been demonstrated to experience longer periods of wound healing (Kiecolt-Glaser et al., 1995) and poorer control of latent Epstein-Barr virus than non-caregivers (Kiecolt-Glaser et al., 1987).

Recent research has also revealed autonomic nervous system (ANS) dysregulation (Lucini et al., 2008) and lower secretory immunoglobulin (S-IgA) (Gallagher et al., 2008) in caregivers compared to non-caregivers. Also, associations between caregiving and sympathetic neuroendocrine dysregulation appear to be directly related to degree of anxiety, depression and caregiver burden (Aschbacher et al., 2008; Gallagher et al., 2008).

Interactions between genes and environmental stress may also be important when considering the impacts of caregiving on health. For example, Brummett et al. (2008) highlight the role of genes that regulate the activity of neurotransmitters such as serotonin, norepinephrine and dopamine and reveal evidence that allelic variation in one such gene (monoamine oxidase A, or MAOA) may moderate the impact of caregiving stress on urinary cortisol excretion.

6.5.2 SUMMARY

In general, then, caregivers may be considered an 'at risk' group in terms of their susceptibility to disease, although the impacts of caregiving on health are likely to be moderated by a range of factors, including the nature of caregiving (such as dementia v. non-dementia-related caregiving), psychological responses to caregiving (level of depression, anxiety, caregiver burden, benefit-finding and so on) and genetically mediated differences in sensitivity to chronic stress. The careful control of confounding variables is necessary when considering the impacts of caregiving on health since caregivers may differ from non-caregivers in terms of other sociodemographic risk factors for disease.

SUMMARY AND CONCLUSIONS

6.6
The research reviewed in this chapter suggests that psychobiological processes may be relevant to not only understanding individual variations in health and illness but also why particular groups are at greater risk of morbidity. For all of the groups reviewed, a high risk of physical illness is paralleled by a high risk of psychological morbidity and dysregulation of systems linking psychological processes with physiological damage (such as the sympathetic, neuroendocrine and immune systems).

Further, these processes appear to be interrelated within high-risk groups, so that greater *psychological* morbidity is associated with greater *physiological* dysregulation and poorer health. Although behavioural factors (such as smoking and exercise) are implicated, these relationships remain even when behaviour is taken into account. It is likely that psychobiological mechanisms (such as allostatic load and gene by environmental stress interactions) account for at least some of the remaining variance. The influence of psychobiological processes may be particularly evident when measures are taken across multiple parameters.

The research reviewed in this chapter has important implications for interventions. First, it is evident that, although being a member of a high-risk group places the individual at greater risk of disease, that risk is modifiable. For example, older people as a group are at greater risk of most major diseases, but that may be ameliorated by interventions that oppose the forces contributing to age-related illness (using interventions expressing parasympathetic activation in order to oppose an age-related shift towards sympathetic activation, for example). This means that, although an individual cannot change his or her age, genetic make-up or life circumstances, the risk associated with these factors need not be accepted as inevitable.

Second, it is evident from the research reviewed in this chapter that the same end result could be achieved by a number of different types of intervention. For example, parasympathetic activation may be achieved via pharmaceutical or lifestyle interventions. Similarly, development of coronary atherosclerosis is likely to be impacted by changes in working conditions, health-related behaviours, social support and coping, as well as via pharmaceutical interventions.

These findings are consistent with the biopsychosocial model of health, which identifies the need for a more holistic approach to illness, considering the multitude of factors that may culminate in disease (see Chapter 1). Psychobiological interventions are considered further in Chapter 7.

KEY TERMS

altered homeostatic theory, coronary atherosclerosis, endocrinosenescence, inflamma–ageing, population ageing, replicative senescence, serotonin, telomere hypothesis, telomeres, thymic involution

■Discussion questions

1 To what extent might social gradients in health be addressed via individual, organisational or societal interventions?

2 Is psychological well-being an individual issue or a societal issue?

3 Is it useful to classify disorders as psychological or physical?

4 How might different dimensions of socio-economic status relate to health and well-being?

FURTHER READING

Clark, B.F.C. (2008). Healthy human ageing. *New Biotechnology,* *25,* 13–15.

Hellstrom, H.R. (2006). The altered homeostatic theory: a hypothesis proposed to be useful in understanding and preventing ischemic heart disease, hypertension, and diabetes – including reducing the risk of age and atherosclerosis. *Medical Hypotheses,* *68,* 415–433.

Marmot, M. (2006). Health in an unequal world. *The Lancet,* *368,* 2081–2094.

Roy-Byrne, P.P., Davidson, K.W., Kessler, R.C., Asmundson, G.J.G., Goodwin, R.D., Kubzansky, L., Lydiard, R.B., Massie, M.J., Katon, W., Laden, S.K. & Stein, M.B. (2008). Anxiety disorders and comorbid medical illness. *General Hospital Psychiatry, 30,* 208–225.

Szanton, S.L., Gill, J.M. & Allen, J.K. (2005). Allostatic load: a mechanism of socio-economic health disparities? *Biological Research for Nursing, 7,* 7–15.

PSYCHOBIOLOGICAL INTERVENTIONS

7

OVERVIEW

In the previous chapters we illustrated psychobiological processes in health and illness with respect to links between the CNS, immune and endocrine systems, impacts of emotional states on physical and psychological functioning, gene–environment and gene–behaviour interactions and psychobiological processes implicated in the experience of pain.

In this chapter, we will consider how knowledge of these psychobiological processes can help to develop interventions to improve health. Knowledge of the theories and processes discussed in previous chapters (and relevant terminology) is assumed.

LEARNING OUTCOMES

By the end of this chapter you should be able to:

- describe coping-based interventions for patients with chronic illness

- discuss links between intervention approaches and theories of emotion, coping and self-regulation

- discuss evidence for the effectiveness of interventions and consider the strengths and limitations of alternative approaches

- describe cognitive and behavioural therapies for patients with chronic illness or pain and evaluate the potential mechanisms of these
- describe the process and principles of operant conditioning and compare with those of classical conditioning
- discuss 'third wave' therapies and compare and contrast these with cognitive and behavioural therapies
- discuss ways in which evidence from intervention studies may feed back into the development of theories and hypotheses for research.

7.1 INTRODUCTION

The research reviewed in the previous chapters indicates that:

- psychological processes influence the functioning of physiological systems previously believed to operate without direction from the brain
- these psychobiological interactions may have important implications for understanding individual variations in susceptibility to illness, the progression of disease and mortality
- the experience of pain, once thought to result entirely from nerve stimulation, is also shaped by complex interactions between psychological and biological processes
- this body of research has the potential to inform the development of interventions to improve health (to reduce the risk of disease in at risk populations, improve the physical and psychological functioning of patients with chronic illness, reduce the suffering of patients in pain and so on).

While this research is useful for identifying potential targets for intervention (such as emotion, coping, appraisals, illness representations, perceived control/outcome expectancies), it is also necessary to demonstrate that deliberate manipulation of these targets has the capacity to change outcomes. In this chapter, therefore, we shift attention from theory to application and take a look at studies that have evaluated the impact of interventions designed to alter psychological processes relevant to health. In the first section, we focus on coping-based interventions for patients with chronic illness, including approaches such as coping skills training, social support interventions and interventions designed to enhance benefit-finding or meaning-based coping and alter perceptions of the illness. In the second section, we consider research relating to behavioural and cognitive therapies, since these approaches also involve manipulation of psychological processes and are increasingly used in the treatment of patients with chronic illness and, particularly, chronic pain. The mechanisms underlying these therapies are considered in relation to emotion and coping theory.

Throughout this chapter we consider not only how research evidence and psychological theory can inform development of interventions but also how intervention studies feed back into the development of theories and hypotheses for research.

7.2 COPING-BASED APPROACHES

7.2.1 COPING SKILLS TRAINING FOR PATIENTS WITH CHRONIC ILLNESS

De Ridder and Schreurs (2001) write that, despite the extensive exploration of the coping concept in studies of chronic disease, it is surprising how little the concept has been picked up by psychologists involved in developing interventions for the chronically ill. In a review of the literature, they identified only three studies that addressed the process of coping itself, labelled it as such and evaluated it with specific coping measures. These included coping effectiveness training for HIV patients (Folkman et al., 1991) and studies on chronic pain by Fry and Wong (1991) and Keefe et al. (1990).

These studies reported improvements in coping, depression, anxiety, pain and psychological disability among individuals receiving training and/or practice in the use of coping strategies. In addition to coping training, Folkman et al. (1991) included training in appraisals and social support, in order that patients could learn to recognise the changeability of situations, use problem-focused strategies for dealing with such situations when possible, use emotion-focused strategies when aspects of situations appeared beyond their control, and mobilise social support when appropriate.

Although few studies addressed coping explicitly, a larger number of studies could be identified that addressed conceptual equivalents of coping, such as behaviours and/or cognitions intended to deal with a situation appraised as stressful, including problemsolving, seeking social support or positive thinking.

Restricting the review to seven chronic diseases (cancer, cardiovascular disease, AIDS and HIV infection, asthma, diabetes, rheumatoid arthritis and chronic pain), De Ridder and Schreurs (2001) identified 35 relevant studies. An overview of the studies showed a promotion of both problem-focused coping (such as self-management, making lifestyle changes and problem solving skills) and emotion-focused coping (relaxation, distraction, venting emotions, scheduling pleasant activities and so on), with a particular emphasis on problem-focused coping.

Eight of the studies reviewed included attempts to improve the appraisal of disease-related stressors, and 13 studies reported how patients could learn to make use of their coping resources (by mobilising support or improving communication with friends and family, for example). A range of both disease-specific and generic outcome measures were used.

De Ridder and Schreurs (2001) concluded that, regardless of the outcome measure, most of the interventions appeared to be effective, although small sample sizes and comparison of conditions did not allow for rigorous testing of the effects. Some of these coping approaches (self-management, venting emotions, social support and so on) have now developed a strong evidence base, as we discuss further below.

7.2.2 SELF-MANAGEMENT INTERVENTIONS

Coster and Norman (2009) point out that there is no universally agreed definition of self-management, but, in general, interventions of this kind aim to increase patients' interest and involvement in their own care and, by doing so, empower them to manage their conditions. Wilson, Kendall and Brooks (2005) highlight that **self-management interventions** may also involve therapeutic adjustment – for example, asthma patients may adjust their inhaler medication or commence oral steroids (Lahdensuo et al., 1996), while diabetes patients may be trained to adjust their own insulin dosage to enable them to have dietary freedom (DAFNE Study group, 2002).

Self-management training may be delivered by healthcare professionals (particularly nurses) or trained laypeople (Lorig, Gonzalez & Laurent, 1997). Evidence indicates that self-management interventions delivered by nurses and other healthcare professionals have definite benefits for asthma patients and are promising for patients with other forms of chronic disease, including diabetes, epilepsy and mental health problems (Coster & Norman, 2009). Lay-led programmes have been adopted in a number of countries and demonstrated to improve psychological outcomes, although critics point out that they have not resulted in anticipated improvements in disease outcomes or reduction in the use of healthcare services (see Box 7.1).

BOX 7.1

Controversies: the expert patient programme – are lay-led self-management interventions effective?

In the 1970s, Kate Lorig, a nurse working in arthritis care, developed a structured programme of self-management training designed to improve patients' self-efficacy. The arthritis self-management programme has been evaluated in a number of randomised controlled trials and become the prototype for several subsequent programmes, including a generic chronic disease self-management programme and others focusing on chronic pain and diabetes (see http://patienteducation.stanford.edu/programs). In the UK this model has been adopted as the expert patient programme (EPP) (see www.nhs.uk/conditions/Expert-patients-programme-/Pages/Introduction.aspx). Similar programmes have also been adopted in other European countries, as well as parts of Australia and the USA.

A key feature of expert patient programmes is that they are lay-led – that is, patients are trained in self-management techniques not by health professionals but by lay (patient) educators. The courses run for six weeks and cover topics such as dealing with the symptoms of the illness and negative emotions, communication with family and health professionals and planning for the future. Using lay educators provides a mechanism for modelling self-management behaviours. Lay-led programmes also appeal to policymakers because they are consistent with prevailing ideologies regarding inclusiveness, choice and shared decisionmaking and are considered to offer potential cost savings (Greenhalgh, 2009).

Greenhalgh (2009) writes, however, that the widespread adoption of lay-led self-management programmes is based on several misconceptions of Lorig's work. For example, self-management training is often believed to improve disease outcomes and reduce the use of healthcare services, but there is little evidence for improvement in disease outcomes (most studies have only evaluated *psychological* outcomes, particularly self-efficacy), and studies suggest that greater engagement in health may actually *increase* the use of health services. There is also no evidence as yet to demonstrate that self-management reduces the overall cost of healthcare and it is not clear whether lay-led self-management training is effective for all social and ethnic groups (see Griffiths et al., 2007, for a more detailed discussion).

Other reviews of self-management interventions (not restricted to lay-led programmes) suggest that interventions can provide benefits for some participants, although the reviews also highlight the fact that there is considerable variation in the format, content and mode of delivery of these interventions. At present, there is insufficient evidence available to evaluate the comparative effectiveness of different approaches, determine at what point (in the disease course) self-management may be optimally effective, or identify the 'active ingredients' of successful self-management programmes (Barlow, Wright, Sheasby, Turner & Hainsworth, 2002; Coster & Norman, 2009).

The Coster and Norman (2009) review revealed that the benefits of self-management interventions are more evident for some conditions (asthma and diabetes, for example), than others (such as arthritis and back pain), although this may reflect differences in the focus of interventions across disease states. Coster and Norman (2009) point out that educational and self-management programmes for conditions such as asthma and diabetes have tended to focus on the monitoring of symptoms, with patients being encouraged to learn pre-emptive strategies to identify symptoms and prevent or reduce the frequency of exacerbations. For conditions such as arthritis and back pain, however, interventions tend to focus on the psychosocial problems of living with the illness and aim to improve patients' psychological and social functioning. These benefits are harder to capture, but may be of great significance to the patients.

De Ridder and colleagues (2008) point out that both emotional and physiological effects of chronic disease may act as barriers to effective self-management. Major depression, for example, has been highlighted as a risk factor for non-adherence and symptoms of depression, such as lack of energy or motivation, can interfere with self-management. Andersen, Golden-Kreutz, Emery and Thiel (2009) also highlight the effects of distress on health-related behaviours. Distressed people experience changes in sleep and dietary habits, for example, and are more likely to self-medicate using alcohol or drugs. De Ridder et al. (2008) further highlight that poor self-management and depression can even themselves be regarded as outcomes, resulting from cytokines and other pathogenic mechanisms (cytokines are discussed in further detail in Chapter 2).

Self-management interventions are therefore likely to be most effective when the patients' psychological needs are also taken into account. Andersen and colleagues (2004, 2007) have described a biobehavioural intervention for breast cancer patients that aims to enhance self-management behaviours while both tackling the impacts of cancer-related distress on health-related behaviours and also training patients in relaxation methods. This intervention produced significant gains across psychosocial, behavioural and biological outcomes (Andersen et al., 2004, 2007). After 11 years of follow-up, the participants also had reduced risk of both the recurrence of breast cancer and death from breast cancer (Andersen et al., 2008). The intervention is described in Research in focus box 7.1. Relaxation therapies are considered further in Section 7.3.

RESEARCH IN FOCUS BOX 7.1

Andersen and colleagues (2009) describe a biobehavioural intervention (BBI) developed and evaluated in studies with cancer patients. The intervention was developed on the basis of the biobehavioural model of cancer-stress and disease course (Andersen, Kiecolt-Glaser & Glaser, 1994). As specified by the model, the intervention was designed to reduce patients' stress, enhance their quality of life, increase their positive health behaviours, decrease their negative ones and improve compliance with medical treatment.

Methodology

The intervention was provided in groups of 8 to 12 patients. Sessions lasted 1.5 hours, with an intensive phase of 18 weekly sessions during the first 4 months, followed by a maintenance phase of 8 monthly sessions, for a total of 16 sessions, over 12 months.

Therapists followed a session-by-session manual and patients received a treatment hand-book. The components of the intervention included education (in relation to stress and coping, the disease and treatment, diet and exercise, and sleep hygiene – overcoming poor sleep habits) and training (in progressive muscle relaxation, problemsolving, communication and drawing on social support).

Patients were supported through the process of changing health-related behaviours (such as setting goals for exercise, identifying triggers or cues for unhealthy eating, referral to stopping smoking therapy) and encouraged to maintain contact with the other patients between sessions to enhance the level of social support they had.

Results

As reported in previous studies (Andersen et al., 2004, 2007) the intervention produced significant gains in terms of enhanced T cell immunity and secondary outcomes (regarding distress, social adjustment, health behaviours (such as improving diet and stopping smoking) adhering to treatment). Patients reported high levels of satisfaction with each of the components of the intervention. After 11 years of follow-up, the intervention patients had a reduced risk of the disease recurring and death from breast cancer (Andersen et al., 2008).

Conclusions and implications

This multicomponent intervention was acceptable to patients and produced significant benefits in relation to psychological and biological outcomes, as well as a reduced risk of the disease recurring and cancer-related mortality. Andersen et al. (2008) report that relaxation, complying with treatment and lifestyle (health behaviour) changes function as complementary strategies to reduce stress, speed recovery and improve patients' quality of life. Interventions provided over a period of several months afford opportunities to address stressors associated with different stages in the course of the disease and provide support for maintaining behaviour changes, so are likely to be more appropriate than short-term psychosocial interventions.

Although self-management in patients with chronic disease can be considered a form of problem-focused coping (De Ridder & Schreurs, 2001), the process of self-management can be usefully considered in relation to **self-regulation** theory. For example, according to Carver and Scheier (1982), behaviour is modified with reference to a *system concept* (to be healthy, for example), which specifies goals for *principles* (such as to eat a balanced diet) that, in turn, specify goals for *scripts*.

Scripts are more specific than general principles and involve a series of 'if x, then y' decisions ('If I am hungry between meals, then I will eat fruit', for instance). They specify goals for successively lower-level systems until the specific behaviours necessary to achieve the system concept can be produced. At the lowest levels, these behaviours involve physiological alterations, such as change in muscle tension in certain parts of the body. Self-regulation within this hierarchical model is dependent on the focus of attention and expectancy. Focusing attention on the self is required to compare our current state with relevant goals, while expecting favourable outcomes is necessary to motivate us to produce the effort required to achieve these goals. Carver and Scheier (1982) point out that actions such as taking a blood pressure reading only make sense within this hierarchical model, since the information obtained is only meaningful when compared to a reference value, and discrepancy from the reference value leads to actions to reduce this discrepancy (provided those actions are associated with the expectation of positive outcomes).

Research evidence suggests that self-regulation depends on limited resources, since efforts to control thoughts, emotions or behaviour impair performance of subsequent control tasks and self-regulation strength (or 'will power') tends to diminish over time. This may explain why stress tends to interfere with behaviours such as dieting or quitting smoking, since coping with negative emotions and resisting temptation both draw on the same, limited resources (Muraven & Baumeister, 2000). Glucose appears to be important for self-regulation, and lack of it is associated with difficulty in overriding urges, thoughts, emotions or habitual response tendencies (Baumeister Vohs & Tice, 2007).

7.2.3 SOCIAL SUPPORT INTERVENTIONS

Studies evaluating social support as a psychosocial intervention have mainly reported benefits relative to either no treatment or active controls (Hogan, Linden & Najarian, 2002). For example, Fife and colleagues (2008) demonstrated that improvements in coping, mood and the meaning HIV patients constructed from their illness could be achieved via a patient–partner intervention model in which patients' cohabiting partners attended four two-hour psychosocial education sessions with the patient. Those who participated in this intervention fared better in terms of these outcomes than a control group in which the person living with HIV received supportive telephone calls alone.

Van Dam et al. (2005) conducted a systematic review of controlled intervention studies testing the effects of social support interventions on health outcomes in primary and outpatient care for type 2 diabetes. Six studies were included and these used a range of intervention approaches, including Internet-based and telephone support, social support groups and support from fellow patients jointly participating in group visits to the physician.

 The findings indicated that social support from peers and fellow patients in group consultations, peer group sessions, telephone peer contacts or Internet-based peer communications may enhance lifestyle adjustments and outcomes of care. Worsening of diabetes control was only prevented in the study that involved group visits to the physician. Involving spouse, peers and peer counsellors had positive results for some patients, although negative effects of social support were found in men when spouses participated in their education group for weight loss.

Social support is also an important component of psychosocial treatment for addiction. For example, in addition to medication (such as nicotine replacement therapy), smokers attempting to quit may be offered telephone, group or one-to-one support. The validated contents of these psychosocial treatments are intra-session and extra-session social support and behavioural skills training (Hughes, 2008). Treatment for alcohol and narcotics addiction includes individual and group counselling as well as 12-step programmes, such as Alcoholics or Narcotics Anonymous (Volkow & Li, 2005a).

Several studies have found that combining medications with psychosocial treatments improves outcomes for patients with addictions to tobacco, alcohol or other substances (Hughes, 2008; Volkow & Li, 2005a).

7.2.4 VENTING EMOTIONS

A wide body of research indicates that expression of emotion is associated with better outcomes for patients than avoidance and inhibition of emotions, with **emotional disclosure** interventions providing the most compelling evidence that expression can improve psychological and physiological functioning (De Ridder et al., 2008).

The emotional disclosure paradigm developed by Pennebaker and colleagues (Pennebaker & Beall, 1986, for example) involves writing about a stressful experience for 15 to 20 minutes on 3 or 4 consecutive days. This task has been demonstrated to result in improvements in a wide range of outcomes, including immune function, self-reported health, physician visits and psychological well-being, with meta-analyses supporting the assertion of benefits for both patient and non-patient populations (Frattaroli, 2006; Frisina, Borod & Lepore, 2004; Smyth, 1998). These effects do not always hold up (Meads, Lyons & Carroll, 2003), however, the mechanisms underlying the intervention's effects are poorly understood and they may vary according to the population taking part. For example, catharsis may be an important mediator of intervention effects for individuals who face social constraints on self-expression (de Moor et al., 2008), but less so for other groups. In addition to catharsis, though, the other positive mechanisms may include habituation to negative emotional memories, changes in the cognitive and emotional processing of stressful experiences and improvements in working memory, resulting from the reduced impact of intrusive thoughts (Smyth & Pennebaker, 2008).

Emotional writing exercises have also been used to enhance patients' ability to find benefits or positive meaning in their experiences. For example, King and Miner (2000) found that, compared with control participants, college students who wrote about the benefits they had experienced as a result of a negative life event made fewer visits to a health centre over the following five months. Stanton et al. (2002) reported that women who wrote about their positive thoughts and feelings concerning their breast cancer had fewer medical appointments for cancer-related morbidities than women in a control group. In this last study, writing about positive thoughts and feelings (benefit-finding) was more useful for women who showed low levels of avoidance coping, while women who exhibited high levels of avoidance coping benefited from writing about their deepest thoughts and feelings concerning breast cancer (written emotional expression).

Cameron and Nicholls (1998) found that written emotional expression was beneficial only for optimists. In their study, a self-regulating version of the writing task was also developed, in which participants wrote down their thoughts and feelings about the event, generated strategies for coping and appraised the outcomes of these strategies. This task reduced illness-related clinic visits for both optimists and pessimists.

Cameron and Jago (2008) suggest that pessimists may respond to undirected emotional expression by developing maladaptive representations that promote avoidance rather than active engagement in the task. Pessimists or avoidant copers may therefore require more structured interventions than optimists in which emotional regulation is accompanied by a focus on cognitive and behavioural regulation.

7.2.5 INTERVENTIONS BASED ON THE COMMONSENSE MODEL

A number of studies have evaluated interventions based on the commonsense model of illness representations (CSM; Leventhal, Meyer & Nerenz, 1980). For example, Petrie and colleagues (2002) evaluated a brief hospital intervention designed to alter patients' perceptions of their myocardial infarction (heart attack). The intervention resulted in a significant reduction in their symptoms of angina and a faster return to work, compared to patients in the control group (Research in focus box 7.2).

Interventions based on the CSM have also produced positive outcomes in relation to hypertension adherence (Theunissen, de Ridder, Bensing & Rutten, 2003) and perceptions of psoriasis (Fortune, Richards, Griffiths & Main, 2004). Peyrot and Rubin (2007) suggest that a consideration of patients' perceptions of illness is an essential first step for any interventions that include a focus on changing behaviour, since perceptions of the identity of the illness, consequences and control of it, are likely to influence their adherence to treatment plans and motivation to change health-related behaviour.

RESEARCH IN FOCUS BOX 7.2

Petrie and colleagues (2002) examined whether or not a brief hospital intervention designed to alter patients' perceptions about their myocardial infarction (MI) would result in a better recovery process and a reduction in any disability.

Methodology

Sixty-five consecutive patients with their first MI were assigned to receive either an intervention designed to alter perceptions of their MI or the usual care from rehabilitation nurses. In contrast to other interventions that typically deliver the same cognitive or behavioural intervention to *all* patients, this study based the content of each patient's intervention on his or her perception of the MI (using the illness perceptions questionnaire (IPQ); Weinman, Petrie, Moss-Morris & Horne, 1996).

The intervention involved three sessions. The first explored patients' beliefs about the cause of the MI and addressed the common misconception that stress was singularly responsible for the MI. The second built on the causes identified by the patient and focused on developing a plan of minimising future risk by altering risk factors relevant to the patient and increasing his or her beliefs about control. The linkage the timeline and the consequences of the illness was achieved by explaining in the second session that, as patients recovered from the illness, they could expect to return to work and normal activities. The third session reviewed the action plan and distinguished symptoms that are a normal part of healing and recovery from symptoms that may be warning signs of another MI.

Results

The intervention resulted in significant positive changes in patients' views of their MI. Patients in the intervention group reported that they were better prepared for leaving hospital and they returned to work faster than those in the control group. At the three-month follow-up, patients in the intervention group reported a significantly lower rate of angina symptoms than did the controls.

Conclusions and implications

A brief in-hospital intervention was successful at changing patients' perceptions of their MI. The intervention allowed for misperceptions and negative beliefs to be modified early in the recovery process, and it has considerable potential for reducing work-related disability.

BEHAVIOURAL AND COGNITIVE THERAPIES

7.3 While the interventions discussed above are largely based on theories of emotion and coping, therapeutic approaches have also been developed on the basis of learning theory. For example, as discussed in Chapters 1 and 2, humans and animals can learn to produce a physiological response (such as salivation) to a previously neutral stimulus (such as a bell), provided that the stimulus is paired repeatedly with an unconditioned stimulus (such as food). This process of associative learning – referred to as 'classical conditioning' – also has clinical applications, such as conditioning immune responses, resulting in a reduced requirement for drugs that have adverse side-effects (see Chapter 2 for further discussion).

7.3.1 CLASSICAL CONDITIONING AND PLACEBO THERAPIES

Classical conditioning may also explain some of the reported effects of **placebo therapies** – therapies which involve the administration of dummy pills or sham treatments in place of active therapies. Placebo therapies may take a number of forms including the use of inert 'dummy' pills (typically a sugar pill), 'sham' surgery or other forms of sham therapy (including physical and psychological manipulations).

Placebo effects can be clinically relevant and some even come close to effects achieved by actual treatments (Pacheco-Lopez, Engler, Niemi & Schedlowski, 2006). Although patients offered placebo therapy in the clinical context do not typically undergo a period of associative learning, Wager and Nitschke (2005) suggest that conditioned associations between the treatment context and physiological responses may exist due to prior experience with actual treatments.

The underlying mechanisms are not well understood, although the effects of placebo therapies on self-reported symptoms, physiological pain and motor mechanisms are believed to be mainly mediated by conscious expectations (Benedetti et al., 2003;

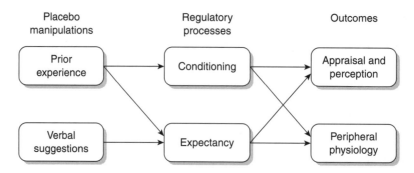

FIGURE 7.1 The relationships between placebo treatments, internal regulatory processes and their outcomes

Source: Wager and Nitschke (2005)

Enck, Benedetti & Schedlowski, 2008), while the effects of placebo therapies on unconscious processes (such as the release of hormones or immune function) may be explained by classical conditioning (Enck et al., 2008), shown in Figure 7.1.

Recent research also suggests that different neurobiological and neuropsychological mechanisms may underlie placebo responses mediated by expectancy and those mediated by conditioning. In particular, it is likely that dopamine and endogenous opioid activation in the nucleus accumbens are implicated in expectation-induced placebo responses, since these neurotransmitters are activated by both the administration of the placebo treatment and the expectation of reward (Enck et al., 2008).

Cytokines might be an important factor in the associative processes occurring during the behavioural conditioning of immune functions, since cytokines seem to play an important role in the pathways between the immune system and CNS (Pacheco-Lopez et al., 2006). Other mechanisms are also possible – for example, placebo analgesia may involve changes in the endogenous pain inhibitory systems affecting spinal and cortical nociceptive responses (Goffaux, Redmond, Rainville & Marchand, 2007).

7.3.2 OPERANT CONDITIONING AND BEHAVIOUR THERAPY

Other forms of learning are also relevant to the development of patient interventions. For example, many therapeutic approaches are based on the principles of **operant conditioning**, which was first described by B.F. Skinner in the 1930s. Skinner demonstrated that behaviour could be modified by providing reinforcement (to increase the likelihood of the behaviour recurring) or punishment (to decrease the likelihood of this happening) – see Box 7.2.

This research gave rise to the development of **behaviour therapy** techniques aimed at eliminating problem behaviours (including problem emotional responses) by manipulating the relationship between responses and their outcomes. For example, **graded exposure therapy** involves repeatedly presenting a feared stimulus under conditions in which the stimulus will not result in unfavourable consequences. This eventually results in the **extinction** of fear responses.

Exposure therapy is also often mentioned in relation to a process called **habituation**. Habituation may be defined as 'a learning process where an animal learns to ignore a stimulus that does not predict anything of value to it' (Balkenius, 2000: 3). If the animal (or person) is repeatedly exposed to a stimulus without experiencing any particular outcome, the response to the stimulus will gradually become weaker. Habituation is often described as a form of 'non-associative learning', since learning can take place in relation to a specific stimulus without reference to the situation or other stimuli that are present (Balkenius, 2000).

BOX 7.2

Operant conditioning

In the 1930s, B.F. Skinner conducted a number of studies in which rats were rewarded with food pellets for pressing a lever. Skinner discovered that rats increased the rate of lever-pressing after a food reward, but that the rate of lever-pressing decreased when subsequent lever presses were not rewarded, with fewer and fewer lever presses for each hour without a food reward. Skinner referred to this pattern as an 'extinction curve'.

Skinner then varied the reward schedule so that rats were reinforced at intervals. He found that the rate of lever-pressing would rise after each lever press and the behaviour would gradually decrease again until the next reward, which prompted a renewed increase in the rate of lever-pressing. Skinner found that, if the next reinforcement occurred before the first reinforcement had completely extinguished, the response rate could be summed, so that each reinforcement added to the response rate in a cumulative manner.

Later, Skinner reinforced 'successive approximations' to the target behaviour, so that, if a rat did *not* press the lever spontaneously, it could still be rewarded for steps towards that behaviour – approaching the site of the lever, touching the lever with its feet and so on. After each step was rewarded, the next reward became contingent on the next approximation towards the lever-pressing behaviour. In this way, the rat could be trained to press the lever.

Skinner used the same method to train a rat to carry out a complex chain of behaviours – to release a marble by pulling a chain, carry the marble across the cage and deposit it in a slot that would release a food pellet.

This form of learned behaviour became known as **operant conditioning**, a process that differs from the previously described process of classical conditioning (Pavlov, 1927) in that behaviour is conditioned not by what precedes it but by what follows it. While classical conditioning involves repeated pairings of a conditioned stimulus (such as a bell) with an unconditioned stimulus (such as food) in order to produce a conditioned response (that is, salivation to the bell), operant conditioning involves pairing an unconditioned response (such as spontaneously pressing a lever) with an unconditioned stimulus (such as food) in order to produce a conditioned response (that is, pressing the lever to obtain food; for a more detailed discussion see: Iversen, 1992).

7.3.3 COGNITIVE THERAPY

Although behaviour therapy techniques remain widely used today, the behaviourist principles on which they are based have been challenged. For example, therapists have questioned the notion that emotional responses (such as fear) result directly from exposure to specific stimuli, and suggest that it is the individual's interpretation of the meaning of their experiences that determines their response (this conceptualisation is also consistent with theories of stress and coping discussed previously). Therefore, **cognitive therapy** techniques have also been developed to challenge problem thinking.

Cognitive therapy was originally developed to treat depression (Beck, 1964), but has since been extended to other patient populations, including those with chronic pain and physical health problems (Butler, Chapman, Forman & Beck, 2006). According to the cognitive model underlying cognitive therapy, depression results from dysfunctional thoughts that arise automatically, without deliberation or reasoning – **negative automatic thoughts (NATs)**. The individual may be barely aware of these thoughts, but is more likely to be aware of the emotion that follows. NATs may also result in dysfunctional behaviours (such as avoiding people, places or situations associated with negative thoughts or feelings). Cognitive therapists therefore train people to be able to identify their NATs and subject them to rational reflection in order to change emotions and behaviour. Behavioural interventions (such as graded exposure) may also be used to overcome avoidance and promote habituation to feared stimuli (Beck, 1995).

When cognitive *and* behavioural therapy techniques are used in combination, the resulting therapeutic approach is referred to as **cognitive behavioural therapy (CBT)**. CBT has been widely supported as an intervention for patients with both physical and mental health problems. CBT is the psychological approach that is most widely used to treat patients living with chronic pain (Lewandowski, 2004); it is supported by evidence from systematic reviews and meta-analyses (Eccleston, Morley, William, Yorke & Mastryannopoulou, 2002) and is often a component of multidisciplinary pain programmes (Gatchel & Rollings, 2008).

7.3.4 MECHANISMS UNDERLYING COGNITIVE BEHAVIOURAL THERAPY

The mechanisms underlying the effects of CBT, however, have been subject to debate. For example, Burns and Spangler (2001) found that changes in dysfunctional attitudes during therapy were not causally related to changes in depression and anxiety during therapy (as the cognitive model predicts). Instead, their findings suggest that a third, unmeasured variable resulted in changes in both dysfunctional thinking and mood.

A more recent review concluded that 'the evidence that cognitive variables mediate cognitive change in CBT is somewhat limited' (Longmore & Worrell, 2007: 184).

The authors suggest that cognitive change may be part of the change resulting from treatment rather than the cause of treatment effects.

Other research indicates that the effects of CBT may be explained, at least in part, by changes in self-efficacy. For example, Turner, Holtzman and Mancl (2007) evaluated cognitive mediators of CBT for temporomandibular (TMD) pain and found that self-efficacy had an independent effect on outcomes that could not be explained by association with pain-specific beliefs (such as perceived pain control, catastrophising and belief that pain signals harm).

CBT may also operate via **somatic marking**. According to the somatic marker hypothesis (Damasio, 1996), threats to homeostasis are 'somatically marked' in that they activate feeling states which allow us to know how we feel about novel events without resorting to deliberate reasoning. These feeling states activate attempts at self-regulation – that is, attempts to achieve homeostasis by monitoring and adjustment of parameters away from an undesired state and towards a desired state or goal.

Deary (2008) suggests that CBT may also result in a cognitive shift away from what the patient is feeling and towards what the patient can do despite these feelings. In self-regulation terminology, this may shift the reference value (desired state or goal) from symptom avoidance towards general well-being.

It is likely that CBT operates on more than one level. For example, Brewin (1996) suggests that CBT operates at both a conscious level – altering verbally accessible cognitions (assumptions or beliefs) – and a non-conscious level – deactivating emotional memories. While assumptions and beliefs may be deliberately interrogated and retrieved, emotional memories are triggered automatically when environmental inputs match the stored memories. Change at the non-conscious level is unlikely to be achieved via cognitive interventions and necessitates associative learning – that is, repeated pairings of the feared stimulus with positive outcomes, culminating in habituation and mastery.

7.3.5 BIOFEEDBACK AND RELAXATION THERAPIES

Cognitive and behavioural therapies may also involve training in **biofeedback** – a technique that is used to produce learned control of a wide range of physiological responses, including systolic and diastolic pressure, peripheral vascular responses and various brain rhythms.

Gatchel and colleagues (2003) explain that, although these physiological processes were long believed to be involuntary, research in the 1960s demonstrated that, if individuals are given feedback about their internal physiological processes (such as blood flow, muscle tension), they can, over time, learn to exert conscious control over these processes.

Feedback is commonly provided using technologies such as **electroencephalography (EEG)**, which provides information on brainwave activity, **electromyography (EMG)**, which provides feedback on muscle tension, and **electrodermal response (EDR)**, which provides information on the activity of sweat glands. Gatchel et al. (2003: 56) write that, 'receiving feedback serves to remove the "blindfold" over physiological responses, enabling individuals to voluntarily control a response.' Also, for pain patients, CBT combined with biofeedback 'increases the patient's sense of self-efficacy by providing clear unequivocal feedback about a person's ability to gain control over certain physiological responses' (Gatchel et al., 2003: 56). Indeed, changes in self-efficacy may be more important than the ability to voluntarily control physiological responses (for some outcomes at least). For example, Holroyd et al. (1984) demonstrated that the effects of biofeedback on tension-type headaches were more closely related to participants' beliefs that they were performing the procedure successfully than to their actual success in reducing muscle tension. Changes in measures of the locus of control and self-efficacy were also associated with reductions in headache activity following treatment.

Lehrer (2003) highlights that, in addition to biofeedback, operant conditioning (learned control) of physiological responses may be achieved via techniques such as Jacobson's (1938) **progressive relaxation** method (and 'derivative' progressive muscle relaxation (PMR) methods) and Eastern meditative techniques such as yoga, Qigong and Zen. For example, Jacobson used deliberate muscle tension, which was progressively lessened to almost imperceptible levels, to teach patients more sensitive perceptions of muscle sensation and help them to acquire control. Eastern masters in meditative practice teach people to modulate their respiration rate in ways that naturally produce large increases in low-frequency heart rate variability, similar to the heart rate variability achieved with biofeedback (Lehrer, 2003). As with behavioural self-regulation, the regulation of physiological responses (either via biofeedback or relaxation training) may be explained in relation to Carver and Scheier's (1982) hierarchical model of self-regulation – that is, awareness of physiological processes at the lowest levels of the hierarchy allows the individual to modify these parameters to achieve goals specified at higher levels of the hierarchy. In order to self-regulate successfully, the individual must maintain a focus on the self and develop expectations of positive outcomes.

7.3.6 IS LEARNED CONTROL ALWAYS ADAPTIVE?

Although the techniques described above have proved successful in producing learned control of cognitive, behavioural and physiological processes, researchers and therapists have started to question whether or not efforts to control these processes should always be considered adaptive. For example, the control of pain is useful when it can be achieved, and it leads to an overall improvement in long-term functioning for the patient, but efforts to control, avoid or find a 'cure' for pain can result in pain becoming more central, more dominant and more disruptive and result in the patient abandoning other meaningful activities (Hayes & Duckworth, 2006; McCracken, Carson, Eccleston & Keefe, 2004). Similar problems can arise as a result of attempting to avoid or control other symptoms – for example, patients with epilepsy may avoid social situations and stick to rigid, restrictive routines owing to fear of seizures (Robinson, Gregg, Dahl & Lundgren, 2004).

An alternative to controlling and avoiding experiences that is becoming increasingly incorporated into behavioural and cognitive therapies is the notion of acceptance. **Acceptance and commitment therapy (ACT),** for example, encourages patients to abandon the struggle to avoid or reduce pain (or other troubling emotions or sensations), disentangle from illness-related thought, develop deepened, conscious contact with the present moment and construct larger and larger patterns of effective action linked to chosen values (Hayes & Duckworth, 2006). For example, rather than focusing *only* on the illness, patients are encouraged to consider valued directions in relation to life domains, including work, leisure, family and friends (Robinson et al., 2004).

ACT differs from CBT in that it does not adopt a tripartite model, distinguishing between overt behaviours (actions), emotions (subjective experience) and cognitions (thought processes), but subsumes cognitions under the more general term 'behaviour', as it is used in traditional behaviour analysis (in which 'behaviour' includes 'private' behaviours (thoughts) as well as public behaviours). Also, where CBT targets avoidance of emotion-eliciting stimuli, ACT targets *experiential avoidance* – an unwillingness to experience a negative thought or sensation (Hoffmann & Asmundson, 2008).

ACT has not yet been extensively evaluated for patients with chronic illness, although the preliminary evidence indicates that it can result in reductions in sick leave and use of medical services in patients with chronic pain (Dahl, Wilson & Nilsson, 2004).

In emphasising acceptance and contact with the present moment, ACT also shares similarities of approach with techniques such as **mindfulness-based stress reduction (MBSR)** and **mindfulness-based cognitive therapy (MBCT).** Fletcher and Hayes (2005) write that MBSR, developed by Kabat-Zinn in 1979, was one of the first techniques to integrate Eastern practices such as meditation and yoga into treatments for chronic pain and illness, while MBCT is an adaptation of MBSR for treating chronic depression.

MBSR is a clinical group intervention that involves extensive training in mindfulness meditation and its applications for daily living and coping with stress, pain and illness (Reibel, Greeson, Brainard & Rosenzweig, 2001). A number of studies have demonstrated positive impacts of MBSR on well-being and daily functioning in patients with pain (Kabat-Zinn, Lipworth & Burney, 1985; Kabat-Zinn, Lipworth, Burney & Sellers, 1986; Kaplan, Goldberg & Galvin-Nadeau, 1993), and a meta-analysis of studies over a wide spectrum of clinical populations (pain, cancer, heart disease, depression, anxiety and so on), as well as non-clinical groups, suggested that MBSR may help individuals to cope with clinical and non-clinical problems.

Mindfulness-based therapies may operate, in part, via alterations in physiological arousal. For example, Esch and colleagues (2004) write that techniques such as meditation, tai chi and yoga have been demonstrated to elicit a **relaxation response (RR)** that has been identified as the physiological counterpart of the fight or flight response – that is, a *lowered* heart rate, blood pressure and respiratory rate – and regular elicitation of RR has been reported to alleviate stress-related medical disorders (see also altered homeostatic theory, discussed in Chapter 6).

Therapies including meditation and related techniques have been reported to activate areas of the brain involved in processing positive emotion and exert physiological effects involving both the endocrine and autonomic nervous system (Esch et al., 2004). These therapies may also impact health and well-being via their impacts on patients' inner resources. For example, Fredrickson, Cohn, Coffey, Pek and Finkel (2008) demonstrated that regularly practising meditation produced increases in participants' daily experiences of positive emotions, which produced increases in a wide range of personal resources, which in turn predicted increases in their satisfaction with life and reduced their depressive symptoms. These findings are consistent with the 'broadening' hypothesis (see broaden and build theory, Chapter 3).

Although acceptance and mindfulness approaches are often referred to as 'third wave' therapies, succeeding behavioural and cognitive behavioural therapies, Hoffmann and Asmundson (2008) suggest that ACT techniques are fully compatible with CBT and that improved interventions for some disorders may result from integrating experiential avoidance techniques with conventional CBT techniques based on stimulus avoidance. They further propose that both CBT and ACT can be considered in relation to Gross' process model of emotions, which emphasises the evaluation of external or internal emotional cues (Gross & John, 2003; Gross & Levenson, 1997).

According to this latter process model, strategies to regulate emotions may include *antecedent-focused* strategies, occurring *before* the emotional response has been fully activated (such as situation modification, attention deployment and cognitive reframing), and *response-focused strategies*, involving attempts to alter the expression or experience of emotions once the response has been fully activated (such as suppression and other experimental avoidance strategies). Hoffmann and Asmundson (2008) suggest that CBT promotes adaptive antecedent-focused strategies, while ACT counteracts maladaptive response-focused strategies. Therefore, the two therapies both target the regulation of emotions, but intervene at different stages of the process of generating these emotions.

SUMMARY

7.4 Psychobiological research has important implications for not only the way we conceptualise relationships between psychological and biological processes with respect to health and illness but also for the development of approaches to treatment. As we have discussed in this chapter, however, the link between theory and practice is not always clear. In some cases the development of intervention approaches predates the development of theory, and in some cases intervention approaches are informed by theory, but without drawing explicit links between the methods employed and specific theoretical constructs. This means that the mechanisms underlying psychological therapies are often difficult to identify and, as a consequence, the methods employed may vary considerably between studies.

Despite these limitations, a wide body of research provides support for interventions that enable patients to gain conscious control over physiological and/or psychological processes. Some processes, however, may not be accessible to cognitive processing and will require different intervention approaches (such as conditioning, habituation or somatic remarking). Some interventions may target both conscious and non-conscious processes – for example, graded exposure may change conscious beliefs and expectations by providing experience of mastery, while also allowing stimuli to be somatically remarked as benign.

Research also highlights that efforts to achieve control may not always be adaptive. For uncontrollable stressors (physical or psychological), acceptance may be more adaptive.

In relation to emotion and coping theory, acceptance may represent activation of the emotion regulating arm of the commonsense model, a shift from problem-focused coping to emotion-focused coping or a change in reference value away from avoiding symptoms and towards general well-being.

For many psychosocial interventions, it is evident that effects may be moderated by individual differences, including gender, personality and coping style. Further research is therefore needed to both shed light on the mechanisms underlying the effects of psychological interventions and determine the circumstances under which particular approaches are most likely to be effective. These methodological issues will be considered in greater detail in Chapter 8.

KEY TERMS

acceptance and commitment therapy (ACT), behaviour therapy, biofeedback, cognitive behavioural therapy (CBT), cognitive therapy, coping skills training, electrodermal response (EDR), electroencephalography (EEG), electromyography (EMG), emotional disclosure, extinction, graded exposure therapy, habituation, mindfulness-based cognitive therapy (MBCT), mindfulness-based stress reduction (MBSR), negative automatic thoughts (NATs), operant conditioning, placebo therapies, progressive relaxation, relaxation response, self-management interventions, self-regulation, somatic marking

■Discussion questions

1   What types of difficulties do you think patients with diabetes might face in relation to self-management? How could these difficulties be addressed via psychosocial interventions?

2   Is it *always* a good thing to express emotions? Can you think of any circumstances in which it might be better to not express emotions or circumstances in which expression would be more difficult?

3   If there is good evidence to support the use of a specific technique for treating stress or pain, does it matter if the underlying mechanisms are not understood?

FURTHER READING

Carver, C.S. & Scheier, M.F. (1982). Control theory: a useful conceptual framework for personality, social, clinical, and health psychology. *Psychological Bulletin, 92*, 111–135.

Coster, S. & Norman, I. (2009). Cochrane reviews of educational and self-management interventions to guide nursing practice: a review. *International Journal of Nursing Studies, 46*, 508–528.

De Ridder, D., Greenen, R., Kuijer, R. & van Middendorp, H. (2008). Psychological adjustment to chronic disease. *The Lancet, 372*, 246–255.

Lehrer, P. (2003). Applied psychophysiology: beyond boundaries of the biofeedback (mending a wall, a brief history of our field and applications to control of the muscles and cardiorespiratory systems). *Applied Psychophysiology and Biofeedback, 28*, 291–304.

METHODOLOGICAL ISSUES IN PSYCHOBIOLOGICAL RESEARCH

8

OVERVIEW

In this chapter we discuss methodological issues in psychobiological research. For example, how can we determine conclusively if and how psychobiological processes influence health? Might these processes explain the influence of other individual or demographic differences on health? How can psychobiological research be translated into effective patient interventions?

Drawing on the research and theories presented in previous chapters, we present a more detailed discussion of factors acting as barriers and drivers of achieving a biopsychosocial approach to disease management. The biopsychosocial model (presented in Chapter 1) is revisited here as we consider whether or not this is really a model at all.

LEARNING OUTCOMES

By the end of this chapter you should be able to:

- describe the conditions necessary to demonstrate a causal inference
- discuss the issue of multifactorial causality

- describe the principles of experimental design

- discuss alternative research designs and consider the relative advantages and disadvantages of each approach

- explain the terms 'mediator' and 'moderator' and describe the conditions necessary to demonstrate mediation and moderation

- explain the term 'randomised controlled trial'

- describe other methods for evaluating intervention effects and discuss the advantages and disadvantages of each approach

- explain the term 'systematic review' and describe the role of systematic reviews in evidence-based medicine

- explain what is meant by the term 'complex intervention' and describe procedures for evaluating complex interventions

- discuss the gap between theory and practice and describe the reasons for this gap

- describe the RE-AIM framework.

INTRODUCTION

8.1

In the previous chapters we discussed interrelationships between psychological and biological processes that have relevance for health, and considered how psychobiological research can be used to inform the development of interventions. In this chapter we turn our attention to methodological issues.

In the first section, we will consider how we can demonstrate not only that psychological and biological processes are related but also that they are *causally* related. That is, what is the nature of the evidence necessary to demonstrate that psychological processes (such as stress) actually produce alterations in physical functioning (change in heart rate, blood pressure, immune function and so on) or that psychobiological processes (such as allostatic load, stress-mediated immune alteration) actually produce changes in health outcomes?

We will consider whether or not observed associations between psychological and biological processes could be explained in other ways – by association with other individual differences or demographic variables, for example. We will also consider how research can be designed to account for alternative explanations and test for causal (as opposed to coincidental) relationships.

In the second section, we will consider how psychological interventions can be evaluated – that is, how can we be certain that interventions designed to target psychological processes actually result in a change in health outcomes? If we observe a change in health in relation to psychological intervention, can we be certain that this change is due to the intervention itself? Would patients have shown the same degree of change if they were given a placebo treatment or no treatment at all? We will also consider both whether or not psychological interventions can really be evaluated in the same way as drug treatments and the extent to which the effects of interventions reported in clinical trials are likely to translate to the real world.

HOW CAN WE DETERMINE WHETHER OR NOT PSYCHOLOGICAL FACTORS INFLUENCE HEALTH?

8.2

In psychobiological research we are interested in demonstrating not only that psychological and biological variables are related but also that they are *causally* related. For example, if we find a relationship between stress and number of colds, we need to determine whether stress actually results in increased susceptibility to colds or if the relationship between stress and number of colds could be explained in another way. It could be the case, say, that having a cold causes people to experience stress – those with a cold might find it difficult to perform the duties expected of them at work or at home or might miss out on enjoyable activities which would normally buffer against stress.

Alternatively, it could be the case that both stress and colds are influenced by a third variable and it is this variable which accounts for the association between stress and colds. For example, we might be more prone to both stress and colds during the winter or some people might be more susceptible to both stress and colds owing to their genetic make-up or living conditions.

Therefore, it is evident that demonstrating a relationship between two variables is insufficient to demonstrate causation. What the criteria for determining causality are, though, is a question that has been debated for centuries. Rutter (2007) points out that the first systematic analysis, provided by John Stuart Mill (1843), argued that three conditions must be met. In addition to demonstrating statistical association, we must demonstrate that the proposed causal factor *precedes* the outcome variable and that there is *no other plausible explanation* for the observed association. Alternative explanations for observed associations between variables are considered further in Box 8.1.

BOX 8.1

Causality

Rutter (2007) lists a number of possible alternative explanations for statistical relationships between risk factors and outcomes:

- there is a possibility of *genetic mediation* of the risk stemming from an environmental feature – parents may pass on risky genes and risky environments, for example
- there is the possibility of *social selection* or *allocation bias*, which suggests that the association between risk factor and outcome reflects the origin of the risk factor rather than its effects – that is, there may be reasons for certain individuals being more likely to find themselves in a high-risk group than others, and these reasons may explain the increase in their level of risk
- there is a possibility of *reverse causation* – that is, the 'outcome' causes the 'risk factor'
- there is a possibility that the risk feature has been misidentified (for an example, see Box 8.2)
- the association might reflect the presence of a *confounding variable* – that is, a variable that is related to both the risk factor *and* the outcome.

Added to this complexity is the issue of **multifactorial causality**. As discussed in previous chapters (particularly Chapter 4), most outcomes we are interested in do not have a single cause, but multiple causal inferences, and several different causal pathways may lead to the same outcome. It is evident that, when we investigate an association between a psychobiological process and the outcome in the form of disease (such as allostatic processes contributing to CVD or stress-mediated immune alteration contributing to infectious disease), we demonstrate not that this process is *the* cause of the disease under investigation, but that it is *one component of the overall causal nexus*.

Rutter (2007) points out that researchers aim not to identify a single cause of any outcome, but, instead, identify causes that are Insufficient but Necessary components of Unnecessary but Sufficient causes – referred by the acronym **INUS** (Mackie, 1965, 1974). The causal nexus is referred to as 'unnecessary but sufficient' since it may result in the disease (CVD, for example) in some cases, but it is not necessary, because other causal pathways are also possible.

8.2.1 EXPERIMENTAL DESIGN

A number of designs are available to examine causal inference. One approach is to utilise an **experimental design** in which variable A is deliberately manipulated and the effect on variable B is observed, while other variables that could influence the relationship between variables A and B (**confounding variables**) are controlled.

Random assignment is used to prevent **allocation bias** (see Box 8.1), by ensuring that the probability of being assigned to either the experimental or control condition is the same for each participant. Ketterer Mahr and Goldberg (2000) point out, however, that even with randomisation it is possible that the two groups may not be equivalent in relation to demographic or other characteristics, so it is important to conduct a **randomisation check** to ensure equivalence at baseline. Further, equivalent groups at baseline may not be equivalent at the end of the study if drop-outs occur more frequently in one group than the other. If this happens, though, it is possible to use statistical correction to account for these problems.

To take one example of how these issues affect experiments, in a number of studies, the effects of stress on immune function have been evaluated by exposing participants to psychological stressors under experimental conditions, then measuring changes in immune response (Kiecolt-Glaser, Cacioppo, Malarkey & Glaser, 1992). Some variables, however, cannot be manipulated experimentally (the effects of chronic stress associated with ongoing life experiences such as stressful working conditions or long-term caregiving, for example). The impact of these stressors on susceptibility to illness, though, can sometimes be investigated under experimental conditions. For example, **viral challenge studies** involve exposing participants to a virus under experimental conditions and then measuring the relationship between the risk factors (assessed prior to exposure) and the subsequent development of symptoms. Using this approach, Cohen et al. (1998) demonstrated that individuals who had recently experienced chronic stress (but not acute stress) were at greater risk of disease (see Chapter 2).

8.2.2 ALTERNATIVE RESEARCH DESIGNS

Although applied to psychobiological research, critics have pointed out that the experimental design developed as a result of the biomedical model and the belief that disease is caused by single, identifiable causal agents – a belief that is at odds with the complex interactions between biological, social and psychological processes highlighted by recent research (Dean, 2004). Manipulating a single causal factor in an experimental setting does not necessarily provide useful information about the way this factor contributes to health and illness in the real world. Hence this approach is said to lack **external or ecological validity**. For example, in the laboratory we can manipulate stress by exposing an individual to a mental arithmetic task or mock job interview. Although these manipulations may be successful in inducing a physiological stress response, they differ considerably from the experience of a person conducting similar tasks in the real world. For example, in the real world, performing badly in a job interview may have significant implications with respect to the individual's income, social status, quality of life and so on. Other types of stressors (such as bereavement) bear little relation to the types of stress we can manipulate in the laboratory.

Further, for practical and ethical reasons, the experimental approach cannot be used to examine the impacts of psychological factors on more serious or long-term conditions – the development of cancer, diabetes or coronary heart disease, for example. These outcomes can, however, be investigated using **naturalistic studies**, in which risk and protective factors (such as depression and social support) are recorded under natural conditions rather than manipulated under experimental conditions.

The impacts of naturally occurring risk and protective factors can be examined at either an inter- or intra-individual level (that is, group differences v. change over time). As with experimental studies, it is important to control for potential confounds. This can be achieved by carefully matching groups for demographic and other potentially confounding variables or measuring potentially confounding variables and controlling for their effects statistically (although it is not possible to control for *unmeasured* variables).

When naturally occurring risk and protective factors are examined using design elements that allow an approximation to experimental conditions, this is referred to as a **natural experiment** (Rutter, 2007). An example is the Whitehall study by Marmot and colleagues (Marmot, Shipley & Rose, 1984; Marmot & Shipley, 1996), who demonstrated differences in health between groups that varied in relation to employment grade, but were similar regarding other demographic and employment variables (see Chapter 6). Similarly, Levav et al. (2000) used this approach to evaluate the impact of bereavement on the incidence of cancer. In this study (also discussed in Chapter 2), a cohort of 6284 Jewish Israelis who had lost an adult son in the Yom Kippur War or in an accident between 1970 and 1977 were followed for 20 years; the incidence of cancer in this cohort was compared with that for non-bereaved members of the population. Confounders associated with the incidence of cancer in Israel (age, sex, period of immigration and region of birth) were statistically controlled. Rutter (2007) also highlights the utility of twin studies in evaluating naturally occurring risk and protective factors, since such studies allow for consideration of the extent to which the effects of a particular risk factor may be environmentally or genetically mediated (twin studies are discussed further in Chapter 4).

Studies evaluating associations at the intra-individual level necessitate the measurement of risk and protective factors in relation to change in a health outcome over time. To provide evidence of causality, it is important to measure predictor variables before the outcome we are interested in occurs. This is referred to as a **prospective longitudinal design** (see Research in focus box 8.1).

RESEARCH IN FOCUS BOX 8.1

Wang and colleagues (2005) examined the impact of social support on the progression of coronary artery disease.

Methodology

A total of 102 women hospitalised for coronary artery disease completed questionnaires assessing social support (emotional support, social integration and interpersonal social relations) within three months of hospitalisation. Coronary atherosclerosis was assessed at baseline and three years later. Analyses controlled for conventional clinical and lifestyle factors, such as age, smoking history, body mass index, menopausal status and diagnosis of index event.

Results

Social support was a significant predictor of how the coronary atherosclerosis progressed from three months to three years following hospitalisation. These associations were independent of clinical and lifestyle factors. Similar effects were found for the three types of social support assessed.

Conclusions and implications

The results suggest that social isolation, lack of emotional support and lack of interpersonal social relations are important risk factors for the accelerated progression of coronary atherosclerosis in middle-aged women, and may be important targets for intervention.

In addition to ecological validity, a major advantage of the prospective longitudinal design is that a number of risk and protective factors can be assessed and interactions between predictor variables may be considered. It can be difficult, however, to determine over what time period to assess the variables of interest. For example, is it better to assess mood experienced in the moment or over the past week? How long would it take for changes in mood to translate into changes in symptoms? Would we expect the same time course for different symptoms or disease processes (pain, inflammation or immune function, for example)?

Recent research suggests that moment-by-moment assessments of mood may result in more reliable predictions in relation to physiological measures than retrospective reports of mood over a number of days (Steptoe, Gibson, Hamer & Wardle, 2007). Although **ecological momentary assessments** are more laborious for participants, Stone et al. (2003) report that patients find this method acceptable and that repeated measurements of pain do not appear to influence the level of pain experienced. Repeated measurements of behaviour and related attitudes or cognitions may be more problematic, though, since it is possible to alter a behaviour simply by asking the participant to answer a question – referred to as the **mere measurement effect** (Morwitz, Johnson & Schmittlein, 1993) or **question–behaviour effect** (Sprott et al., 2006).

Just as physicians must recognise that the reality of illness is not merely observed but also created via the process of dialogue, researchers must recognise that completing questionnaires may actually produce the behaviour we aim to predict (for a more detailed discussion, see Ajzen & Fishbein, 2004; Borrell-Carrio et al., 2004; Ogden, 2003).

8.2.3 GENERAL CONSIDERATIONS

Even with careful control of potential confounds, it is not possible to rule out third-factor causes in naturalistic studies, whether the research considers naturally existing group differences or within-person associations between risk factors and outcomes. For example, as highlighted in Box 8.1, there may be reasons for people finding themselves in different groups and these reasons may explain the increased risk. Differences may also be due to unmeasured variables.

In relation to prospective designs, it is possible that reverse causation may account for the observed relationships, even when the risk factor is measured before the outcome variable. For example, Evans Hucklebridge and Clow (2000) point out that, although studies have reported a link between a depressed state of mind and the occurrence of cancer, cancer takes a long time to develop and be detected, so it is possible that depressive symptoms arise as a result of the immune system's response in the early stages of the development of cancer. At least for some outcomes of interest then, it is possible that the process may have been developing for some time before changes could be detected.

In reality, it is never possible to *prove* causality since 'causal reasoning requires an implicit comparison of what actually happened when an individual experienced the supposed causal inference with what would have happened if simultaneously they had not had that experience' (Rutter, 2007: 378). None of the designs discussed above can achieve this. Carefully designed research studies can help to strengthen or weaken the causal inference, however, and, taken together, empirical studies can build a body of evidence to support or reject hypothesised associations between variables.

In his now classic paper, Hill (1965: 12) points out that we often have to make a decision to act on the evidence available and 'all scientific work is incomplete – whether it be observational or experimental.' Therefore, when we consider the case for causation, we must consider multiple aspects of association between variables (including strength, consistency, specificity, biological plausibility), reach a decision informed by our understanding of the relative merits of these forms of evidence and keep in mind the implications of our decision. For example, we might decide to restrict the use of a drug for morning sickness in pregnant women on the basis of relatively slight evidence, while we would require very strong evidence before requiring people to make changes to their lifestyles that may restrict freedoms or reduce quality of life (Hill, 1965).

8.2.4 MODERATOR AND MEDIATOR VARIABLES

In addition to identifying causal variables, it is often useful to identify **moderator** and **mediator** variables. A moderator is a variable that explains under which conditions a relationship exists, while a mediator explains how or why the relationship exists (Baron & Kenny, 1986). For example, as shown in Figure 8.1, psychological factors

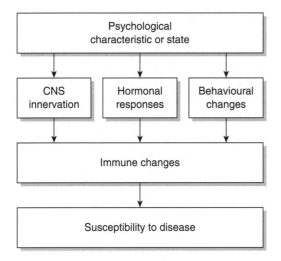

FIGURE 8.1 Psychological factors that might influence the onset and progression of immune system-mediated diseases via a variety of routes, not all of which are included here

Source: Cohen and Herbert (1996: 118)

might influence immune change (with implications for susceptibility to disease) via a number of routes, including innervation of the central nervous system, hormonal responses and behavioural changes (such as smoking, poor diet, poor sleeping habits). The magnitude of the changes in each of these mediator variables (and hence the impact on immune-mediated disease), however, is likely to differ from individual to individual, owing to individual differences in HPA reactivity or social or contextual resources, for example (see Chapter 2). These individual difference variables therefore *moderate* the impacts of psychological factors on immune-mediated disease

MacKinnon and Leucken (2008) write that, for mediation to exist, the following conditions must be met:

1 there must be a substantial relation between the independent (predictor) variable and the mediating variable
2 there must be a substantial relation between the mediating variable and the dependent (outcome) variable
3 the independent variable must precede and be a cause of the mediator
4 the mediator must precede and be a cause of the dependent variable.

They explain that other important conditions also exist, including the use of valid and reliable measures, sufficient sample size and accurate modelling of the distribution of the variables (MacKinnon, 2008).

For the assessment of moderation effects, the relation between the independent and dependent variable must be different at different levels of a third variable, such as for people of different ages, personality types or in different situations. Moderation may be particularly important to consider when studying the impacts of personality on health. For example, Segerstrom (2003) points out that optimism has been reported to have both positive and negative impacts on immune function. These different effects can be explained by the moderating effect of situational variables – that is, when the stressor is straightforward or responsive to coping efforts, optimism is associated with higher immune parameters; when the stressor is difficult or non-responsive, optimism is associated with lower immune parameters. Segerstrom (2003) suggests that this pattern is likely to reflect optimists' greater propensity to remain engaged with stressors in the face of lack of progress (Carver & Scheier, 1998). Interactions between person variables (such as optimism) and situation variables are considered further in Chapter 2.

Moderators and mediators are also important to consider when designing and evaluating interventions to improve health. For example, Kraemer, Kieman, Essex and Kupfer (2008) explain that, because an intervention is not equally effective for all participants, it is important to establish moderators of responses to an intervention – who responds and who does not – in order to optimally target the intervention and seek better interventions for those who do not respond. Establishing mediators of responses to interventions – how an intervention works – can prompt researchers to strengthen, add or remove certain components to make the intervention more effective. Methodological issues relating to the development and evaluation of interventions to improve health are considered further in the next section.

DESIGNING AND EVALUATING HEALTH INTERVENTIONS

8.3 Many of the methodological issues discussed above apply equally to the evaluation of the effects of interventions. The 'gold standard' for evaluating interventions is the **randomised controlled trial (RCT)** or **randomly assigned controlled clinical trial (RACC)** (Ketterer, Mahr & Goldberg, 2000). This method involves randomly assigning participants to receive either an active intervention or an inactive control (such as a dummy pill).

Although other types of evidence may contribute to a causal inference, Ketterer et al. (2000: 360) suggest that other designs cannot provide the same degree of certainty regarding the effects of intervention and we should consider the case proven:

> if, and only if, there exists at least one randomly controlled clinical trial targeting the psychological factor, demonstrating modification of that factor and yielding a statistically significant reduction in an objective outcome measure of disease state (ideally death) relative to the control group.

Bearing in mind the advantages and disadvantages of different research designs, Ketterer et al. (2000) provide a hierarchy of scientific evidence for inferring causality, which, in addition to prospective studies (discussed above), includes:

Natural observation ('clinical experience')

- Cannot control for selective perception/recall
- Cannot control for third factor possibility or other historical confounds (such as changes in concomitant treatments)
- Cannot control for causal directionality (A > B v. B > A)
- Cannot control for spontaneous remission or placebo effect.

Correlational (cross-sectional/retrospective association studies)

- Can control for known/suspected confounding factors, but cannot control unknown, and therefore uncontrolled, factors
- Directionality not determinable
- Cannot rule out the third factor possibility
- Sample skewing can weaken/strengthen association (such as death prior to study, refusal to participate, drop-outs)
- Can make non-randomised comparisons (such as male v. female).

Prospective correlational

- Adds element of forwardness-in-time (consistent with directionality hypothesis)
- Avoids/minimises sample skewing
- Cannot control for unknown factors
- Cannot rule out third factor possibility
- Sample skewing can weaken/strengthen association
- Can make non-randomised comparisons.

Pre-/post-intervention trials

- Add element of temporal coincidence with therapy
- Cannot control for unknown factors
- Cannot rule out spontaneous remission, placebo effect or other historical confounds, but likelihood of these *can* be reduced by use of a baseline observation as control.

Controlled intervention

- Are groups truly equivalent at baseline? (Cannot control for unknown/unanticipated factors)
- Cannot control unknown factors.

Randomised controlled intervention ('gold standard')

- Unknown/uncontrolled factors can legitimately be assumed equivalent across groups, particularly in large samples
- Problems remain for any selection biases: refusers and drop-outs
- Control group: defines the question you are answering
- Outcome measures: distress, disability, death (or a surrogate of disease progression)
- Analyses: representativeness of sample; baseline and historical confounding/mediating factors ('randomisation check'); outcome measures; adjusted outcome measures.

Systematic reviews of healthcare interventions use similar hierarchies to rank reviewed studies according to the quality of the evidence provided, with RCTs providing the highest-quality evidence. Systematic reviews combine evidence from several studies, using explicit scientific methods, in order to allow decisionmakers to select interventions on the basis of the available evidence and determine where evidence is lacking (Centre for Reviews and Disseminations, 2009; Higgins & Green, 2009). Thus, systematic reviews play a key role in **evidence-based medicine (EBM)** (Manchikanti, 2008).

Many systematic reviews also contain **meta-analyses**. These use statistical methods to summarise the results of a number of relevant studies and facilitate an examination of the consistency of evidence across studies (Higgins & Green, 2009).

Meta-analyses and systematic reviews of the same literature often yield different conclusions (as we have discussed in previous chapters), owing to differences in the ways studies are identified and selected for review. For example, systematic reviews often involve a very thorough search for relevant studies and may therefore identify studies not included in meta-analyses of the same literature. Equally, studies included in meta-analyses may be rejected from systematic review if they fail to meet quality criteria. For further discussion, see Greenhalgh (2007).

8.3.1 LIMITATIONS OF RANDOMISED CONTROLLED TRIALS

Although randomised controlled trials appear at the top of the hierarchy given above, this does not mean that they are without limitations. Many of these limitations are the same as those for experimental research – possible non-equivalence of groups at baseline or at the end of the trial due to unequal attrition in the two groups, for example. External/ecological validity may also be questionable, particularly since trials often recruit highly selective samples (such as within a specific age range, without co-morbidities), so it is not possible to determine to what extent the results will generalise to the wider population.

RACCs raise other problems, including the spontaneous utilisation of the therapy under consideration by participants in the control group (Ketterer et al., 2000).

Inadequate reporting of trials is also common, despite the publication of guidelines to improve standards of reporting – namely, the **Consolidated Standards of Reporting Trials (CONSORT) Statement**, which was first published in 1996 and revised in 2001 (Altman et al., 2001; Moher, Schulz & Atman, 2001; full details are available online at: www.consort-statement.org).

A number of researchers have also questioned the applicability of clinical trial methods to an evaluation of non-pharmacological interventions. For example, clinical trials use **blinding** to assign patients to experimental or control conditions. This means that patients do not know whether they are receiving an active drug or a placebo and, in **double blind** trials, the clinician or care provider does not know which groups the patients are in either (in **triple blind** trials, those evaluating the intervention *also* do not know how participants have been assigned).

Blinding is used to ensure that expectancies regarding outcomes are equivalent in both the active and placebo drug conditions. Non-pharmacological interventions (such as surgery, rehabilitation, psychological interventions), however, are difficult to evaluate under blind conditions since patients are typically aware of, and often consciously engaged in, the intervention procedures. Patients may also have had prior experience of the treatments being evaluated and have pre-existing expectations or preferences for particular treatments. Patients' preferences may influence their decisions to enter a trial (that is, since they are aware that they may be randomised and receive a non-preferred intervention), or they may result in resentment among patients randomised to non-preferred interventions and, therefore, represent a threat to the validity of the clinical trials concerned (Bower, King, Nazareth, Lampe & Sibbald, 2005).

Providing no treatment to the control group may be unacceptable to patients. One possible solution is a **randomised waiting list study**, in which all patients eventually receive the treatment being evaluated (Campbell et al., 2000). This type of study still has limitations, however, in that the outcome data can only be collected shortly after the intervention (before the control group receives the intervention), and it is important to determine whether or not patients randomised to the waiting list experience dissatisfaction or resentment.

Partially randomised **patient preference trials** have also been proposed. These involve randomising participants without strong preferences and allowing those *with* a strong preference to receive their preferred treatment. With this type of design, however, outcomes may be affected by uncontrolled confounders in the non-randomised groups (see Tilbrook, 2008, for a more detailed discussion).

In recognition of the specific issues raised by non-pharmacological interventions, an extension of the original CONSORT Statement was recently published. This includes a modified checklist for reporting non-pharmacological treatments (Boutron, Moher, Altman, Schulz & Ravaud, 2008).

8.3.2 EVALUATING COMPLEX INTERVENTIONS

A further complication (and one that is acknowledged in the CONSORT extension) is that non-pharmacological intervention trials often involve evaluation of **complex interventions** involving several components that may be difficult to describe and standardise (pain clinics, stroke units, cognitive behavioural therapy for depression and so on). Campbell et al. (2000) therefore suggest that development and evaluation of such interventions should be considered to involve a number of distinct phases (see Figure 8.2).

First, it is necessary to identify the evidence that an intervention might have a desired effect by reviewing the theoretical basis for it and examining previous research. This is the 'preclinical' or 'theoretical' phase.

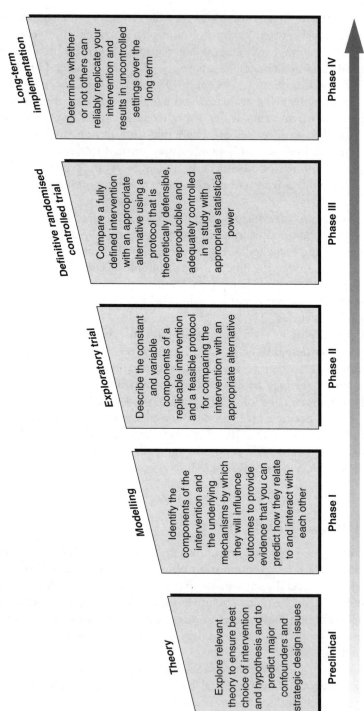

Theory

Explore relevant theory to ensure best choice of intervention and hypothesis and to predict major confounders and strategic design issues

Preclinical

Phase I

Modelling

Identify the components of the intervention and the underlying mechanisms by which they will influence outcomes to provide evidence that you can predict how they relate to and interact with each other

Phase II

Exploratory trial

Describe the constant and variable components of a replicable intervention and a feasible protocol for comparing the intervention with an appropriate alternative

Phase III

Definitive randomised controlled trial

Compare a fully defined intervention with an appropriate alternative using a protocol that is theoretically defensible, reproducible and adequately controlled in a study with appropriate statistical power

Phase IV

Long-term implementation

Determine whether or not others can reliably replicate your intervention and results in uncontrolled settings over the long term

Continuum of increasing evidence

FIGURE 8.2 The sequential phases of developing randomised controlled trials of complex interventions

Source: Campbell et al. (2000)

Next, it is necessary to identify the relevant components of the intervention and the mechanisms via which they will influence outcomes – 'phase I'.

In phase II, the information gathered in phase I is used to develop the optimum intervention and study design. This involves identifying the standard and variable components of the intervention (components which may be relevant to some patients but not others) and a relevant comparison treatment for the control group (or, alternatively, using a no treatment or waiting list as the comparison). Relevant outcome measures also need to be identified at this stage. Once the intervention study methods have been fully described, it is possible to move to Phase III. Phase III is the randomised controlled trial. This involves addressing issues such as sample size, inclusion/exclusion criteria, methods for randomising patients and blinding. Individual randomisation may not always be possible, so patients may, instead be randomised in clusters (all patients attending a particular medical practice being entered into the intervention or control condition, for example) or blocks (allocating patients to the intervention or control condition in sets of four, say) (see Altman & Bland, 1999, for further discussion of randomisation methods).

According to Campbell et al. (2000) the development and evaluation of an intervention should not end with the RCT since it is also necessary to examine the implementation of the intervention in practice – paying attention to the rate of uptake and possible adverse effects, for example. This should form the basis of phase IV.

In practice, however, there is often little information available to determine how best to target components of theory-based interventions since theories only tell us *what* to target not *how* to go about changing these determinants (Michie, Johnston, Francis, Hardeman & Eccles, 2008). This gap between theory and practice must be bridged before a theory can be effectively mapped to intervention (Bartholomew, Parcel, Kok & Gottlieb, 2001; Kok, Schaalma, Ruiter & Van Empelen, 2004). Craig et al. (2008) also point out that, although it is useful to think in terms of phases in evaluating complex interventions, in practice these may not always follow a linear sequence.

8.3.3 IS KNOWLEDGE OF MECHANISMS NECESSARY?

Although Campbell et al. (2000) suggest that a consideration of the mechanisms via which interventions are expected to produce an effect should be an integral part of intervention development and evaluation, Ketterer, Mahr and Goldberg (2000) argue that knowledge of underlying mechanisms is not necessary to demonstrate efficacy of an intervention and that causality can be proven in clinical trials without knowledge of the underlying mechanisms.

For example, they point out that Semmelweis' discovery and validation of antiseptic technique during obstetrical delivery by controlled clinical trials in the 1800s predated a mechanistic understanding of infection by about 50 years. These findings were not accepted by mainstream medical practice, however, until the process of infection was understood, resulting in thousands of potentially avoidable deaths (see Box 8.2). Similarly, as discussed in Chapter 5, many interventions for pain were developed years (or even centuries) before the mechanisms underlying these interventions were understood.

BOX 8.2

Controversies: do we need to understand the mechanisms underlying the effects of interventions? The case of Ignaz Semmelweis

In 1846, Ignaz Semmelweis was working as an assistant in the Vienna Maternity Hospital, where he noticed a strange pattern in the rates of maternal deaths due to puerperal fever.

The hospital was divided into two clinics – one used for the instruction of medical students and one for the instruction of midwives. Women were allocated to these clinics on alternate days, thereby creating a system of random allocation. The death rate in the clinic attended by student doctors was more than twice that for the midwife clinic.

Semmelweis considered a number of theories for this phenomenon, weighing up the evidence for each. The dominant theory of the time was the *miasma theory*. According to this theory, disease was caused by a putrid environment or atmosphere. This theory had much evidence to support it. For example, diseases were more likely to occur in overcrowded slums and workhouses, where the atmosphere was often foul-smelling. This theory, however, could not explain the difference in the death rates for the two clinics, since both were in the same building and shared an anteroom.

After rejecting a number of hypotheses, including the miasma theory, Semmelweis proposed that the difference in death rates was due to particles carried on the hands of the student doctors who attended women in labour shortly after dissecting dead bodies. Although the students washed their hands after dissections with soap and water, Semmelweis proposed that some particles may have remained present on their hands after washing. To test this theory, he implemented a programme of handwashing using disinfectant. This resulted in a dramatic decline in the number of deaths.

Despite these dramatic effects, Semmelweis' findings were not accepted by mainstream medicine until the mechanisms underlying the process of infection were understood – some 50 years later. Gillies (2004: 180) writes that the Semmelweis case highlights:

> that any new practice which can be shown statistically to be better than alternative practices as regards either prevention or cure, and which does not have any harmful side-effects, should be adopted even if it is based on a theory which contradicts the dominant paradigm. In fact in such a case, attempts should be made either to explain the success of the new practice using the dominant paradigm, or to modify the dominant paradigm to accommodate the new practice.

Sources: Gillies (2004) and Ketterer Mahr and Goldberg (2000)

For a further example, consider the work of Ader and Cohen (1975). These researchers demonstrated that the immune system could be influenced by the brain even though it was widely believed that the immune system operated autonomously (see Chapter 2).

What these lessons from history teach us is that knowledge of underlying mechanisms is *not* necessary to demonstrate intervention effects, but, also, that empirical evidence may be met with a degree of scepticism until the underlying mechanisms are fully understood, particularly when the effects of interventions appear to conflict with the contemporary understanding of biological processes.

8.3.4 TRANSLATING RESEARCH EVIDENCE INTO CLINICAL PRACTICE

> Malaise pervades the secret meeting places of the biopsychosocial community, a sense that a concept of overwhelming appeal has proved inordinately difficult to apply.
>
> Herman (2005: 372)

It is important to determine not only how theoretical models are supported by empirical evidence but also the extent to which these models and methods can be translated into clinical practice. For example, Alonso (2004: 243) writes that although:

> the biopsychosocial model has been successfully applied to obtain a better understanding of the disease processes and their causes ... medical practitioners are still reluctant to incorporate it into treatment plans.

Similarly, Zimmermann and Tansella (1996) report that research has highlighted the general difficulty physicians have in considering psychosocial factors in their clinical practice.

Biderman, Yeheskel and Herman (2005: 380) also highlight difficulties with the uptake of the biopsychosocial approach – pointing to a need for adequate training, a suitable setting and sufficient 'time during the doctor–patient encounter for "being" biopsychosocial'. Suls and Rothman (2004) suggest that the biopsychosocial model is best viewed as 'work in progress' and is really more of a conceptual framework than a model.

Part of the problem faced by care-providers in applying the biopsychosocial model is that many commonly used psychological interventions can result in inequitable and limited participation by patients and poor implementation and maintenance. Further, there is often limited evidence as to the best choice of treatment modality, and choices are often guided by convenience or the results of randomised controlled trials rather than their impact in practice settings (Glasgow, McKay, Piette & Reynolds, 2001).

TABLE 8.1   RE-AIM evaluation dimensions

Evaluation dimension	Assessment level
Reach (what proportion of the target population participated in this intervention?)	Individual level
Efficacy (what is success rate if implemented as in protocol?)	Individual level
Adoption (what proportion of setting, practices, and plans will adopt this intervention?)	Organization level
Implementation (to what extent is the intervention implemented as intended in the real-world?)	Organization level
Maintenance (to what extent is the program sustained over time?)	Individual and Organization level

It is evident, then, that evidence from clinical trials is not sufficient to achieve wide-spread implementation in practice. To achieve this, it is necessary to demonstrate long-term effectiveness in real-world settings. Glasgow et al. (2001) suggest that this can be best considered in relation to five dimensions:

- Reach
- Efficacy
- Adoption
- Implementation
- Maintenance.

These dimensions give the **RE-AIM framework** its name. They incorporate both individual-level factors (such as cost, transport, inconvenience to patients) and organisational-level factors (such as level of resources or expertise required, fit with current practice) acting as potential barriers to the effectiveness of interventions (see Table 8.1).

SUMMARY

8.4

As discussed in this chapter, demonstrating interrelationships between psychological and biological processes is not enough to engender a shift from the biomedical to the biopsychosocial model of health.

The biopsychosocial model raises a number of methodological issues that must be addressed if research evidence is to be translated into practice. For example, according to the biopsychosocial model (Engel, 1980), processes cannot be meaningfully isolated from their natural contexts. Experimental findings obtained in laboratory settings must therefore be considered with a degree of caution. For example, as discussed in Chapter 2, it was long believed that the immune system operates autonomously without direction from the brain since cells of the immune system could be removed from the body and examined in the laboratory. Research in the field of psychoneuroimmunology, however, has now established that, when they are in the body, immune cells *can* be influenced by the brain. This principle applies equally to observations at each level of the biopsychosocial model – the behaviour of human beings, like that of cells, is shaped by the context in which it takes place.

Naturalistic studies raise a different set of methodological issues. For example, how can we be certain that associations we observe are not due to the influence of unmeasured variables? If a psychological variable appears to cause a change in an outcome measure, can we conclude that manipulation of the proposed causal influence will change this outcome? In reality, all study designs have both advantages and disadvantages. The challenge for researchers is to:

1 build up a body of evidence for (or against) proposed causal associations
2 demonstrate that these causal associations exist outside the laboratory (that is, in the natural context)
3 determine the underlying (mediating) mechanisms linking cause and outcome variables
4 determine under which conditions the causal association exists (identify moderator variables)
5 determine how best to target underlying mechanisms to effect change (bearing in mind moderators)
6 develop protocols to implement interventions in the real world, considering the context in which the intervention is to be applied.

When considering the context in which psychological interventions are to be applied, we must also be mindful that, in Western countries at least, this context has been largely shaped by the biomedical model. Complex, individualised treatments addressing biological, psychological *and* social aspects of illness are challenging to incorporate into a system that developed to provide medical responses to biological changes. Interventions must therefore be designed to also include both a consideration of organisational-level factors that may act as barriers to their effectiveness and how best to address or accommodate them.

KEY TERMS

allocation bias, blinding, complex interventions, confounding variables, Consolidated Standards of Reporting Trials (CONSORT) Statement, double blind trials, ecological momentary assessments, evidence-based medicine, experimental design, external or ecological validity, INUS, mediator, mere measurement effect or question–behaviour effect, meta-analysis, moderator, multifactorial causality, natural experiment, naturalistic studies, patient preference trials, prospective longitudinal design, random assignment, randomisation check, randomised controlled trial (RCT) or randomly assigned controlled clinical trial (RACC), randomised waiting list study, RE-AIM framework, systematic review, triple blind trials, viral challenge studies

■Discussion questions

1 Consider the wide range of treatment approaches available for patients with chronic pain (discussed in Chapters 5 and 7). What factors should therapists and practitioners take into account before selecting a treatment approach?

2 How can complex interventions be designed to take into account patients' expectations and prior experience of treatments?

3 Are placebo therapies ethical?

4 How would you design a study to evaluate the impact of stress on outcomes for patients with type 2 diabetes? What variables would you measure or manipulate?

5 Is it ethical to offer therapies without a strong evidence base, provided there is no evidence of harmful effects?

FURTHER READING

Campbell, M., Fitzpatrick, R., Haines, A., Kinmonth, A.L., Sandercock, P., Spielgelhalter, D. & Tyrer, P. (2000). Framework for design and evaluation of complex interventions to improve health. *British Medical Journal, 321*, 694–696.

Glasgow, R.E., McKay, H.G., Piette, J.D., & Reynolds, K.D. (2001). The RE-AIM framework for evaluating interventions: what can it tell us about approaches to chronic illness management? *Patient Education and Counselling, 44*, 119–127.

Greenhalgh, T. (1997). How to read a paper: papers that summarise other papers (systematic reviews and meta-analyses). *British Medical Journal, 315*, 672–675.

Ketterer, M.W., Mahr, G. & Goldberg, A.D. (2000). Psychological factors affecting a medical condition: ischemic coronary heart disease. *Journal of Psychosomatic Research, 48*, 357–367.

Michie, S., Johnston, M., Francis, J., Hardeman, W., & Eccles, M. (2008). From theory to intervention: mapping theoretically derived behavioral determinants to behaviour change techniques. *Applied Psychology: An International Review*, 57, 660–680.

SUMMARY AND FUTURE DIRECTIONS

9

OVERVIEW

In this chapter we look into the future in order to consider new opportunities and challenges to psychobiological research and practice, reviewing what we have learned so far and what questions we have yet to adequately address.

In addition, we consider how psychobiological research and practice could benefit from recent technological advances, including those in information and communication technologies, brain imaging technologies and virtual reality applications.

We end with a consideration of ethical issues relevant to the future development of the field.

LEARNING OUTCOMES

By the end of this chapter you should be able to:

- describe advances in research methods across a number of fields relevant to health

- consider how these advances have contributed to our current understanding of associations between psychological, social and biological processes with respect to their implications for health

- discuss the implications of this research for the treatment and prevention of illness

- describe psychological, biological and social conditions associated with optimal functioning, as well as conditions that may be considered 'toxic'

- consider how psychobiological processes might be influenced by macro-level determinants of health

- consider how these macro-level determinants might influence the effectiveness of psychological interventions

- consider the methodological and practical difficulties researchers might face in delineating relationships between variables at the macro, meso and micro levels

- consider how technological advances might influence the future development of the field

- consider how technological advances might influence the development and delivery of therapeutic interventions

- discuss the limitations of new technologies and consider ethical issues associated with their application.

9.1 WHAT HAVE WE LEARNED SO FAR?

This book set out to consider:

- how advances in research are helping us to uncover the true complexity of links between psychological, social and biological processes with respect to their implications for health
- how such advances may inform the development of new approaches to the treatment and prevention of illness.

Before looking to the future, we will summarise what we have learned so far in relation to these two points.

9.1.1 ADVANCES IN RESEARCH: METHODS, MODELS AND SPECIALIST FIELDS

As discussed throughout this book, research evidence from a number of fields (psychology, endocrinology, immunology, epidemiology, genetics and so on) has provided support for Engel's assertion that disease cannot be fully explained by deviations from the norm of biological variables and has contributed towards a greater understanding of the biopsychosocial processes in health and illness.

Within each of these fields, methods have been developed to measure and/or manipulate variables of interest, and theoretical models have been introduced to account for relationships between these variables and implications for health. The recognition of complex interrelationships between biological, psychological and social processes has also resulted in the development of specialist fields of enquiry (health psychology, psychoneuroimmunology (PNI), psychoneuroendocrinology (PNE) and behavioural genetics, for example). Research conducted within these new fields is beginning to build knowledge of not only relevant processes within social, psychological and biological systems but also the linkages between these systems.

Advances in research and their implications for understanding are summarised below.

9.1.1.1 Psychological research

Psychological research has identified personality constructs that are relevant to physical health and psychological well-being, situational determinants of psychological well-being and cognitive, emotional and behavioural processes intervening between adverse environmental conditions and their implications for health.

Reliable methods have been developed to measure each of these psychological constructs, and theoretical models have been presented to account for interrelationships between cognitive, emotional and behavioural processes that are relevant to health.

Researchers have also developed methods for *manipulating* psychological processes. For example, outcome expectancies (and behaviour) may be manipulated by pairing a response with a negative, neutral or positive outcome; emotions may be manipulated by completing a stressful task (such as public speaking) or via exposure to emotion-inducing stimuli (such as watching a frightening or amusing film). These experimental manipulations have also contributed to our understanding of associations between psychological variables and their implications for health.

Much of the research in this field that is relevant to health has focused on the concept of 'stress', but it has proved difficult to define. Selye (1956) defined stress as the rate of wear and tear on the body, while Lazarus and Folkman (1984) have defined it as a transaction between the individual and the environment that is perceived as taxing or exceeding the individual's coping resources. Alternatively, Ursin and Eriksen (1994) define stress as a discrepancy between one's current state and what 'should be'.

These definitions probably describe different aspects of the phenomenon that we refer to as 'stress'. For example, Selye's definition is consistent with the concept of allostatic load, which describes (chronic) stress in relation to wear and tear. Lazarus and Folkman's definition is consistent with the findings of research focusing on 'at risk' populations, which has revealed that individuals experiencing high levels of demand and low levels of control or resources are at greater risk of a wide range of health problems than individuals with more balanced situations. Ursin and Eriksen's definition is consistent with theories of self-regulation, which suggest that individuals are engaged in a constant process of monitoring deviations between their current and desired states and adjusting cognition, emotion and behaviour towards valued goals.

Models of psychological well-being also address different aspects of the phenomenon, describing not only what distinguishes a happy person from an unhappy person (self-acceptance, positive relations with others, autonomy, environmental mastery, purpose in life and personal growth) but also the conditions most conducive to experiencing moments of happiness (such as level of challenge matched to resources, clear proximal goals, immediate feedback, loss of reflective self-consciousness, sense of control).

9.1.1.2 PNI and PNE research

PNI and PNE research has identified mechanisms by which emotional and cognitive processes influence physical health, drawing attention to links between the CNS, neuroendocrine and immune systems. This research has identified chemical mediators of the stress response, which have wide-ranging effects throughout the body.

Theoretical models have been presented to account for the protective and damaging effects of stress mediators, as well as similarities between physiological responses to stress, depression, infection and injury. Of these, the allostatic load model has particularly important implications for research. This model is relevant to understanding the physical effects of chronic stress (such as changes in blood pressure, glucose, cholesterol and hip–waist ratio), as well as psychological effects (including changes in cognition, emotion and behaviour). These changes may culminate in the development of physical and mental disorders (such as cardiovascular disease, type 2 diabetes, depression, anxiety disorders and substance abuse). Although allostatic load is an indicator of chronic stress, processes culminating in physiological dysregulation are also shaped by genetic, developmental and experiential factors.

PNI and PNE research also has important implications for the study of psychological well-being since research in this field has reported the protective effects of positive psychological or relational experiences across multiple physiological systems. Well-being is also determined by a combination of genetic and experiential factors, as well as social–environmental influences (access to clean water, shelter, healthcare and so on).

Psychological well-being and allostatic load may represent opposite sides of the same coin, since the well-being concept describes both a situation of optimal psychological functioning and the conditions most likely to promote vitality and longevity, while the allostatic load concept describes a situation of severely compromised psychological functioning and the conditions most likely to promote physical and psychological disorders.

9.1.1.3 Epidemiological evidence

Experimental research in PNI and PNE is supported by evidence from epidemiological studies. These have revealed differences between groups in terms of rates of illness and mortality, with a higher risk being reported for people with psychiatric illness and groups exposed to chronic stress over a number of years (owing to stressful working conditions, caregiving or low socio-economic status and so on). Within these groups, a high risk of physical illness is paralleled by a high risk of psychological morbidity and the dysregulation of systems linking psychological processes with physiological damage (sympathetic, neuroendocrine, immune). Further, these processes appear to be interrelated within high-risk groups, so that greater psychological morbidity is associated with greater physiological dysregulation and poorer health.

The cumulative effects of psychological stressors may also account (at least in part) for age-related functional decline and morbidity. Indeed, research indicates that many age-related diseases share common pathogenic mechanisms, including neuro-immune-endocrine dysregulation, a shift from parasympathetic to sympathetic activation and loss of maintenance and repair capacities, culminating in damage accumulation and loss of homeostasis. Stress processes may mimic or exacerbate these effects.

Research focusing on at risk populations indicates that the influence of biological and psychological processes on health must be considered in relation to the wider social context. Social and environmental factors that are relevant to both physical health and psychological well-being include lack of social engagement, social stigmatisation and discrimination.

9.1.1.4 Genetic research

The field of genetics has seen considerable advances in research methods over recent years, with discoveries and techniques derived from the Human Genome Project providing opportunities for researchers to examine naturally occurring DNA differences in order to identify mutations associated with specific traits. These advances are important for not only identifying single gene disorders but also investigating gene–environment and gene–behaviour interactions (the term 'environment' here is used to refer to the psychosocial environment as well as the physical environment).

Research conducted within this field suggests that, although there are thousands of single-gene disorders, these are typically rare disorders, affecting only a small proportion of the population. Most major diseases have a complex multifactorial aetiology. While genetic factors contribute significantly to the variations seen at population level in relation to complex diseases, this does not rule out a role for psychological variables since psychological factors can induce disease in both carriers of disease gene variants (by influencing gene expression) and otherwise healthy individuals (via DNA damage resulting from unhealthy behaviours or the biological effects of stress).

Gene–environment interactions culminating in disease can be considered in relation to an imbalance between demands (imposed by psychological stress or exposure to toxins) and resources (the capacity for maintenance and repair). When environmental demands exceed the organism's capacity to maintain and repair itself, disease results.

Genetic research is also important for understanding individual differences in personality and behaviour. For example, twin studies suggest that genetic influences underlie the association between personality and alcohol use and that most of the genetic vulnerability to different addictive substances is shared. Genetic discoveries have important implications beyond the field of genetics, impacting all professions concerned with health-related research, the prevention of disease (at an individual or population level) and patient care.

One major implication of all this is that researchers cannot assume that environmental and genetic influences can be separated since genes can influence 'environmental' factors (drinking, smoking, lack of exercise, for example) and environmental factors can induce change in the genome. Researchers are only beginning to investigate the health implications of specific epigenetic changes.

9.1.1.5 Summary

Research evidence drawn from a wide range of fields therefore supports a biopsychosocial conceptualisation of health and illness. Each of these areas of research provides a different piece of the jigsaw puzzle and, since research is ongoing, the jigsaw is as yet incomplete. It is possible, however, to draw some general conclusions regarding the conditions associated with optimal functioning as well as conditions that may be considered 'toxic' – that is, most likely to result in damage or disorder. These conditions are summarised in Table 9.1.

TABLE 9.1 Conditions associated with optimal functioning and ones that may be considered 'toxic'

Optimal conditions	Toxic conditions
Social functioning	
Basic needs are met (eg. Clean water, shelter, health care)	Insufficient resources/ opportunity to meet basic needs (e.g. due to poverty)
Psychological needs are met: self-acceptance, positive relations with others, autonomy, environmental mastery, purpose in life, personal growth)[i]	Insufficient resources/ opportunity to meet psychological needs (e.g. due to stigmatization, discrimination, lack of social engagement, unemployment, lack of education)
Social environment provides level of demand commensurate with the individual's level of resources (including social, psychological and biological resources)	Social (e.g. work/home) environment characterized by high demands and low control[ii]. Environment requires high effort expenditure, with insufficient opportunity for reward[iii].
Psychological Functioning	
Individual is engaged in meaningful activities, experiences positive relations with others, high positive affect, low negative affect, high levels of energy, motivation and life satisfaction[iv].	Individual lacks energy/ motivation, does not engage in meaningful activities, experiences inadequate relations with others, high negative affect, low positive affect, and low levels of life satisfaction.

(Cont'd)

TABLE 9.1   (Continued)

Optimal conditions	Toxic conditions
Individual is able to maintain psychological equilibrium by modifying emotion, cognition and behaviour according to changes in the external (social) and internal (biological) environmental.	Individual is unable to regulate emotion, cognition or behaviour (e.g. due to lack of resources/energy)[vi]
Individual engages in novel, creative thoughts and actions, takes a 'big-picture' view and is able to find varied and adaptive ways to use their social support network[v].	Narrow thought-action repertoire dominated by automatic behavioural scripts. Unable to take a 'big picture' view. Limited use of social support networks.

Biological Functioning

Optimal conditions	Toxic conditions
Adequate sleep, nutrition, exercise, limited exposure to toxins (e.g. alcohol, tobacco, radiation, hazardous substances)[vii].	Inadequate sleep, poor nutrition, limited (or excessive) exercise, high levels of exposure to toxins (e.g. alcohol, tobacco, radiation, hazardous substances).
Normal maintenance and repair capacity, lack of damage accumulation, genomic stability	Loss of maintenance and repair capacity, damage accumulation, genomic instability[viii]
Physiological systems maintain equilibrium in relation to normal set point (homeostasis), able to respond to stress by changing homeostatic set-point (allostasis)	Physiological systems unable to maintain equilibrium (loss of homeostasis), impaired ability to respond to stress.

[i]The core dimensions of psychological well-being according to Ryff's six-factor model - discussed in chapter 3.
[ii]The demand-control model (Karasek & Theorell, 1990) - discussed in chapter 6.
[iii]The effort-reward imbalance model (Siegrist & Marmot, 2006) - discussed in chapter 6.
[iv]Determinants of subjective well-being (SWB; Diener et al., 1999) and eudaimonic well-being (Ryan & Deci, 2000; Ryff, 1989) – discussed in chapter 3.
[v]The 'Broaden and Build Theory' of positive emotions (Fredrickson, 1998) – discussed in chapter 3.
[vi]Self-regulation depends on limited resources (Muraven & Baumeister, 2000) – discussed in chapter 7.
[vii]Factors responsible for DNA damage, or 'acquired mutations' (Gidron et al., 2006) – discussed in chapter 4.
[viii]The 'telomere hypothesis' (Gilley et al., 2007) – discussed in chapter 6.

9.1.2 IMPLICATIONS FOR INTERVENTIONS

Advances in research bring with them opportunities to not only develop the knowledge base but also apply this knowledge to the development of new treatment approaches. Thus, the research reviewed in previous chapters has led (directly or indirectly) to the development of a number of treatment approaches, summarised in Table 9.2.

As discussed in Chapter 7, the link between theories and the development of interventions is not always clear, and their effects can often be explained in relation to more than one theory or construct.

Potential mediators are also indicated in Table 9.2, which relate broadly to four types of theory – coping theory, self-regulation theory, learning theory and/or emotion theory.

Evidence of the effects of interventions can also feed back into the development of theories and hypotheses for research. For example, within the transactional model, social support is considered a resource for coping, so interventions that boost social support should have positive implications for coping and, consequently, outcomes in patients' health. Intervention studies, however, have demonstrated that social support is not *always* beneficial, and the implications for health may be moderated by individual differences (particularly gender differences). Certain forms of coping (such as venting emotions) also appear to be beneficial for some people but not others. Intervention studies can be useful, therefore, for highlighting the conditions under which hypothesised relationships between a psychological process and implications for health hold up.

TABLE 9.2 Psychobiological intervention approaches and associated theoretical constructs

Intervention approach	Theoretical constructs (potential mediators)
Self-management interventions for patients with chronic illness	Problem-focused coping/ social support/ self-regulation (CT/SRT)
Social support interventions	Social support (CT)
Emotional disclosure interventions	Emotion-focused coping (CT)
Benefit-finding interventions	Emotion-focused coping/positive emotion (CT/ET)
Placebo treatments	Outcome expectancy/ conditioning (SRT/CT/LT)
Behaviour therapy techniques (e.g. Exposure therapy) and cognitive therapy techniques (e.g. Challenging dysfunctional attitudes)	Habituation/ operant conditioning/ somatic remarking/ outcome expectancy (LT/ET/SRT)
Biofeedback	Operant conditioning/outcome expectancy/ self-regulation (LT/SRT)
Relaxation therapies	Emotion-focused coping, self-regulation, positive emotion (CT/SRT/ET)
Mindfulness-based therapies	Emotion-focused coping, positive emotion, personal resources (CT/ET)

CT = coping theory, SRT = self-regulation theory, LT = learning theory, ET = emotion theory.

Intervention studies also indicate that it is not only the intervention approach that matters but also the ways in which different approaches are combined. For example, self-management interventions are likely to be most effective when patients' psychological needs are taken into account, and emotional expression may be most effective when combined with self-regulation strategies. These findings are consistent with the notion that emotional and cognitive processes are closely interrelated and work together to influence outcomes.

The interactive effects of the components of interventions raise challenges for the reporting and evaluation of psychological interventions. Reporting standards and guidelines originally developed for drug trials have been modified to reflect the complexities of non-pharmacological treatments.

Psychobiological research also points to the potential to *prevent* disease. For example, as noted above, psychobiological mechanisms (allostatic load, gene by environmental stress interactions and so on) account for at least some of the excess risk associated with certain sociodemographic characteristics. This research suggests that, although risk factors such as age or socio-economic status cannot necessarily be altered, the risk associated with these factors may be modifiable. Further, advances in genetic research point to the potential to prevent disease in individuals identified as high risk as a result of predictive genetic testing. Psychological approaches to disease prevention may also benefit from advances in pharmacogenetic research – supplementing psychological support for those stopping smoking with individually tailored nicotine replacement therapy, for example. This potential is yet to be realised, however, and researchers have pointed out that the process for translating genomic discoveries from bench to bedside is likely to be a long one.

In general, then, it can be seen that psychobiological research has important implications for developing interventions to improve health, but the link between theory and the development of interventions is not always clear, and psychological interventions can be difficult to evaluate. The development of reporting standards and evaluation guidelines for non-pharmacological interventions should help to overcome these limitations. Psychobiological research may also have important implications for preventing ill health in at risk populations, although more work is needed to realise this potential.

WHAT QUESTIONS HAVE WE YET TO ADEQUATELY ADDRESS?

9.2

Although research conducted over the past few decades has advanced our understanding of associations between psychological, biological and social processes that have implications for health, there are still many questions that research has yet to adequately address. These questions are discussed below in relation to four main themes:

- macro-level determinants of health
- measurement issues
- the development of interventions
- interdisciplinary working.

9.2.1 MACRO-LEVEL DETERMINANTS OF HEALTH

Although research has demonstrated connections between psychological processes and levels of analysis at the micro level, reviewers have emphasised that future research will need to devote greater attention to the macro level, considering the influence of cultural, religious and spiritual variables on psychobiological processes (Nicassio, Meyerowitz & Kerns, 2004). For example, Taylor and colleagues (1997) point out that substantial race differences exist in health and these can be largely explained by socio-economic differences as well as those in the more immediate environments in which people live – their communities, work, family and social life. These environments determine not only the level of stress that individuals are exposed to but also coping skills, resources, health habits and behaviours.

Geronimus (1992) suggests that racial and ethnic differences in health may be explained by 'weathering' – that is, the cumulative impact of repeated experience with social and economic adversity and marginalisation. The 'weathering' concept is very closely related to the concept of allostatic load and has even been operational-ised using the cumulative measures of physiological dysregulation proposed by McEwen and colleagues (Geronimus, Hicken, Keene & Bound, 2006).

Seeman, Dubin and Seeman (2003) point out that religion and spirituality are likely to have important implications for physiological functioning since research has supported associations between religious practices (including Judaeo-Christian religious practices and Zen, yoga meditation and relaxation practice) and a range of physiological indices (such as blood pressure, lipids profiles, cholesterol, immune function and stress hormone levels) as well as effects on health. Others, however, have highlighted the difficulties researchers are likely to face in considering the influence of cultural, religious or spiritual variables. For example, Keefe and Blumenthal (2004) suggest that, among minorities, there remains a distrust of the research enterprise and a concern that individuals' rights may be violated. Researchers must therefore identify barriers to participating in research among minorities and tailor their approach to overcome these barriers.

9.2.2 MEASUREMENT ISSUES

Closer attention to measurement issues will also be needed. For example, as noted above, there is no universally agreed definition of 'stress'. As a consequence, stress has been operationalised in a number of ways. In many psychobiological investigations, caregiving (such as caring for a relative with dementia) has been used as an indicator of chronic stress. Major life events, stressful working conditions and daily hassles have also been studied and, in some studies, participants are exposed to stressful manipulations in experiments. This means that, although we can aggregate across studies in order to form conclusions regarding the physiological effects of stress, we must also be mindful that such aggregation may obscure important differences between these studies in the types of stress measured.

This issue relates equally to the measurement of socio-economic status, religion and spirituality. For example, low socio-economic status may impair functioning owing to an inability to meet basic needs (due to lack of clean water, shelter or healthcare, for example) and/or specific psychological needs (the conditions necessary for psychological well-being), and different measures of socio-economic status may influence well-being for different reasons. For example, discrimination or stigmatisation may act as a barrier to self-acceptance, lack of education or unemployment may act as barriers to the development of autonomy, environmental mastery or personal growth (see Table 9.1).

In relation to culture, it is evident that researchers have used a wide range of proxy variables (nationality, place of birth, region of residence, race, religion and so on) and these are also likely to be related to health for different reasons (Rudell & Diefenbach, 2008).

Regarding spirituality, most research has focused on the frequency with which participants go to church, with little attention being paid to other aspects of religious practice (Seeman et al., 2003). Research undertaken in the future will need to use more sensitive methods to assess socio-economic, cultural and religious and spiritual influences on health, as well as developing models delineating relationships between variables at the macro, meso and micro levels.

9.2.3 THE DEVELOPMENT OF INTERVENTIONS

Another important direction for future research is the development of theory-based interventions. As discussed previously, many interventions for pain were developed long before the mechanisms underlying these interventions were understood. Also, many psychological interventions for patients with chronic illness appear to be informed by theory, although the link between specific theoretical constructs and specific components of the interventions is not made explicit. Therefore, these approaches may be more accurately described as 'theory-inspired' rather than 'theory-based' (Michie & Abraham, 2004). This issue is not peculiar to psychological interventions, since medical interventions may also be developed or implemented before the underlying mechanisms are fully understood (see Box 8.2, Chapter 8).

It is evident, however, that a better understanding of the mechanisms underlying the effects of interventions would facilitate the development of more effective interventions, and that evaluations of such interventions could feed back to refine theory.

A greater understanding of cultural, religious and spiritual influences will also be important for the development of interventions. For example, Nicassio et al. (2004) point out that cultural background and other individual differences (such as the duration of an illness, age, gender and disposition) are likely to be important moderators of the effects of an intervention, and that cultural, religious and spiritual variables are likely to influence patients' preferences for particular modes of intervention. The immediate environment (that is, the organisation or setting in which the intervention is implemented) is also important to consider since organisational factors may act as barriers to the effectiveness of an intervention. Nicassio et al. (2004) suggest that intervention research should shift from a primary focus on *efficacy* studies, which determine whether or not a treatment leads to gains relative to appropriate controls, to a greater consideration of *effectiveness* studies, which determine the clinical significance of an intervention in applied settings.

It will also be important in future research to consider issues of dose and timing – that is, how much and what type of intervention should be delivered and at what point? For example, research involving cancer patients has revealed that interventions provided over a period of several months afford opportunities to address stressors associated with different stages in the course of the disease and are likely to be more appropriate than short-term psychosocial interventions. Other interventions (such as written emotional disclosure) are provided for a brief time period, so it is important to determine when they should be delivered – immediately after a stressful experience, after diagnosis of an illness, during an ongoing stressful experience or medical treatment, or after cessation of a stressor or treatment programme.

Unwanted effects of psychological interventions (and self-directed changes in behaviour) must also be considered. For example, interventions involving the expression of emotions have also been demonstrated to result in increases in negative affect in the period immediately afterwards (Fattaroli, 2006). Changes in health-related behaviour (such as quitting smoking or restricting caloric intake) may also have unwanted effects in the short-term, interfering with the regulation of emotion, cognition and behaviour (see Chapters 2 and 7).

9.2.4 INTERDISCIPLINARY WORKING

In the future, it is also likely that psychobiological research and practice will require greater interdisciplinary collaboration. For example, as discussed in Chapter 5, pain researchers have suggested that a greater understanding of the mechanisms underlying the development of chronic pain could be achieved by incorporating expertise in endocrinology and immunology, and this interdisciplinary working could help to develop treatments to prevent unrelenting suffering.

Combining expertise in PNI and PNE and pharmacology may also lead to the development of new treatment approaches. For example, Volkow and Li (2005) explain that corticotropin releasing factor (CRF) receptor antagonists have been shown to block the initiation of the stress response in the brain and that evidence of links between stress and substance addiction has led to the evaluation of these compounds in the treatment of drug abuse. These trials have revealed a remarkable ability of CRF receptor antagonists to block the initiation of drug taking in animals as well as the stress-induced reinstatement of drug-seeking behaviour. The most promising among these compounds (a drug called 'Antalarmin') is now being studied in preclinical trials to evaluate its therapeutic effects (Volkow & Li, 2005). Increased understanding of the chemical mediators of the stress response may therefore contribute to the development of not only psychological interventions but also drug treatments.

McBeth and Cordingley (2009: 864) suggest that epidemiology and health psychology may be usefully combined since 'supplementing the population-level viewpoint that epidemiology offers with the theory-rich understanding of individual-level processes that psychology describes will enhance both traditions'. Also, Keefe and Blumenthal (2004) suggest that there is a pressing need for health psychologists to become more involved in the area of behavioural genetics since it is increasingly evident that genetic background may be an important individual difference factor that can affect clinical outcomes, and it is likely that information about genetic factors will, in the future, be used to tailor behavioural interventions.

The emerging field of public health genomics is likely to have important implications for health psychology (Brand & Crutzen, 2009). Rudell and Diefenbach (2008) suggest that, in order to build on current health psychology theorising, it will be necessary to incorporate models and advances from neighbouring disciplines, such as anthropology, cultural psychology, sociology and other health professions.

As discussed above, research conducted within each of these and other disciplines contributes a different piece of the jigsaw puzzle. As we move towards a more sophisticated understanding of the interrelationships between biological, psychological and social variables with respect to their implications for health, it will become increasingly important to find and fit these pieces together.

9.2.5 SUMMARY

A number of key questions may be identified in relation to the themes discussed above. It will be important that these questions are addressed in future research.

1 What are the pathways (biological, behavioural and so on) by which socio-economic, cultural, religious and spiritual variables influence health?
2 How can researchers overcome methodological and practical barriers to investigate macro-level determinants of health and their relationship with processes at the meso and micro levels?
3 How can researchers best assess the broadranging physiological effects of adverse environmental conditions?

4 Should the same measures be used to assess the physiological effects of socio-economic status, culture, religion and spirituality?

5 Can theory-based interventions produce clinically meaningful changes in health? If so, for which conditions, under what circumstances?

6 How much and what types of interventions should be delivered and at what point?

7 How can we address unwanted short-term effects of psychological interventions and self-directed behaviour change?

8 What benefits might be gained (for research and practice) from closer interdisciplinary collaborations?

TECHNOLOGICAL ADVANCES

9.3

As we look to the future, it is also important to consider how *techno-logical* advances might influence the development of this field.

In this section we consider the relevance for psychobiological research of advances in information and communication technologies and brain imaging technologies. We then consider how technological advances might influence the development and delivery of therapeutic interventions. We end with a consideration of ethical issues relevant to the future development of this field.

9.3.1 INFORMATION AND COMMUNICATION TECHNOLOGIES

According to the 2008 Annual Report of the Policy and Planning Board of the American Psychological Association (APA), technology has a profound impact on human interaction. For example, whereas the family was once the most important environment for shaping attitudes and beliefs, individuals are now exposed to diverse role models and ways of thinking via TV and the Internet. People may also use technology to remain connected to others, by e-mail, texting, instant messaging or 'twittering' (APA, 2008). This is likely to have many implications for processes relevant to health, by, for example, providing a more diverse range of (more or less reliable) sources of information about health, which people may use to formulate personal models of illness, seek social support, identify strategies for coping and expectations regarding treatment options. This means that researchers must increasingly expand their own models of psychosocial determinants of health to incorporate influences outside the immediate home, family or work environment.

At the same time, these technologies may be harnessed by researchers to facilitate the collection of psychobiological data. For example, ecological momentary assessments may be conducted using online diaries or personal digital assistants (PDAs; APA, 2008). The use of electronic diaries not only helps to reduce retrospective bias and, hence, provide more reliable data for research purposes, but also has the potential to enhance clinicians' understanding of their clients' symptoms and life circumstances (Piasecki, Hufford, Solhan & Trull, 2007).

Other technologies are available to facilitate the assessment of health-related behaviours, such as pill bottles that record the times and dates of when they were opened, portable transducers for measuring smoking topography (that is, how a person smokes cigarettes – the number of puffs, puff volume, duration and velocity) and wearable devices that track blood alcohol concentration by measuring ethanol excretion through the skin (see Piasecki et al., 2007, for a review).

Progress in biosensor technology has also led to portable recording systems that allow for the naturalistic assessment of a range of physiological parameters (cardio-vascular, electrodermal and respiratory activity, for example), while sophisticated computer processing enables confounding variables to be controlled (disentangling emotional activation from effects of physical activity, for example), so that these processes may be studied outside the controlled environment of the laboratory (Ebner-Priemer & Trull, 2009; Houtveen & de Geus, 2009).

9.3.2 BRAIN IMAGING TECHNOLOGIES

Developments in functional brain imaging technology may also have important implications for advancing our understanding of the relationships between psycho-logical and physiological processes (Miller, Elbert, Sutton & Heller, 2007). These advances include the introduction of new technologies, such as **functional magnetic resonance imaging (fMRI)**, as well as ongoing improvements in the performance of technologies such as electroencephalography (EEG) and **magnetoencephalography (MEG)**. Miller et al. (2007), however, urge that, in the face of powerful brain imag-ing technologies, constant vigilance is needed against naïve reductionism. Researchers must keep in mind that, even if brain mechanisms (or gene expression affecting brain mechanisms) are implicated in the aetiology of a specific psychological disorder, it is untenable to assume that the brain mechanism (or gene expression) is not itself driven by psychological events.

The use of brain imaging technologies is not restricted to psychological disorders, but may also be applied to investigation of psychological states. For example, EEG studies of meditative states have been conducted for around 50 years, and fMRI studies are beginning to refine neuroelectric data by suggesting possible neural loci for the effects of meditation (Cahn & Polich, 2006).

Lorig (2009), however, points out that knowing which parts of the brain are active during psychological tasks is not the same as knowing *how* the brain accomplishes these tasks. Further, 'studies have overwhelmingly demonstrated that, whatever task might be accomplished, there are multiple areas of localised brain activity that are active during their execution' (Lorig, 2009: 20). Thus, we can only conclude that these tasks are accomplished *by the brain*. In the future, therefore, it will be impor-tant to utilise brain imaging technologies not only to investigate which parts of the brain 'light up' during particular tasks but also to develop theories of psychological functions (Lorig, 2009).

9.3.3 THE DEVELOPMENT AND DELIVERY OF INTERVENTIONS

Technological advances are pertinent to not only the assessment of psychobiological processes but also manipulation of these processes. For example, research suggests that portable biofeedback devices may be a useful adjunct to CBT for anxiety disorders (Reiner, 2008). **Neurofeedback** (self-regulation of functional brain networks using fMRI feedback) has also been highlighted as a promising therapeutic tool for achieving learned control of emotion networks (see Research in focus box 9.1).

RESEARCH IN FOCUS BOX 9.1

Johnston and colleagues (2010) used fMRI to identify areas of the brain that react to positive and negative emotional stimuli, then fMRI neurofeedback to train participants to up-regulate the target areas associated with processing negative stimuli.

Methodology

A total of 13 participants (4 males, 9 females, aged between 21 and 52) were recruited. A subset of five participants completed psychometric tests (the profile of mood states (POMS), McNair et al., 1971, and positive and negative affect scale (PANAS), Watson et al., 1988) immediately before and after the neurofeedback.

Prior to the neurofeedback, fMRI was used to identify the areas of the brain that respond most to negative stimuli compared to the neutral pictures for each individual.

During the neurofeedback, participants were instructed to up-regulate activity of the target region for periods of 20 seconds, alternating with 14-second rest periods. This was repeated over 12 cycles for each training run. The experimenters suggested that emotional imagery might be employed, and instructed participants to monitor the feedback signal and 'tune' their strategy during each successive training block. For the continuous feedback, a picture of a thermometer was used – the temperature of which reflected increases in the amplitude of the fMRI signal in the target area relative to baseline.

Results

The localising procedure identified a network of brain areas that is commonly found to be active in relation to emotional stimuli. The strongest activation was observed for negative pictures, with activity in the amygdalae, ventrolateral prefrontal cortex (VLPFC) and insula particularly prominent. Note that the amygdala is often associated with fear, and the insula with disgust.

(Cont'd)

All the participants were able to produce greater activation of the target area during 'up' compared to 'rest' periods. Participants reported that imagery of the previously viewed affective scenes was not the most effective strategy, and all participants eventually settled for a strategy that involved personal memories.

The subset of participants who completed psychometric tests showed increased mood disturbance after the neurofeedback, particularly in relation to negative affect.

Conclusions and the implications

The findings indicate that fMRI neurofeedback may be a useful tool for achieving learned control of emotion networks. It is important to determine, however, whether or not similar results could be obtained for inducing a positive mood.

As discussed in Chapter 3, positive emotions are not associated with specific patterns of physiological at activation, and down-regulation of negative emotion will not necessarily result in the up-regulation of positive emotion. Thus, fMRI neurofeedback may represent a useful therapeutic tool, but further work is needed to realise its potential.

Virtual reality (VR) is an emerging technology with a variety of potential benefits. It involves the immersion of the user in a 'virtual environment' – a digital space in which the user's movements are tracked and his or her surroundings digitally composed and displayed to the senses in accordance with those movements. This results in a substitute reality in which the user can interact with objects, people and environments (Fox, Arena & Bailenson, 2009).

One of the commonest applications of this technology is exposure therapy, using virtual environments to treat patients with phobias or anxiety disorders. Exposure to virtual cues has also been shown to stimulate nicotine and alcohol cravings, so it is anticipated that VR may also be used therapeutically for the treatment of addictions (see Fox et al., 2009, for a review).

Pain management methods, integrating VR to distract patients' attention from uncomfortable procedures, have achieved considerable success (Glantz, Rizzo & Graap, 2003; Gold, Belmont & Thomas, 2007; Hoffman et al., 2008).

VR has also been applied in non-clinical situations in order to target stress management and relaxation (Villani, Riva & Riva, 2007) and enhance the psychological benefits of indoor exercise, such as walking on a treadmill (Plante et al., 2003). The studies have reported benefits of VR compared to less technologically advanced alternatives, although these benefits appear to be moderated by individual differences – particularly the individuals' ability to become fully immersed (or achieve a 'sense of presence') in the virtual environment. Less technologically advanced solutions (such as relaxation DVDs) may be as effective if designed to maximise the participants' sense of presence (Villani & Riva, 2008).

The introduction of **telehealth** has implications for the ways in which individuals access healthcare (APA, 2008). Telehealth has been defined (Nickelson, 1996: 444) as:

> the use of advanced telecommunications to provide access to assessment, diagnosis, intervention, consultation, supervision, education, and information to underserved populations and isolated practitioners.

> Telehealth relies on a wide range of technologies to connect individuals and transmit information, ranging from a desktop computer connected to the Internet to search for references to two-way interactive audio and video.

Computer-mediated communication may even be used to deliver psychotherapy – an application referred to as **teletherapy** (also called **e-therapy, telepsychotherapy** or **telepsychology**; Castelnuovo, Gaggioli, Mantovani & Riva, 2003). Procedures of this kind currently in use include online treatment programmes (such as weight management, pain management, stopping smoking, support for dementia caregivers), self-help chat rooms, neuropsychological assessments and adherence-enhancing strategies, (such as e-mail reminders, Web-based appointments and follow-up (Saab et al., 2004)). Teletherapy has also been successfully applied to the treatment of anxiety and eating disorders (Castelnuovo et al., 2003).

9.3.4 ETHICAL CONSIDERATIONS

While technological advances confer a number of potential benefits on research and practice, it is also important to consider the ethical implications of these advances. For example, what would happen if electronic communications between a patient and practitioner (or between a client and therapist) were accessed by a third person, or electronic records were lost owing to a computer failure? Is it ethically acceptable to research online communications (via chat rooms, for example) without informed consent? How can we be certain that individuals completing online studies or receiving therapy via the Internet are not at risk of harm?

McMinn and colleagues (1999) surveyed several hundred psychologists to determine the frequency with which they engaged in a wide range of behaviours involving the use of communication and information technologies (such as providing consultation via telephone or the Internet or sending confidential information via fax or e-mail). The respondents were also asked to rate each behaviour in terms of its ethical acceptability. Only two behaviours occurred for 90 per cent or more of respondents – providing consultation for a colleague on the telephone and crisis intervention by telephone – and both of these were considered to be ethical by the vast majority of respondents. A number of behaviours were identified as rare and unethical, including allowing professionals other than psychologists access to computerised assessment tools, listening to a confidential message from one client in the presence of another client, and allowing unauthorised access to client records (such as by a computer hacker).

The researchers also highlighted a number of 'equivocal' behaviours – those for which a significant proportion indicated 'don't know' or 'not sure' on the ethics rating or for which there was an equal proportion of respondents indicating 'never/rarely ethical' and 'unquestioningly ethical/ethical under many circumstances'. These behaviours included storing therapy records on a computer network, failing to receive clients' messages because of technical problems, losing clients' records owing to a technology failure, using computers to take notes during therapy and using computers as an adjunctive tool during therapy.

McMinn, Buchanan, Ellens & Ryan (1999) point out that it is difficult for ethical guidelines to keep pace with technological advances and that many psychologists are uncertain about the ethical uses of particular technologies.

A survey of several hundred psychologists conducted by VandenBos and Williams (2000) also reported that the telephone was the most widely used form of communication technology, while only 2 per cent provided services via the Internet or satellite technology. Barnett and Scheetz (2003) highlight a number of ethical issues and concerns arising from the use of telephone interactions. For example, it is not possible to observe body language, eye contact or general appearance, and risk management issues also arise, such as working with suicidal patients or issues of dangerousness or abuse.

Conducting research via the Internet also raises ethical issues. Nosek, Banaji and Greenwald (2002) highlight three differences between Internet and traditional laboratory research that have implications for ethics:

- absence of a researcher
- uncertainty regarding adequate informed consent
- debriefing and the potential loss of the anonymity or confidentiality of participants.

The APA Board of Scientific Affairs Advisory Group on the Conduct of Research on the Internet (Kraut et al., 2004: 108) concluded that:

> online research poses no more risk to human subjects than comparable research conducted through other means, but conducting research online changes the nature of the risks and investigators' ability to assess it.

For example, determining whether an individual is identifiable or anonymous has implications for the risks subjects are exposed to, and there are circumstances under which Internet communications (via online forums, say) may or may not be considered exempt from informed consent requirements.

Further, experimental manipulations (such as altering beliefs or emotions) may present a risk to some subjects, particularly if participants are not adequately debriefed (due to leaving a study before its completion, for example).

It is possible to minimise these risks by means of careful research design (Nosek, Banaji & Greenwald, 2002). Kraut et al. (2004) write, however, that it will be important for ethical review boards to have access to expertise relevant to judging the risks of online research.

SUMMARY AND CONCLUSIONS

9.4 Advances in research methods and the technologies available to facilitate research and practice will undoubtedly yield greater understanding of the complex interrelationships between biological, psychological and social processes with respect to their implications for health, and also improve the effectiveness of preventative and therapeutic interventions. It is likely, however, that ethical and practical considerations will also become increasingly complex. Researchers and clinicians will need to keep abreast of new developments within their own fields and call on expert knowledge from other relevant disciplines when needed. Interdisciplinary collaboration is also likely to be important for the development of guidelines for the conduct and evaluation of research, as well as its delivery and the evaluation of therapeutic interventions.

As the knowledge base develops, we must also remember to constantly feed this knowledge back to refine theory, in order that we may understand not only if particular social or psychological processes influence physiological functioning but also how and when they do so and with what implications for health.

KEY TERMS

functional magnetic resonance imaging (fMRI), magnetoencephalography (MEG), neurofeedback, telehealth, teletherapy (also called e-therapy, telepsychotherapy or telepsychology), virtual reality (VR)

■Discussion questions

1 Apart from those outlined above, what questions have we yet to adequately address?

2 What do you think the key priorities for future research should be?

3 How could greater interdisciplinary integration help to address the health challenges facing us today? (Consider this question in relation to smoking, alcohol, obesity or chronic illness.)

4 How do you think technological advances will change the way patients are treated in the future? Are changes likely to be more positive than negative?

FURTHER READING

American Psychological Association (2008). How technology changes everything (and nothing) in psychology: 2008 annual report of the APA Policy and Planning Board. *American Psychologist, 64*, 454–463.

Castelnuovo, G., Gaggioli, A., Mantovani, F. & Riva, G. (2003). New and old tools in psychotherapy: the use of technology for the integration of traditional clinical treatments. *Psychotherapy: Theory, Research, Practice, Training, 40*, 33–44.

Lorig, T.S. (2009). What was the question? fMRI and inference in psychophysiology. *International Journal of Psychophysiology*, 73, 17–21.

Nicassio, P.M., Meyerowitz, B.E. & Kerns, R.D. (2004). The future of health psychology interventions. *Health Psychology*, 23, 132–137.

Piasecki, T.M., Hufford, M.R., Solhan, M. & Trull, T.J. (2007). Assessing clients in their natural environments with electronic diaries: rationale, benefits, limitations, and barriers. *Psychological Assessment, 19*, 25–43.

GLOSSARY

A-beta fibres Rapidly conducting non-nociceptive fibres. *See* gate control theory.

Acceptance and commitment therapy (ACT) A mindfulness-based therapy that encourages patients to disentangle from troubling thoughts or sensations, develop deepened conscious contact with the present moment and construct patterns of action linked to chosen values.

Acupressure Stimulation of acupuncture points without piercing the skin, applying pressure instead. Used to relieve pain.

Acupuncture Involves insertion of solid needles at acupuncture points. Used to relieve pain.

Acute pain Pain elicited by substantial injury to body tissue and activation of nociceptive transducers.

Adaptive immunity (also called acquired or specific immunity) Highly targeted immune response to overcome specific foreign invaders.

A-delta fibres Fast, myelinated fibres carrying information about intense, sharp pain. *See* gate control theory.

Alleles Alternative forms of a gene at a specific chromosomal location.

Allocation bias Deviation from random assignment in which group allocation is related to (known or unknown) risk factors or confounding variables.

Allodynia *See* stimulus-evoked pain.

Allostasis The process of maintaining stability through change.

Allostatic load The biological 'cost' associated with allostatic systems.

Altered homeostatic theory Suggests that age-associated diseases result from a shift from parasympathetic to sympathetic regulation and loss of maintenance and repair functions.

Appraisal Cognitive evaluation of a situation or stimulus.

Autonomic nervous system (ANS) The division of the peripheral nervous system responsible for controlling the functioning of a number of organs and glands.

Autosomal dominant inheritance A mutant gene from one parent is sufficient to cause the disease, even if a normal copy is inherited from the other parent.

Autosomal recessive inheritance Each individual must inherit two copies of the mutant gene (one from each parent) to develop the disease.

Autosome Any chromosome other than a sex chromosome.

Behaviour therapy A therapeutic approach involving the use of a range of techniques aimed at eliminating problem behaviours by manipulating response contingencies.

Behavioural genetics The genetic study of behaviour.

Behavioural medicine An interdisciplinary field concerned with the integration and application of behavioural, environmental and biomedical knowledge relevant to health and disease.

Benefit-finding Finding positive meaning (benefit) in stressful experiences.

Biochemical theory of pain Describes biochemical mechanisms implicated in pain.

Biofeedback A technique used to produce learned control of a wide range of physiological responses, including systolic and diastolic blood pressure, peripheral vascular responses and various brain rhythms.

Biomedical model Considers disease to be fully explained by deviations from the norm of biological variables.

Biopsychosocial model Considers health to result from complex interactions between biological, social and psychological factors.

Blinding Withholding information from the participant about the assigned intervention (drug v. placebo, for example). Information may also be withheld from the person delivering the intervention ('double blind trial') and from the person responsible for analysing the data ('triple blind trial').

Broaden and build theory Suggests that positive emotions perform an important adaptive function by broadening the thought–action repertoire and building resources.

Catastrophising A coping strategy aimed at increasing attention or empathy from others.

Cellular immunity, cell-mediated immunity, Th1 response Involves the use of killer T cells and NK cells to destroy infected cells.

Central nervous system (CNS) The brain and spinal cord.

Central sensitisation Increased excitability of neurons in the central nervous system.

C fibres Slow, unmyelinated fibres carrying information about dull, throbbing pain. *See* gate control theory.

Chromosomal disorders Result from an abnormal chromosome number or structural rearrangement of chromosomes.

Chromosome Large stretches of DNA.

Chronic pain Pain that persists beyond the normal time of healing.

Circadian pattern A rhythmic, 24-hour cycle in relation to sleep.

Classical conditioning An associative learning process resulting in a conditioned response to a previously neutral stimulus, such as dogs salivating in response to a bell.

Cognitive activation theory (CAT) Conceptualises stress and coping in terms of expectancy.

Cognitive behavioural therapy (CBT) A therapeutic approach involving the use of behaviour therapy and cognitive therapy techniques. *See* behaviour therapy and cognitive therapy.

Cognitive therapy A therapeutic approach involving the use of a range of techniques developed to challenge problem thinking.

Commonsense model of illness representations Proposes that individuals hold cognitive and emotional representations of illness, and these guide their attempts to cope.

Complex interventions Interventions involving several components that may be difficult to describe and standardise, such as in pain clinics and stroke units.

Complex or multifactorial disorders Result from complex interactions between genes and the environment.

Conditioned immunomodulation Alteration of immune function via classical conditioning.

Confounding variables Variables that could influence the relationship between an independent (manipulated or measured) variable and a dependent (outcome) variable.

Consolidated Standards of Reporting Trials (CONSORT) Statement A set of evidence-based guidelines for reporting randomised controlled trials.

Coping skills training A psychological intervention based on coping theory.

Coping *Either* efforts to alter a stressful situation, and/or minimise resulting distress (*see* transactional model of coping) or positive outcome expectancy (*see* cognitive activation theory).

Coronary atherosclerosis A progressive disease involving a gradual thickening of the walls of the coronary arteries.

Corticosteroids Steroid hormones produced by the adrenal glands (cortisol in humans, corticosterone in rats and mice).

Cytokines Chemical messengers released by cells of the immune system.

Deep brain or motor cortex stimulation Electrical stimulation of the brain. Used to treat refractory neuropathic pain states.

Deoxyribonucleic acid (DNA) The primary material (in most organisms) containing the information for all hereditary traits of the organism.

Disease An organising construct for explaining and responding to constellations of symptoms.

Dizygotic (DZ) twins Derive from two distinct fertilised eggs and, therefore, have the same genetic relationship as non-twin siblings.

Double blind trials *See* blinding.

Ecological momentary assessments Involve the use of methods by which a participant in research can report on his or her emotions, cognitions or behaviours as they are experienced.

Electroacupuncture Weak, pulsed electric current passed through acupuncture needles. Used to relieve pain.

Electrodermal response (EDR) A technique used to monitor sweat gland activity.

Electroencephalography (EEG) A technique used to monitor brainwave activity.

Electromyography (EMG) A technique used to monitor muscle tension.

Emotional disclosure A psychological intervention that involves expressing negative thoughts and feelings. Typically, it involves writing in a diary for three to four days.

Endocrine system A system of glands that produce and secrete hormones.

Endocrinosenescence Age-related changes in endocrine function.

Endophenotype Higher-order variables explaining individual variability in self-reported and observed behaviour.

Endorphins Endogenous, morphine-like substances that attach to pain receptors to modulate or decrease pain.

Enteric nervous system Division of the autonomic nervous system responsible for controlling intestinal functions.

Environmental epigenomics A new field of study that aims to determine which human genes are likely to be involved in susceptibility to disease when epigenetically deregulated.

Epidural block Injection of anaesthetic into the epidural space near the spinal cord to relieve pain.

Epigenetic landscape A theoretical model that explains phenotypic variance in terms of environmental forces acting on an organism, represented by a ball rolling over a landscape.

Epigenetics Localised changes in gene expression that take place without a change in the DNA sequence.

Epigenomics Changes in gene expression across many genes in a cell or organism.

Evidence-based medicine (EBM) The process of systematically reviewing, appraising and using research evidence to guide the delivery of clinical care.

Experimental design Involves manipulating one or more independent variable(s) in order to observe changes in the outcome (dependent) variable, while controlling for potential confounding variables.

External or ecological validity The extent to which the results of a study may be generalised beyond the study sample or experimental setting.

Extinction Lack of reinforcement for a previously reinforced (conditioned) response, resulting in cessation of the conditioned response.

Fight or flight response Bodily changes associated with fear and rage, as described by Walter Cannon (1871–1945). *See* relaxation response.

Flow A state of optimal psychological functioning in which challenges are matched to the individual's level of skill.

Functional magnetic resonance imaging (fMRI) A non-invasive brain imaging technique used to map brain activity, evidenced by changes in blood flow.

Gamma-aminobutyric acid (GABA) The primary inhibitory neurotransmitter of the nervous system.

Gate control theory (GCT) A theory of pain that incorporates both physiological and psychological dimensions.

Gene Unit of genetic material made up of deoxyribonucleic acid (DNA).

Gene expression How and when genes are 'switched on'.

Gene therapy An experimental technique that uses genes to prevent or treat disease.

General adaptation syndrome (GAS) A three-stage response to prolonged stress, as described by Hans Selye (1907–1982).

Genome The entire complement of genetic material of a cell.

Genotype The individual's unique set of genes.

Graded exposure therapy Involves repeatedly presenting a feared stimulus under conditions in which the stimulus will not result in unfavourable consequences.

Habituation The process by which an animal (or person) learns to ignore a stimulus that does not predict anything of value.

Hardiness A personality construct characterised by commitment, control and challenge.

Health An evaluative notion based on adherence to physical, social and mental 'normality'.

Health psychology An applied branch of psychology concerned with understanding and improving health and the healthcare system.

Health psychology interventions Psychological (cognitive, emotional, behavioural) interventions designed to improve health or target processes contributing to illness and disease.

Homeostasis The process of maintaining physiological equilibrium.

Humoral immunity, antibody-mediated immunity, Th2 response Involves the use of molecules that bind with an antigen in order to clear it from the body.

Hyperalgesia *See* stimulus-evoked pain.

Hypothalamic-pituitary-adrenal (HPA) axis Refers to interactions between the hypothalamus, pituitary gland and adrenal gland.

Illness A deviation from physical, social or mental 'normality' that is perceived by the patient as distressing and a title to special treatment.

Immune surveillance hypothesis Suggests that tumours develop when the normal surveillance function of the immune system is suppressed.

Immune system A network of cells, tissues and organs responsible for defending the organism against attack by 'foreign' invaders, such as bacteria, fungi, parasites, viruses.

Inflamma-ageing An increased inflammatory immune response with advancing age.

Innate immunity (also called natural immunity) Non-specific immune response that acts near entry points into the body.

INUS Stands for causes that are Insufficient but Necessary components of Unnecessary but Sufficient causes.

Leukocytes White blood cells of the immune system.

Local anaesthetic A drug that causes reversible local anaesthesia.

Lymphocytes Cells of the immune system responsible for identifying and eliminating foreign invaders.

Lymphoid organs Organs of the immune system.

Magnetoencephalography (MEG) A non-invasive brain imaging technique used to map brain activity, evidenced by changes in magnetic fields.

Mediator A variable that explains how or why the relationship between two other variables exists.

Mere measurement effect or question–behaviour effect The phenomenon in which behaviour is altered simply by asking the participant to answer a question.

Meta-analysis The use of statistical methods to summarise the results of a number of relevant studies and examine the consistency of evidence across studies.

Mindfulness-based cognitive therapy (MBCT) An adaptation of mindfulness-based stress reduction (MBSR), used for treating chronic depression.

Mindfulness-based stress reduction (MBSR) A group intervention that involves training in mindfulness meditation and its applications in daily living and coping with stress, pain and illness.

Moderator A variable that explains under which conditions a relationship between two other variables exists.

Monozygotic (MZ) twins Derive from a single egg and, therefore, inherit identical genetic material.

Multifactorial causality Outcomes that are produced by multiple causal inferences for which several different causal pathways may lead to the same outcome.

Mutations Changes in DNA sequence with an effect on gene function.

Natural experiment A study design that involves examination of naturally occurring risk and protective factors using design elements that allow an approximation to experimental conditions.

Naturalistic studies Studies that involve recording risk and protective factors under natural (rather than experimental) conditions.

Negative automatic thoughts (NATs) Dysfunctional thoughts that arise automatically, without deliberation or reasoning, and have the capacity to produce dysfunctional behaviours.

Neurofeedback Self-regulation of functional brain networks using functional magnetic resonance imaging (fMRI) feedback. See fMRI.

Neuromatrix theory of pain A theory of pain that incorporates genetic, cognitive neurohormonal and neural mechanisms.

Neuropathic pain Pain that is not thought to indicate tissue damage, but results from changes to the nervous system.

Neuropeptides See neurotransmitters.

Neurosignature The characteristic pattern of nerve impulses produced by the pattern of synaptic connections in the neuromatrix.

Neurotransmitters Chemical messengers released by neurons. Includes small molecule neurotransmitters (such as ACTH, GABA) and neuropeptide neurotransmitters (such as CRH, ACTH).

Nociception The physiological response to tissue injury.

Nociceptive transducers Peripheral terminals of nociceptors.

Nociceptors Nerves that transmit pain signals to the brain.

Non-steroidal anti-inflammatory drugs (NSAIDS) Non-steroid drugs used to treat inflammation.

Normal distribution A bell-shaped distribution of measurements or scores, with the highest frequency around the average value for the group.

Obesity epidemic A term used to refer to the rapid rise in obesity levels recorded by the World Health Organisation in the late twentieth and early twenty-first century.

Operant conditioning Involves pairing an unconditioned response (such as spontaneously pressing a lever) with an unconditioned stimulus (such as food) in order to produce a conditioned response (pressing the lever to obtain food).

Opiate drugs Drugs that bind to opioid receptors, used in the treatment of pain.

Opioid receptors Receptors that bind opiates or opioid substances.

Parasympathetic nervous system (PNS) Division of the autonomic nervous system responsible for rest and storing energy.

Patient preference trials Involve randomising participants without strong preferences, and allowing those with a strong preference to receive their preferred treatment.

Patient-centred care Emphasises the role of the patient in their own care.

Pattern theory One of the main theories of pain until the 1960s. Suggested that the intensity of the stimulus and central summation are the main determinants of pain.

Perceived control The individual's belief that he or she is able to alter the outcome of a situation.

Peripheral nerve stimulation Non-noxious stimulation of peripheral nerves, used to relieve pain.

Peripheral nervous system Nerves that carry information to and from the central nervous system.

Pharmacogenetics or pharmacogenomics The targeting of pharmaceuticals based on an individual's genetic characteristics.

Phenotype The individual's set of observable characteristics or traits.

Placebo therapies Therapies that involve the administration of dummy pills or sham treatments in place of active therapies.

Polymorphisms Changes in DNA sequence that have no effect on the functioning of the gene.

Population ageing The process by which older individuals become a proportionally larger share of the population.

Positional cloning The process of localising and identifying a disease gene.

Predictive genetic testing The use of a genetic test to predict risk of a disease in the future.

Progressive relaxation A technique used to produce relaxation by first tensing and then releasing muscles.

Prospective longitudinal design A study design that involves the measurement of independent (predictor) variables at time 1 and outcome variables at time 2.

Proteins Large molecules made of one or more chains of amino acids.

Psychological resilience The ability to 'bounce back' from negative emotional experiences and adapt to the changing demands of stressful experiences.

Psychological well-being (PWB) Conceptualisation of well-being in relation to meaning or self-realisation and the degree to which a person is functioning fully.

Psychoneuroendocrinology (PNE) The study of interactions between the brain and endocrine system and resulting implications for health.

Psychoneuroimmunology (PNI) The study of interactions between the brain and immune system and resulting implications for health.

Psychophysiology (PP) The study of relations between psychological manipulations and physiological responses.

Psychosocial threat Sense of threat resulting from the interpretation of changes in the environment.

Psychosomatic medicine The study of relations between the mind, body and health.

Quantitative genetic strategies Methods used to determine if, and to what extent, a disease may be heritable.

Random assignment A process of assigning participants to groups, ensuring that the probability of being assigned to either the experimental or control group is the same for each participant.

Randomisation check A statistical comparison of experimental and control group data performed to test for group equivalence at baseline.

Randomised controlled trial (RCT) or randomly assigned controlled clinical trial (RACC) Involves randomly assigning participants to receive either an active intervention or an inactive control (such as a dummy pill) using an experimental design.

Randomised waiting list study A study design that involves randomly allocating participants to intervention or waiting list conditions (participants in the waiting list condition receive the intervention at a later point in time).

RE-AIM framework A framework used to evaluate the long-term effectiveness of interventions when delivered in real-world settings, considering both individual-level factors (such as cost, transport, inconvenience to patients) and organisation-level factors (such as level of resources, expertise required, fit with current practice).

Referred pain Pain felt at a site remote from the site of origin or stimulation.

Relationship-centred care Emphasises the role of both patients and clinicians (and relationships between patients and clinicians) in the care process.

Relaxation response (RR) The physiological counterpart of the fight or flight response. *See* fight or flight response.

Replicative senescence The characteristic of all normal somatic cells to undergo a limited number of cell divisions (the Hayflick limit).

Self-determination theory (SDT) Suggests that fulfilment of basic psychological needs is essential for well-being.

Self-management interventions Interventions that aim to increase patients' interest and involvement in their own care and empower them to manage their condition.

Self-regulation The process by means of which individuals maintain control over thoughts, feelings and actions.

Serotonin (also called 5-hydroxytryptamine, 5-HT) A neurotransmitter that plays an important role in the regulation of mood and is used in the treatment of depression.

Sex chromosomes Either of a pair of chromosomes that combine to determine the sex of an organism.

Single-gene disorders Caused by a mutation in a single gene.

Somatic marking The process by which threats to homeostasis activate feeling states and initiate attempts at self-regulation.

Specificity theory One of the main theories of pain until the 1960s. Suggested that pain signals are carried to the brain by specific types of fibres in the spinal nerves.

Spinal cord stimulation (SCS) Non-noxious stimulation of the spinal cord, used to relieve pain.

Spontaneous pain Pain arising owing to spontaneous activity in the primary sensory neurons.

Statistical normality A statistically defined concept of 'normality' based on the distribution of scores for a particular group or population. *See* normal distribution.

Steroids Anti-inflammatory substances that occur naturally in the body (such as cortisol) or are produced synthetically in order to treat inflammation.

Stimulation-produced analgesia (SPA) Pain relief via nerve stimulation.

Stimulus-evoked pain Heightened reaction to a painful stimulus evoked by brushing or pressure (hyperalgesia) or tactile pain to an innocuous stimulus (allodynia).

Stressful life events Events that normally demand readjustment of the average person's routine.

Subjective well-being (SWB) Conceptualisation of well-being as a subjective construct, dependent on the individual's personal evaluation of their own life circumstances.

Sympathetic nervous system Division of the autonomic nervous system responsible for arousal and energy release.

Sympathetic-adrenal-medullary axis (SAM) Links between the sympathetic nervous system and adrenal medulla.

Systematic review A methodically rigorous review of relevant literature using explicit scientific methods to synthesise findings of individual studies in an unbiased manner.

Telehealth The use of advanced telecommunications to provide access to healthcare, such as assessment, diagnosis and intervention, to underserved or isolated populations.

Teletherapy (also called e-therapy, telepsychotherapy or telepsychology) The use of computer-mediated communication to deliver psychotherapy.

Telomere hypothesis Suggests that the counting mechanism for replicative senescence is provided by progressive shortening of telomeres.

Telomeres Specialised DNA or protein structures at the ends of chromosomes that act to protect chromosome caps.

Thymic involution Age-related degeneration of the thymus.

Transactional model (TM) of coping Conceptualises stress and coping in relation to dynamic interactions between the individual and environment.

Transcutaneous electrical nerve stimulation (TENS) A non-invasive method of applying electrical stimulation to the skin for pain control.

Tricyclic antidepressants Antidepressant drugs that prevent the reabsorption of noradrenalin and serotonin. Also used as frontline therapies for neuropathic pain states.

Triple blind trials *See* blinding.

Type A personality A personality construct characterised by impatience, competitiveness and hostility.

Undoing effect A reduction in physiological arousal to negative emotion resulting from exposure to positive emotion stimuli. *See* broaden and build theory.

Viral challenge studies Involve exposing participants to a virus under experimental conditions and then measuring the relationship between risk factors (assessed prior to exposure) and the subsequent development of symptoms.

Virtual reality (VR) The use of technologies that involve immersion of the user in a virtual environment.

X-linked dominant inheritance Diseases linked to the X chromosome. Individuals need inherit only one copy of the mutant gene to inherit the disease.

X-linked recessive inheritance Disease linked to the X chromosome. Females must inherit two copies of the mutant gene to inherit the disease, but males will inherit the disease if only one mutant gene is inherited.

REFERENCES

Abramson, L.Y., Metalsky, G.I., & Alloy, L.B. (1989). Hopelessness depression: a theory based subtype of depression. *Psychological Review, 96*, 358–372.

Abramson, L.Y., Seligman, M.E.P., & Teasdale, J.D. (1978). Learned helplessness in humans: critique and reformulation. *Journal of Abnormal Psychology, 87*, 49–74.

Adams, P., Hurd, M.D., Merrill, A., & Ribeiro, T. (2003). Healthy, wealthy, and wise? Tests for direct causal paths between health and socioeconomic status. *Journal of Econometrics, 112*, 3–56.

Adda, J., Chandola, T., & Marmot, M. (2003). Socio-economic status and health: causality and pathways. *Journal of Econometrics, 112*, 57–63.

Ader, R. (2003). Conditioned immunomodulation: research needs and directions. *Brain, Behavior and Immunity, 17*, 51–57.

Ader, R., & Cohen, N. (1975). Behaviourally conditioned immunosuppression. *Psychosomatic Medicine, 37*, 333–340.

Ader, R., & Cohen, N. (1982). Behaviorally conditioned immunosuppression and murine systemic lupus erythematosus. *Science, 215*, 1534–1536.

Ajzen, I., & Fishbein, M. (2004). Questions raised by a reasoned action approach: comment on Ogden (2003). *Health Psychology, 23*, 431–434.

Ajzen, I., & Madden, T.J. (1986). Prediction of goal-directed behavior: attitudes, intentions and perceived behavioral control. *Journal of Experimental Social Psychology, 22*, 453–474.

Alonso, Y. (2004) The biopsychosocial model in medical research: the evolution of the health concept over the last two decades. *Patient Education and Counseling, 53*, 239–244.

Altman, D.G., & Bland, J.M. (1999). Statistics notes: how to randomise. *British Medical Journal, 319*, 703–704.

Altman, D.G., Schulz, K.F., Moher, D., Egger, M., Davidoff, F., Elbourne, D., Gotzsche, P.C., & Lang, T. (2001). The revised CONSORT statement for reporting randomized trials: explanation and elaboration. *Annals of Internal Medicine, 134*, 663–694.

Alzheimer's Society (2007). Dementia UK 2007: full dementia UK report, available online at: http://alzheimers.org.uk/site/scripts/download_info.php?fileID=2

American Academy of Pediatrics (2006). Prevention and management of pain in the neonate: an update. *Pediatrics, 118*, 2231–2241.

American Psychological Association (2008). How technology changes everything (and nothing) in psychology: 2008 annual report of the APA policy and planning board. *American Psychologist, 64*, 454–463.

Anagnostopoulos, F., & Spanea, E. (2005). Assessing illness representations of breast cancer: a comparison of patients with healthy and benign controls. *Journal of Psychosomatic Research, 58*, 327–334.

Anand, K.J., & Craig, K.D. (1996). New perspectives on the definition of pain. *Pain, 67*, 3–6.

Andersen, B.L., Kiecolt-Glaser, J.K., & Glaser, R. (1994). A biobehavioral model of cancer stress and disease course. *American psychologist, 49*, 389–404.

Anderson, B.L., Farrar, W.B., Golden-Kreutz, D., Emery, C.F., Glaser, R., Crespin, T., & Carson, W.E. (2007). Distress reduction from a psychological intervention contributes to improved health for cancer patients. *Brain Behavior and Immunity, 21*, 953–961.

Anderson, B.L., Farrar, W. B., Golden-Kreutz, D.M., Glaser, R., Emery, C.F., Crespin, T.R., Shapiro, C.L., & Carson, W.E. (2004). Psychological, behavioral, and immune changes after a psychological intervention. *Journal of Clinical Oncology, 22*, 3570–3580.

Anderson, B.L., Golden-Kreutz, D.M., Emery, C.F., & Thiel, D.L. (2009). Biobehavioral intervention for cancer stress: conceptualization, components, and intervention strategies. *Cognitive and Behavioral Practice, 16*, 253–265.

Anderson, B.L., Yang, H.C., Farrar, W.B., Golden-Kreutz, D.M., Emery, C.F., Thornton, L.M., Young, D.C., & Carson, W.E. (2008). Psychological intervention improves survival for breast cancer patients: a randomized clinical trial. *Cancer, 113*, 3450–3458.

Andreassi, J.L. (2000). *Psychoneuroimmunology: human behavior and physiological response*. Mahwah, NJ: Lawrence Erlbaum Associates.

Arendt-Nielsen, L., & Svensson, P. (2001). Referred muscle pain: basic and clinical findings. *Clinical Journal of Pain, 17*, 11–19.

Armstrong, D., Michie, S., and Marteau, T. (1998) Revealed identity: a study of the process of genetic counselling. *Social Science and Medicine, 47*, 1653–1658.

Aschbacher, K., Mills, P.J., von Kanel, R., Hong, S., Mausbach, B.T., Roepke, S.K., Dimsdale, J.E., Patterson, T.L., Ziegler, M.G., Ancoli-Israel, S., & Grant, I. (2008). Effects of depressive and anxious symptoms on norepinephrine and platelet P-selectin responses to acute psychological stress among elderly caregivers. *Brain, Behavior and Immunity, 22,* 493–502.

Assal, J. (1999). Revisiting the approach to treatment of long-term illness: from the acute to the chronic state. A need for educational and managerial skills for long-term follow-up. *Patient Education and Counselling, 37,* 99–111.

Bakker, A.B. (2005). Flow among music teachers and their students: the crossover of peak experiences. *Journal of Vocational Behavior, 66,* 26–44.

Balkenius, C. (2000). Attention, habituation and conditioning: toward a computational model. *Cognitive Science Quarterly, 1,* 171–204.

Bandura, A. (1977). Self-efficacy: toward a unifying theory of behavioral change. *Psychological Review, 84,* 191–215.

Bandura, A. (1986). *Social foundations of thought and action: a social cognitive theory.* Englewood Cliffs, NJ: Prentice Hall.

Bandura, A. (1989). Human agency in social cognitive theory. *American Psychologist, 44,* 1175–1184.

Bandura, A. (1991). Social cognitive theory of self-regulation. *Organizational Behaviour and Human Decision Processes, 50,* 248–287.

Bandura, A. (1997). *Self-efficacy: the exercise of control.* New York: W.H. Freeman.

Bandura, A. (2001). Social cognitive theory: an agentic perspective. *Annual Review of Psychology, 52,* 1–26.

Barlow, J., Wright, C., Sheasby, J., Turner, A., & Hainsworth, J. (2002). Self-management approaches for people with chronic conditions: a review. *Patient Education and Counselling, 48,* 177–187.

Barnett, J.E., & Scheetz, K. (2003). Technological advances and telehealth: ethics, law, and the practice of psychotherapy. *Psychotherapy: Theory, Research, Practice, Training, 40,* 86–93.

Baron, R.M., & Kenny, D.A. (1986). The moderator–mediator variable distinction in social psychological research: conceptual, strategic, and statistical considerations. *Journal of Personality and Social Psychology, 51,* 1173–1182.

Bartholomew, L.K., Parcel, G.S., Kok, G., & Gottlieb, N. (2001). *Intervention Mapping: A process for designing theory- and evidence-based health promotion programs.* Mountain View, CA: Mayfield Publishing.

Bartlett, D. (1998). *Stress perspectives and processes.* Philadelphia, PA: Open University Press.

Bauer, M., Vedhara, K., Perks, P., Wilcock, G., Lightman, S., Shanks, N. (2000). Chronic stress in caregivers of dementia patients is associated with reduced lymphocyte sensitivity to glucocorticoids. *Journal of Neuroimmunology, 103,* 84–92.

Baum, A., & Posluszny, M.D. (1999). Health psychology: mapping biobehavioral contributions to health and illness. *Annual Review of Psychology, 50,* 137–163.

Baumeister, R.F., Vohs, K.D., & Tice, D.M. (2007). The strength model of self-control. *Current Directions in Psychological Science, 16,* 351–355.

Beck, A.T. (1964). Thinking and depression: II. Theory and therapy. *Archives of General Psychiatry, 10,* 561–571.

Beck, J.S. (1995). *Cognitive therapy: basics and beyond.* New York: Guilford Press.

Becker, M.H. (1974). The health belief model and sick role behavior. *Health, Education Monographs, 2,* 409–419.

Benedetti, F., Pollo, A., Lopiano, L., Lanotte, M., Vighetti, S., & Rainero, I. (2003). Conscious expectation and unconscious conditioning in analgesic, motor, and hormonal placebo/nocebo responses. *Journal of Neuroscience, 23,* 4315–4323.

Biderman, A., Yeheskel, A., & Herman, J. (2005). The biopsychosocial model: have we made any progress since 1977? *Families, Systems & Health, 23,* 379–386.

Bieri, D., Reeve, R.A., Champion, G.D., Addicoat, L., & Ziegler, J.B. (1990). The Faces Pain Scale for the self-assessment of the severity of pain experienced by children: development, initial validation, and preliminary investigation for ratio scale properties. *Pain, 41,* 139–150.

Bijttebier, P., Vertommen, H., & Vander-Steene, G. (2001). Assessment of cognitive coping styles: a closer look at situation–response inventories. *Clinical Psychology Review, 21,* 85–104.

Bildner, J., & Krechel, S.W. (1996). Increasing awareness of postoperative pain management in the NICU. *Neonatal Network, 15,* 11–16.

Blakemore, C., & Jennett, S. (2001). *The endocrine system.* Oxford: Oxford Reference Online, Oxford University Press.

Blalock, J.E. (1984). The immune system as a sensory organ. *Journal of Immunology, 132,* 1067–1070.

Blalock, J.E., & Smith, E.M. (2007). Conceptual development of the immune system as a sixth sense. *Brain, Behavior and Immunity, 21,* 23–33.

Boomsma, D., Busjahn, A., & Peltonen, L. (2002). Classical twin studies and beyond. *Nature, 3,* 872–882.

Boomsma, D.I., Koopmans, J.R., van Doornen, L.J.P., & Orlebeke, J.F. (1994). Genetic and social influences on starting to smoke: a study of Dutch adolescent twins and their parents. *Addiction, 89,* 219–226.

Boorse, C. (1977). Health as a theoretical concept. *Philosophy of Science, 44,* 542–573.

Boothby, J.L., Beverly, E., Overduin, L.Y., & Ward, L.C. (2004). Catastrophizing and perceived partner response to pain. *Pain, 109,* 500–506.

Borrell-Carrio, F., Suchman, A.L., & Epstein, R.M. (2004). The biopsychosocial model 25 years later: principles, practice and scientific inquiry. *Annals of Family Medicine, 2,* 576–582.

Boutron, I., Moher, D., Altman, G., Schulz, K.F., & Ravaud, P. (2008). Extending the CONSORT statement to randomised trials of nonpharmacological treatment: explanation and elaboration. *Annals of Internal Medicine, 148*, 295–309.

Bower, P., King, M., Nazareth, I., Lampe, F., & Sibbald, B. (2005). Patient preferences in randomised controlled trials: conceptual framework and implications for research. *Social Science & Medicine, 61*, 685–695.

Brambilla, F. (2000). Psychoneuroendocrinology: a science of the past or a new pathway for the future? *European Journal of Pharmacology, 405*, 341–349.

Brand, A., & Crutzen, R. (2009). Public Health Genomics and its potential for health psychology: an interview with Angela Brand. *European Health Psychologist, 11*, 61–63.

Brewin, C.R. (1996). Theoretical foundations of cognitive behaviour therapy for anxiety and depression. *Annual Review of Psychology, 47*, 33–57.

Brickman, P., Coates, D., & Janoff-Bulman, R. (1978). Lottery winners and accident victims: is happiness relative? *Journal of Personality and Social Psychology, 36*, 917–927.

Brummet, B.H., Boyle, S.H., Siegler, I.C., Kuhn, C.M., Surwit, R.S., Garrett, M.E., Collins, A., Ashley-Koch, A., & Williams, R.B. (2008). HPA axis function in male caregivers: effect of the monoamine oxidase-A gene promoter (MAOA-uVNTR). *Biological Psychology, 79*, 250–255.

Burgner, D., Jamieson, S.E., & Blackwell, J.M. (2006). Genetic susceptibility to infectious disease: big is beautiful, but will bigger be even better. *Lancet Infectious Disease, 6*, 653–663.

Burke, W., Olsen, A.H., Pinsky, L.E., Reynolds, S.E., & Press, N.A. (2001). Misleading presentation of breast cancer in popular magazines. *Efficient Clinical Practice, 4*, 58–64.

Burnet, F.M. (1957). Cancer: a biological approach. *British Medical Journal, 1*, 841–847.

Burns, A.B., Brown, J.S., Sachs-Ericsson, N., Plant, E.A., Curtis, J.T., Fredrickson, B.L., & Joiner, T.E. (2008). Upward spirals of positive emotion and coping: replication, extension, and initial exploration of neurochemical substrates. *Personality and Individual Differences, 44*, 360–370.

Burns, D.D., & Spangler, D.L. (2001). Do changes in dysfunctional attitudes mediate changes in depression and anxiety in cognitive behavioral therapy? *Behavior Therapy, 32*, 337–369.

Busnach, G., Piselli, P., Arbustini, E., Baccarani, U., Burra, P., Carrieri, M.P., Citterio, F., De Juli, E., Bellelli, S., Pradier, C., Rezza, G., & Serraino, D. (2006). Immunosuppression and cancer: a comparison of risks in recipients of organ transplants and in HIV-positive individuals. *Transplantation Proceedings, 38*, 3533–3535.

Butler, A.C., Chapman, J.E., Forman, E.M., & Beck, A.T. (2006). The empirical status of cognitive behavioral therapy. *Clinical Psychology Review, 26*, 17–31.

Cahn, B.R., & Polich, J. (2006). Meditation states and traits: EEG, ERP, and neuroimaging studies. *Psychological Bulletin, 132*, 180–211.

Cameron, L.D., & Jago, L. (2008). Emotion regulation interventions: a common-sense model approach. *British Journal of Health Psychology, 13*, 215–221.

Cameron, L.D., & Nicholls, G. (1998). Expression of stressful experiences through writing: effects of a self-regulation manipulation for pessimists and optimists. *Health Psychology, 17*, 84–92.

Campbell, M., Fitzpatrick, R., Haines, A., Kinmonth, A.L., Sandercock, P., Spiegelhalter, D., & Tyrer, P. (2000). Framework for design and evaluation of complex interventions to improve health. *British Medical Journal, 321*, 694–696.

Cannon, W.B. (1925). *Bodily changes in pain, hunger, fear and rage: an account of recent researches into the function of emotional excitement.* New York: Appleton.

Cannon, W.B. (1939). *The wisdom of the body* (2nd ed.). New York: Norton.

Cano, A., Johansen, A.B., & Geisser, M. (2004). Spousal congruence on disability, pain and spousal responses to pain. *Pain, 109*, 258–265.

Capuron, L., & Dantzer, R. (2003). Cytokines and depression: the need for a new paradigm. *Brain, Behavior and Immunity, 17*, S119–S124.

Carter, L.L., & Dutton, R.W. (1996). Type 1 and Type 2: a fundamental dichotomy for all T-cell subsets. *Current Opinion in Immunology, 8*, 336–342.

Carter, N.M. (2004). Implications for medicine in the 'post-genomic era'. *Current Anaesthesia and Critical Care, 15*, 37–43.

Carver, C.S., & Scheier, M.F. (1981). *Attention and self-regulation: a control-theory approach to human behavior.* New York: Springer-Verlag.

Carver, C.S., & Scheier, M.F. (1982). Control theory: a useful conceptual framework for personality, social, clinical, and health psychology. *Psychological Bulletin, 92*, 111–135.

Carver, C.S., & Scheier, M.F. (1998). *On the self-regulation of behavior.* New York: Cambridge University Press.

Caspi, A., Sugden, K., Moffitt, T.E., Taylor, A., Craig, I.W., Harrington, H.L., McClay, J., Mill, J., Martin, J., Braithwaite, A., & Poulton, R. (2003). Influence of life stress on depression: moderation by a polymorphism in the 5-HTT gene. *Science, 301*, 386–389.

Cassileth, B.R., & Vickers, A.J. (2004). Massage therapy for symptom control: outcome study at a major cancer center. *Journal of Pain and Symptom Management, 28*, 244–249.

Castelnuovo, G., Gaggioli, A., Mantovani, F., & Riva, G. (2003). New and old tools in psychotherapy: the use of technology for the integration of traditional clinical treatments. *Psychotherapy: Theory, Research, Practice, Training, 40,* 33–44.

Castes, M., Palenque, M., Canelones, P., Hagel, I., & Lynch, N. (1998). Classic conditioning and placebo effects in the bronchodilator response of asthmatic children. *Neuroimmunomodulation 5,* 70.

Castle, S.C. (2000). Clinical relevance of age-related immune dysfunction. *Clinical Infectious Disease, 31,* 578–585.

Centre for Reviews and Dissemination (2009). *Systematic reviews: CRD's guidance for undertaking reviews in health care.* York: University of York.

Chandola, T., Kuper, H., Singh-Manoux, A., Bartley, M., & Marmot, M. (2004). The effect of control at home on CHD events in the Whitehall II study: gender differences in psychosocial domestic pathways to social inequalities in CHD. *Social Science & Medicine, 58,* 1501–1509.

Chrousos, G.P., & Gold, P.W. (1992). The concepts of stress and stress system disorders: overview of physical and behavioral homeostasis. *Journal of the American Medical Association, 267,* 1244–1252.

Ciechanowski, P., Sullivan, M., Jensen, M., Romano, J., & Summers, H. (2003). The relationship of attachment style to depression, catastrophizing and health care utilization in patients with chronic pain. *Pain, 104,* 627–637.

Clark, B.F.C. (2008). Healthy human ageing. *New Biotechnology, 25,* 13–15.

Clow, A. (2001). The physiology of stress. In F. Jones & J. Bright (Eds), *Stress: myth, theory and research.* Harlow: Pearson. Pp. 47–72.

Cohen, F., & Lazarus, R.S. (1979). Coping with the stresses of illness. In G.C. Stone, F. Cohen & N.E. Adler (Eds), *Health psychology: a handbook.* San Francisco, CA: Jossey-Bass.

Cohen, S., & Herbert, T.B. (1996). Health psychology: psychological factors and physical disease from the perspective of human psychoneuroimmunology. *Annual Review of Psychology, 47,* 113–142.

Cohen, S., & Lazarus, R.S. (1979). Coping with the stress of illness. In G.C. Stone, F. Cohen & N.E. Adler (Eds), *Health psychology: a handbook.* San Francisco, CA: Jossey-Bass. Pp. 217–254.

Cohen, S., Frank, E., Doyle, W.J., Skoner, D.P., Rabin, B.S., & Gwaltney, J.M., Jr (1998). Types of stressors that increase susceptibility to the common cold in healthy adults. *Health Psychology, 17,* 214–223.

Cohen, S., Kamarck, T., & Mermelstein, R. (1983). A global measure of perceived stress. *Journal of Health and Social Behavior, 24,* 385–396.

Cohn, M.A., & Fredrickson, B.L. (2006). Beyond the moment, beyond the self: shared ground between selective investment theory and the broaden-and-build theory of positive emotions. *Psychological Inquiry, 17,* 39–44.

Collaziol, D., Luz, C., Dornelles, F., da Cruz, I.M., & Bauer, M.E. (2004). Psychoneuroendocrine correlates of lymphocyte subsets during healthy ageing. *Mechanisms of Ageing and Development, 125,* 219–227.

Colman, A.M. (2006). *A dictionary of psychology.* Oxford: Oxford University Press.

Costa, P.T., & McCrae, R.R. (1980). Influence of extraversion and neuroticism on subjective well-being: happy and unhappy people. *Journal of Personality and Social Psychology, 38,* 668–678.

Coster, S., & Norman, I. (2009). Cochrane reviews of educational and self-management interventions to guide nursing practice: a review. *International Journal of Nursing Studies, 46,* 508–528.

Cousins, N. (1990). *Head first: the biology of hope and the healing power of the human spirit.* London: Penguin.

Coyne, J.C., & Tennen, H. (2010). Positive psychology in cancer care: bad science, exaggerated claims, and unproven medicine. *Annals of Behavioral Medicine, 39,* 16–26.

Craig, P., Dieppe, P., Macintyre, S., Mitchie, S., Nazareth, I., & Petticrew, M. (2008). Developing and evaluating complex interventions: the new Medical Research Council guidance. *British Medical Journal, 337,* a1655.

Csikszentmihalyi, M. (1975). Play and intrinsic rewards. *Journal of Humanistic Psychology, 15,* 41–63.

Csikszentmihalyi, M. (1999). If we are so rich, why aren't we happy? *American Psychologist, 54,* 821–827.

Csikszentmihalyi, M. (2000). *Beyond boredom and anxiety.* San Francisco, CA: Jossey-Bass.

DAFNE Study Group (2002). Training in flexible intensive insulin management to enable dietary freedom in people with type 1 diabetes: dose adjustment for normal eating (DAFNE) randomised controlled trial. *British Medical Journal, 325,* 746–751.

Dahl, J., Wilson, K.G., & Nilsson, A. (2004). Acceptance and commitment therapy and the treatment of persons at risk for long-term disability resulting from stress and pain symptoms: a preliminary randomized trial. *Behavior Therapy, 35,* 785–801.

Damasio, A.R. (1996). The somatic marker hypothesis and the possible functions of the prefrontal cortex. *Philosophical Transactions of the Royal Society B: Biological Sciences, 351,* 1413–1420.

Dantzer, R. (2005). EuroConference on cytokines in the brain: expression and action of cytokines in the brain and pathophysiological implications. *Brain, Behavior and Immunity, 19,* 263–267.

de Moor, J.S., Moye, L., Low, M.D., Rivera, E., Singletart, S.E., Fouladi, R.T., & Cohen, L. (2008). Expressive writing as pre-surgical stress management intervention for breast cancer patients. *Journal of the Society for Integrative Oncology, 6*, 59–66.

De Ridder, D., Greenen, R., Kuijer, R., & van Middendorp, H. (2008). Psychological adjustment to chronic disease. *The Lancet, 372*, 246–255.

De Ridder, D., & Schreurs, K. (2001). Developing interventions for chronically ill patients: is coping a helpful concept? *Clinical Psychology Review, 2*, 205–240.

De Vogli, R., Brunner, E., & Marmot, M.G. (2007). Unfairness and the social gradient of metabolic syndrome in the Whitehall II study. *Journal of Psychosomatic Research, 63*, 413–419.

Dean, K. (2004). The role of methods in maintaining orthodox beliefs in health research. *Social Science & Medicine, 58*, 675–685.

Deary, V. (2008). A precarious balance: using a self-regulation model to conceptualise and treat chronic fatigue syndrome. *British Journal of Health Psychology, 13*, 231–236.

Decruyenaere, M., Evers-Kiebooms, G., Cloostermans, T., Boogaerts, A., Demyttenaere, K., Dom, R., & Fryns, J.-P. (2003). Psychological distress in the 5-year period after predictive testing for Huntington's disease. *European Journal of Human Genetics, 11*, 30–38.

DeNeve, K.M., & Cooper, H. (1998). The happy personality: a meta-analysis of 137 personality traits and subjective well-being. *Psychological Bulletin, 124*, 197–229.

Department of Health (1996). Immunisation against infectious disease: 'The Green Book', available online at: www.dh.gov.uk/en/Publicationsandstatistics/Publications/PublicationsPolicyAndGuidance/DH_113027

Department of Health (2004). The NHS Improvement Plan: Putting people at the heart of public services. Retrieved 12th July 2010, from: www.dh.gov.uk/en/Publicationsandstatistics/Publications/PublicationsPolicyAndGuidance/DH_4084476

Department of Health (2005). Choosing Health: Making healthy choices easier. Retrieved 12th July 2010, from: www.dh.gov.uk/en/Publicationsandstatistics/Publications/PublicationsPolicyAndGuidance/DH_4094550

Department of Health (2006). Immunisation against infectious disease: 'The Green Book', 3rd edition. Available online at: http://www.dh.gov.uk/prod_consum_dh/groups/dh_digitalassets/documents/digitalasset/dh_119557.pdf

Devins, G.M., & Binik, Y.M. (1996). Facilitating, coping and chronic illness. In Zeidner, N. & Endler, N.S. *Handbook of coping.* New York: Wiley. Pp. 640–696.

Diener, E., & Biswas-Diener, R. (2002). Will money increase subjective well-being? A literature review and guide to needed research. *Social Indicators Research, 57*, 119–169.

Diener, E., Diener, M., & Diener, C. (1995). Factors predicting the subjective well-being of nations. *Journal of Personality and Social Psychology, 69*, 851–864.

Diener, E., & Fujita, F. (1995). Resources, personal strivings and subjective well-being: a nomothetic and idiographic approach. *Journal of Personality and Social Psychology, 68*, 926–935.

Diener, E., Suh, E., Lucas, R., & Smith, H. (1999). Subjective well-being: three decades of progress. *Psychological Bulletin, 2*, 276–302.

Diener, E., Wolsic, B., & Fujita, F. (1995). Physical attractiveness and subjective well-being. *Journal of Personality and Social Psychology, 69*, 120–129.

Dunn, G.P., Bruce, A.T., Ikeda, H., Old, L.J., & Schreiber, R.D. (2002). Cancer immunoediting: from immunosurveillance to tumor escape. *Nature Immunology, 3*, 991–998.

Ebner-Priemer, U.W., & Trull, T.J. (2009). Ambulatory assessment: an innovative and promising approach for clinical psychology. *European Psychologist, 14*, 109–119.

Eccleston, C., Morley, S., Williams, A., Yorke, L., & Mastryannopoulou, K. (2002). Systematic review and meta-analysis of randomised trials of psychological therapy for chronic pain in children and adolescents. *Pain, 99*, 157–165.

Effros, R.B., & Pawelec, G. (1997). Replicative senescence of T cells: does the Hayflick limit lead to immune exhaustion? *Immunology Today, 18*, 450–454.

Ekman, P. (1992). Facial expression of emotion: new findings, new questions. *Psychological Science, 3*, 34–38.

Elenkov, I.J., & Chrousos, G.P. (1999). Stress, cytokine patterns and susceptibility to disease. *Best Practice & Research in Clinical Endocrinology & Metabolism, 13*, 583–595.

Elenkov, I.J., & Chrousos, G.P. (1999a). Stress hormones, Th1/Th2 patterns, pro-/anti-inflammatory cytokines and susceptibility to disease. *Trends in Endocrinology and Metabolism, 10*, 359–368.

Enck, P., Benedetti, F., & Schedlowski, M. (2008). New insights into the placebo and nocebo responses. *Neuron, 59*, 195–206.

Engel, G.L. (1977). The need for a new medical model: a challenge for biomedicine. *Science, 196*, 129–136.

Engel, G.L. (1980). The clinical application of the biopsychosocial model. *American Journal of Psychiatry, 137*, 535–544.

Engelhardt, H.T. (1981). The concepts of health and disease. In A.L. Caplan, H.T. Engelhardt, & J.J. McCartney (Eds), *Concepts of health and disease: interdisciplinary perspectives.* Reading, MA: Addison-Wesley. Pp. 31–46.

Epel, E.S. (2009). Telomeres in a life-span: a new 'psychobiomarker'? *Current Directions in Psychological Science, 18*, 6–10.

Epel, E.S., Blackburn, E.H., Lin, J., Dhabhar, F.S., Adler, N.E., Morrow, J.D., & Casthon, R.M. (2004). Accelerated telomere shortening in response to life stress. *Proceedings of the National Academy of Sciences, 107*, 17312–17315.

Eriksen, H.R., Murison, R., Pensgaard, A.-M., & Ursin, H. (2005). Cognitive activation theory of stress (CATS): from fish brains to the Olympics. *Psychoneuroendocrinology, 30*, 933–938.

Ershler, W.B., & Keller, E.T. (2000). Age associated increased interleukin-6 gene expression, late-life disease and frailty. *Annual Review of Medicine, 51,* 245–270.

Esch, T., Guarna, M., Blanchi, E., Zhu, W., & Stefano, G.B. (2004). Commonalities in the central nervous system's involvement with complementary medical therapies: limbic morphinergic processes. *Medical Science Monitor, 10,* MS6–MS17.

Evans, P., Hucklebridge, F., & Clow, A. (2000). *Mind, immunity and health: the science of psychoneuroimmunology.* London: Free Association Books.

Felten, D.L., Felten, S.Y., Carlson, S.L., Olschowka, H.A., & Livnat, S. (1985). Noradrenergic and peptidergic innervation of lymphoid tissue. *Journal of Immunology, 135,* 755–765.

Fife, B.L., Scott, L.L., Fineberg, N.S., & Zwickl, B.E. (2008). Promoting adaptive coping by persons with HIV disease: evaluation of a patient/partner intervention model. *Journal of the Association of Nurses in AIDS Care, 19,* 75–84.

Fletcher, L., & Hayes, S.C. (2005). Relational frame theory, acceptance and commitment therapy and a functional analytic definition of mindfulness. *Journal of Rational–Emotive & Cognitive Behavior Therapy, 23,* 315–336.

Folkman, S. (1997). Positive psychological states and coping with severe stress. *Social Science and Medicine, 45,* 1207–1221.

Folkman, S., & Moskowitz, J.T. (2000). Positive affect and the other side of coping. *American Psychologist, 55,* 647–654.

Folkman, S., & Moskowitz, J.T. (2004). Coping: pitfalls and promise. *Annual Review of Psychology, 55,* 745–774.

Folkman, S., Chesney, M., McKusick, L., Ironson, G., Johnson, D.S., & Coates, T.J. (1991). Translating coping theory into intervention. In J. Eckenrode (Ed.), *The social context of coping.* New York: Plenum. Pp. 239–259.

Fordyce, W.E. (1976). *Behavioral methods for chronic pain and illness.* St Louis, MO: Mosby.

Fortune, D.G., Richards, H.L., Griffiths, C.E.M., Main, C.J. (2004). Targeting cognitive behaviour therapy to patients' implicit model of psoriasis: results from a patient preference controlled trial. *British Journal of Clinical Psychology, 43,* 65–82.

Fox, J., Arena, D., & Bailenson, J.N. (2009). Virtual reality: a survival guide for the social scientist. *Journal of Media Psychology, 21,* 95–113.

Franceschi, C., Bonafe, M., Valensin, S., Olivieri, F., de Luca, M., Ottaviani, E., & de Benedictis, G. (2000). Inflamm-aging: an evolutionary perspective on immunosenescence. *Annals of the New York Academy of Sciences, 908,* 244–254.

Frankenhaeuser, M. (1982). Challenge control interaction as reflected in sympathetic and pituitary–adrenal activity: comparison between the sexes. *Scandinavian Journal of Psychology, Supplement 1,* 158–164.

Frankenhaeuser, M. (1986). A psychobiological framework for research on human stress and coping. In M.H. Appley & R. Trumbell (Eds), *Dynamics of stress: physiological, psychological, and social perspectives.* New York: Plenum. Pp. 101–116.

Frattaroli, J. (2006). Experimental disclosure and its moderators: a meta-analysis. *Psychological Bulletin, 132,* 823–865.

Fredrickson, B.L. (1998). What good are positive emotions? *Review of General Psychology, 2,* 300–319.

Fredrickson, B.L., Cohn, M.A., Coffey, K., Pek, J., & Finkel, S.M. (2008). Open hearts build lives: positive emotions, induced through loving kindness meditation build consequential personal resources. *Journal of Personality and Social Psychology, 95,* 1045–1062.

Fredrickson, B.L., & Joiner, T. (2002). Positive emotions trigger upward spirals toward emotional well-being. *Psychological Science, 13,* 172–175.

Fredrickson, B.L., & Levenson, R.W. (1998). Positive emotions speed recovery from the cardiovascular sequelae of negative emotions. *Cognition and Emotion, 12,* 191–220.

Fredrickson, B.L., Mancuso, R.A., Branigan, C., & Tugade, M.M. (2000). The undoing effect of positive emotions. *Motivation and Emotion, 24,* 237–258.

Fredrickson, B.L., Tugade, M.M., Waugh, C.E., & Larkin, G.R. (2003). What good are positive emotions in crises? A prospective study of resilience and emotions following the terrorist attacks on the United States on September 11th, 2001. *Journal of Personality and Social Psychology, 84,* 365–376.

Frijda, N.H. (1986). *The emotions.* New York: Cambridge University Press.

Frisina, P.G., Borod, J.C., & Lepore, S.J. (2004). A meta-analysis of the effects of written emotional disclosure on the health outcomes of clinical populations. *Journal of Nervous and Mental Disease, 192,* 629–634.

Fry, P.S., & Wong, P.T. (1991). Pain management training in the elderly: matching interventions with subjects' coping style. *Stress Medicine, 7,* 93–98.

Gallagher, S., Phillips, A.C., Evans, P., Der, G., Hunt, K., & Carroll, D. (2008). Caregiving is associated with low secretion rates of immunoglobulin A in saliva. *Brain, Behavior and Immunity, 22,* 565–572.

Gallagher, R.M., & Rosenthal, L.J. (2008). Chronic pain and opiates: balancing pain control and risks in long-term opioid treatment. *Archives of Physical Medicine and Rehabilitation, 89,* S77–S82.

Garn, S.M., Bailey, S.M., Solomon, M.A., & Hopkins, P.J. (1981). Effect of remaining family members on fatness prediction. *American Journal of Clinical Nutrition, 34,* 148–153.

Garssen, B., & Goodkin, K. (1999). On the role of immunological factors as mediators between psychosocial factors and cancer progression. *Psychiatry Research, 85,* 51–61.

Gatchel, R.J., & Rollings, K.H. (2008). Evidence-informed management of chronic low back pain with cognitive behavioral therapy. *Spine Journal, 8*, 40–44.

Gatchel, R.J., Robinson, R.C., Pulliam, C., & Maddrey, A.M. (2003). Biofeedback with pain patients: evidence for its effectiveness. *Seminars in Pain Medicine, 1*, 55–66.

Geronimus, A.T. (1992). The weathering hypothesis and the health of African-American women and infants: evidence and speculations. *Ethnicity & Disease, 2*, 207–221.

Geronimus, A.T., Hicken, M., Keene, D., & Bound, J. (2006). 'Weathering' and age patterns of allostatic load scores among blacks and whites in the United States. *American Journal of Public Health, 96*, 826–833.

Giamberardino, M.A., Affaitati, G., Lerza, R., & Vecchiet, L. (2004). Referred muscle pain and hyperalgesia from viscera: clinical and pathophysiological aspects. *Basic Applied Myology, 4*, 23–28.

Gidron, Y., Russ, K., Tissarchondou, H., & Warner, J. (2006). The relation between psychological factors and DNA damage: a critical review. *Biological Psychology, 72*, 291–304.

Gilley, D., Herbert, B.-S., Huda, N., Tanaka, H., & Reed, T. (2008). Factors impacting human telomere homeostasis and age-related disease. *Mechanisms of Aging and Development, 129*, 27–34.

Gilron, I., Watson, P.N., Cahill, C.M., & Moulin, D. (2006). Neuropathic pain: a practical guide for the clinician. *Canadian Medical Association Journal, 175*, 266–275.

Glantz, K., Rizzo, A., & Graap, K. (2003). Virtual reality for psychotherapy: current reality and future possibilities. *Psychotherapy: Theory, Research, Practice, Training, 40*, 55–67.

Glaser, R. (2005). Stress-associated immune dysregulation and its importance for human health: a personal history of psychoneuroimmunology. *Brain, Behavior and Immunity, 19*, 3–11.

Glasgow, R.E., McKay, H.G., Piette, J.D., & Reynolds, K.D. (2001). The RE-AIM framework for evaluating interventions: what can it tell us about approaches to chronic illness management? *Patient Education and Counselling, 44*, 119–127.

Godoy-Izquierdo, D., Lopez-Chicheri, I., Lopez-Torrecillas, F., Velez, M., & Godoy, J.F. (2007). Contents of lay illness models dimensions for physical and mental diseases and implications for health professionals. *Patient Education and Counseling, 67*, 196–213.

Goebel, M.U., Meykadeh, N., Kou, W., Schedlowski, M., & Hengge, U.R. (2008). Behavioral conditioning of antihistamine effects in patients with allergic rhinitis. *Psychotherapy and Psychosomatics, 77*, 227–234.

Goffaux, P., Redmond, W.J., Rainville, P., & Marchand, S. (2007). Descending analgesia – when the spine echoes what the brain expects. *Pain, 130*, 137–143.

Gold, J.I., Belmont, K.A., & Thomas, D.A. (2007). The neurobiology of virtual reality pain attenuation. *CyberPsychology & Behavior, 10*, 536–544.

Gonzalez-Bono, E., Rohleder, N., Hellhammer, D.H., Salvador, A., & Kirschbaum, C. (2002). Glucose but not protein or fat load amplifies the cortisol response to psychosocial stress. *Hormones and Behavior, 41*, 328–333.

Graff, J.C. (2007). Integrating genetics and genomics into developmental disabilities nursing practice. *International Journal of Nursing in Intellectual and Developmental Disabilities*. 3. Retrieved 12th July 2010, from: http://journal.ddna.org/volumes/volume-3-issue-2/articles/3-integrating-genetics-and-genomics-into-developmental-disabilities-nursing-practice

Greenhalgh, T. (1997). How to read a paper: papers that summarise other papers (systematic reviews and meta-analyses). *British Medical Journal, 315*, 672–675.

Greenhalgh, T. (2009). Chronic illness: beyond the expert patient. *British Medical Journal, 338*, 629–631.

Greer, S., Morris, T., & Pettingale, K.W. (1979). Psychological response to breast cancer: effect on outcome. *The Lancet, 13*, 785–787.

Griffiths, C., Foster, G., Ramsay, J., Eldridge, S., & Taylor, S. (2007). How effective are expert patient (lay led) education programmes for chronic disease? *British Medical Journal, 334*, 1254–1256.

Gross, A.R., Kay, T., Hondras, M., Goldsmith, C., Haines, T., Peloso, P., Kennedy, C., & Hoving, J. (2002). Manual therapy for mechanical neck disorders: a systematic review. *Manual Therapy, 7*, 131–149.

Gross, J.J., & John, O.P. (2003). Individual differences in two emotion regulation processes: implications for affect, relationships, and well-being. *Journal of Personality and Social Psychology, 85*, 348–362.

Gross, J.J., & Levenson, R.W. (1997). Hiding feelings: the acute effects of inhibiting positive and negative emotions. *Journal of Abnormal Psychology, 106*, 95–103.

Grunau, R.E., Oberlander, T., Holsti, L., & Whitfield, M.F. (1998). Bedside application of the neonatal facial coding system in pain assessment of premature neonates. *Pain, 76*, 277–286.

Grunau, R.V., & Craig, K.D. (1987). Pain expression in neonates: facial action and cry. *Pain, 28*, 395–410.

Grunau, R.V., Johnston, C.C., & Kenneth, D. (1990). Neonatal facial and cry responses to invasive and non-invasive procedures. *Pain, 42*, 295–305.

Hagger, M.S., & Orbell, S. (2003). A meta-analytic review of the commonsense model of illness representations. *Psychology & Health, 18*, 141–184.

Hall, W., Madden, P., & Lynskey, M. (2002). The genetics of tobacco use: methods, findings and policy implications. *Tobacco Control, 11*, 119–124.

Hallner, D., & Hasenbring, M. (2004). Classification of psychosocial risk factors (yellow flags) for the development of chronic low back and leg pain using artificial neural network. *Neuroscience Letters, 361*, 15–154.

Hawkley, L.C., & Cacioppo, J.T. (2004). Stress and the aging immune system. *Brain, Behavior and Immunity, 18*, 114–119.

Hayes, N., & Joseph, S. (2003). Big 5 correlates of three measures of subjective well-being. *Personality and Individual Differences, 34*, 723–727.

Hayes, S.C., & Duckworth, M.P. (2006). Acceptance and commitment therapy and traditional cognitive behaviour therapy approaches to pain. *Cognitive and Behavioral Practice, 13*, 185–187.

Hayney, M.S., Dienberg-Love, G., Buck, J.M., Ryff, C.D., Singer, B., & Muller, D. (2003). The association between psychosocial factors and vaccine-induced cytokine production. *Vaccine, 21*, 2428–2432.

Head, J., Kivimaki, M., Siegrist, J., Ferrie, J.E., Vahtera, J., Shipley, M.J., & Marmot, M.G. (2007). Effort–reward imbalance and relational injustice at work predict sickness absence: the Whitehall II study. *Journal of Psychosomatic Research, 63*, 433–440.

Health Survey for England (2008). Trend Tables. The NHS Information Centre, 2009. Available online at: http://www.ic.nhs.uk/webfiles/publications/HSE/HSE08trends/Health_Survey_for_england_trend_tables_2008.pdf

Heath, A.C., Eaves, L.J., & Martin, N.G. (1998). Interaction of marital status and genetic risk for symptoms of depression. *Twin Research, 1*, 119–122.

Hellstrom, H.R. (2006). The altered homeostatic theory: a hypothesis proposed to be useful in understanding and preventing ischemic heart disease, hypertension, and diabetes including reducing the risk of age and atherosclerosis. *Medical Hypotheses, 68*, 415–433.

Herman, J. (2005). The need for a transition model: a challenge for biopsychosocial medicine? *Families, Systems, & Health, 23*, 372–376.

Herr, K.A., Mobily, P.R., Kohout, F.J., & Wagenaar, D. (1998). Evaluation of the faces pain scale for use with the elderly. *Clinical Journal of Pain, 14*, 29–38.

Hettinga, D.M., Hurley, D.A., Jackson, A., May, S., Mercer, C., & Roberts, L. (2008). Assessing the effect of sample size, methodological quality and statistical rigour on outcomes of randomised controlled trials on mobilisation, manipulation and massage for low back pain of at least 6 weeks' duration. *Physiotherapy, 94*, 97–104.

Higgins, J.P.T., & Green, S. (2009). *Cochrane handbook for systematic reviews of interventions*, Version 5.0.2 (updated September 2009). London: The Cochrane Collaboration.

Hill, A.B. (1965). The environment and disease: association or causation? *Proceedings of the Royal Society of Medicine, 58*, 295–300.

Hoffman, H.G., Patterson, D.R., Seibel, E., Soltani, M., Jewett-Leahy, L., & Sam, R. (2008). Virtual reality pain control during burn wound debridement in the hydrotank. *Clinical Journal of Pain, 24*, 299–304.

Hoffmann, S.G., & Asmundson, G.J.G. (2008). Acceptance mindfulness-based therapy: new wave or old hat? *Clinical Psychology Review, 28*, 1–16.

Hogan, B.E., & Linden, W., & Najarian, B. (2002). Social support interventions. *Clinical Psychology Review, 22*, 381–440.

Holahan, C.J., & Moos, R.H. (1987). Personal and contextual determinants of coping strategies. *Journal of Personality and Social Psychology, 52*, 946–955.

Holdcroft, A., & Power, I. (2003). Recent developments: management of pain. *British Medical Journal, 326*, 635–639.

Holman, H., & Lorig, K. (2000). Patients as partners in managing chronic disease: partnership is a prerequisite for effective and efficient health care. *British Medical Journal, 320*, 526–527.

Holmes, T.H., & Rahe, R.H. (1967) The Social Readjustment Rating Scale. *Journal of Psychosomatic Research, 11*, 213–218.

Holroyd, K.A., Penzien, D.B., Hursey, K.G., Tobin, D.L., Rogers, L., Holm, J.E., Marcille, P.J., Hall, J.R., & Chila, A.G. (1984). Change mechanisms in EMG biofeedback training: cognitive changes underlying improvements in tension headaches. *Journal of Consulting and Clinical Psychology, 52*, 1039–1053.

Houtveen, J.H., & de Geus, E.J.C. (2009). Noninvasive psychophysiological ambulatory recordings: study design and data analysis strategies. *European Psychologist, 14*, 132–141.

Huether, G. (1996). The central adaptation syndrome: psychosocial stress as a trigger for adaptive modifications of brain structure and brain function. *Progress in Neurobiology, 48*, 569–612.

Hughes, J. (2008). An algorithm for choosing among smoking cessation treatments. *Journal of Substance Abuse Treatment, 34*, 426–432.

Human Genome Program, US Department of Energy (2003). *Genomics and its impact on science and society: a 2003 primer*. Washington, DC: US Department of Energy.

Imamura, M., Furlan, A.D., Dryden, T., & Irvin, E. (2008). Evidence-informed management of chronic low back pain with massage. *Spine Journal, 8*, 121–133.

Iversen, I.H. (1992). Skinner's early research: From reflexology to operant conditioning. *American Psychologist, 47*, 1318–1328.

Jacobson, E. (1938). *Progressive relaxation*. Chicago, IL: University of Chicago Press.

Jatzko, A., Rothenhofer, S., Schmitt, A., Gaser, C., Demirakca, T., Weber-Fahr, W., Wessa, M., Magnotta, V., &

Braus, D.F. (2006). Hippocampal volume in chronic posttraumatic stress disorder (PTSD): MRI study using two different evaluation methods. *Journal of Affective Disorders, 94*, 121–126.

Jirtle, R.L., & Skinner, M.K. (2007). Environmental epigenomics and disease susceptibility. *Nature Reviews Genetics, 8*, 253–262.

Johnston, S.J., Boehm, S.G., Healy, D., Goebel, R., & Linden, D.E.J. (2010). Neurofeedback: a promising tool for the self-regulation of emotion networks. *NeuroImage, 49*, 1066–1072.

Jones, F., & Bright, J. (2001). *Stress: myth, theory and research*. Harlow: Pearson.

Kabat-Zinn, J., Lipworth, L., & Burney, R. (1985). The clinical use of mindfulness meditation for the self-regulation of chronic pain. *Journal of Behavioral Medicine, 8*, 163–190.

Kabat-Zinn, J., Lipworth, L., Burney, R., & Sellers, W. (1986). Four-year follow-up of a meditation-based program for the self-regulation of chronic pain: treatment outcomes and compliance. *Clinical Journal of Pain, 2*, 159–173.

Kaplan, K., Goldberg, D., & Galvin-Nadeau, M. (1993). The impact of a meditation-based stress reduction program on fibromyalgia. *General Hospital Psychiatry, 15*, 284–289.

Kaplan, S.H., Greenfield, S., & Ware, J.E. (1989). Assessing the effects of physician-patient interactions on the outcomes of chronic disease. *Medical Care, 27*, S110–S127.

Karasek, R., & Theorell, T. (1990). *Healthy work: stress, productivity and the reconstruction of working life*. New York: Basic Books.

Kass, L.R. (1981). Regarding the end of medicine and the pursuit of health. In A.L. Caplan, H.T. Engelhardt & J.J. McCartney (Eds), *Concepts of health and disease: interdisciplinary perspectives*. Reading, MA: Addison-Wesley. Pp. 3–30.

Keefe, F.J., & Blumenthal, J.A. (2004). Health psychology: what will the future bring? *Health Psychology, 23*, 156–157.

Keefe, F.J., Caldwell, D.S., Williams, D.A., Gil, K.M., Mitchell, D., Robertson, C., Martinez, S., Nunley, J., Beckham, J.C., & Helms, M. (1990). Pain coping skills training in the management of osteoarthritic knee pain: II. Follow-up results. *Behavior Therapy, 21*, 435–447.

Kemeny, M.E., & Schedlowski, M. (2007). Understanding the interaction between psychosocial stress and immune-related diseases: a stepwise progression. *Brain, Behavior and Immunity, 21*, 1009–1018.

Kerns, R.D., Haythornthwaite, J., Rosenberg, R., Southwick, S., Giller, E.L., & Jacob, M.C. (1991). The pain behaviour check list (PBCL): factor structure and psychometric properties. *Journal of Behavioral Medicine, 14*, 155–167.

Ketterer, M.W., Mahr, G., & Goldberg, A.D. (2000). Psychological factors affecting a medical condition: ischemic coronary heart disease. *Journal of Psychosomatic Research, 48*, 357–367.

Khoury, M.J., Gwinn, M., Burke, W., Bowen, S., & Zimmern, R. (2007). Will genomics widen or help heal the schism between medicine and public health. *American Journal of Preventive Medicine, 33*, 310–317.

Kiecolt-Glaser, J.K., Cacioppo, J.T., Malarkey, W.B., & Glaser, R. (1992). Acute psychological stressors and short-term immune changes: what, why, for whom, and to what extent? *Psychosomatic Medicine, 54*, 680–685.

Kiecolt-Glaser, J.K., Glaser, R., Shuttleworth, E.C., Dyer, C.S., Ogrocki, P., & Speicher, C.E. (1987). Chronic stress and immunity in family caregivers for Alzheimer's disease victims. *Psychosomatic Medicine, 49*, 523–535.

Kiecolt-Glaser, J.K., Marucha, P.T., Malarkey, W.B., Mercado, A.M., & Glaser, R. (1995). Slowing of wound healing by psychological stress. *The Lancet, 346*, 1194–1196.

Kiecolt-Glaser, J.K., McGuire, L., Robles, T., & Glaser, R. (2002). Psychoneuroimmunology: psychological influences on immune function and health. *Journal of Consulting and Clinical Psychology, 70*, 537–547.

King, T.L., & McCool, W.F. (2004). The definition and assessment of pain. *Journal of Midwifery and Women's Health, 49*, 471–472.

King, L.A., & Miner, K.N. (2000). Writing about the perceived benefits of traumatic events: implications for physical health. *Personality and Social Psychology Bulletin, 26*, 220–230.

Kinlen, L. (2004). Infections and immune factors in cancer: the role of epidemiology. *Oncogene, 23*, 6341–6348.

Knotkova, H., Clark, W.C., Mokrejs, P., Padour, F., & Kuhl, J. (2004). What do ratings on unidimensional pain and emotion scales really mean? A multidimensional affect and pain survey (MAPS) analysis of cancer patient responses. *Journal of Pain and Symptom Management, 28*, 19–27.

Kobasa, S.C. (1979). Stressful life events, personality and health: an inquiry into hardiness. *Journal of Personality and Social Psychology, 37*, 1–11.

Kochar (2006). Cancer Vaccines. Available online at: www.csa.com/discoveryguides/cancer/review.php

Kok, G., Schaalma, H., Ruiter, R.A.C., & van Empelen, P. (2004). Intervention mapping: protocol for applying health psychology theory to prevention programmes. *Journal of Health Psychology, 9*, 85–98.

Kooijman, C.M., Dijkstra, P.U., Geertzen, J.H.B., Elzinga, A., & van der Schans, C.P. (2000). Phantom pain and phantom sensations in upper limb amputees: an epidemiological study. *Pain, 87*, 33–41.

Korte, S.M., Koolhaas, J.M., Wingfield, J.C., & McEwen, B.S. (2005). The Darwinian concept of stress: benefits of allostasis and costs of allostatic load and the trade-offs in health and disease. *Neuroscience and Biobehavioral Reviews, 29*, 3–38.

Kotze, A., & Simpson, K.H. (2008). Stimulation-produced analgesia: acupuncture, TENS and related techniques. *Anaesthesia & Intensive Care Medicine, 9*, 29–32.

Kraemer, H.C., Kiernan, M., Essex, M., & Kupfer, D.J. (2008). How and why criteria defining moderators and mediators differ between the Baron & Kenny and MacArthur approaches. *Health Psychology, 27*, S101–S108.

Kraut, R., Olson, J., Banaji, M., Bruckman, A., Cohen, J., & Couper, M. (2004). Psychological research online: report of board of scientific affairs' advisory group on the conduct of research on the internet. *American Psychologist, 59*, 105–117.

Kristenson, M., Eriksen, H.R., Sluiter, J.K., Starke, D., & Ursin, H. (2004). Psychobiological mechanisms of socio-economic differences in health. *Social Science & Medicine, 58*, 1511–1522.

Kudielka, B.M., & Kirschbaum, C. (2005). Sex differences in HPA axis responses to stress: a review. *Biological Psychology, 69*, 113–132.

Lahdensuo, A., Haahtela, T., Herrala, J., Kava, T., Kiniranta, K., Kuusisto, P., Peramaki, E., Poussa, T., Saarelainen, S., & Svahn, T. (1996). Randomised comparison of guided self-management and traditional treatment of asthma over one year. *British Medical Journal, 312*, 748–751.

Lazarus, R.S. (1991). *Emotion and adaptation.* New York: Oxford University Press.

Lazarus, R.S. (1993). Coping theory and research: past, present, and future. *Psychosomatic Medicine, 55*, 234–247.

Lazarus, R.S. (1999). *Stress and emotion: a new synthesis.* New York, NY: Springer.

Lazarus, R.S., & Folkman, S. (1984). *Stress, appraisal and coping.* New York: Springer.

Lehrer, P. (2003). Applied psychophysiology: beyond boundaries of the biofeedback (mending a wall, a brief history of our field and applications to control of the muscles and cardiorespiratory systems). *Applied Psychophysiology and Biofeedback, 28*, 291–304.

LeMoal, M.L. (2007). Historical approach and evolution of the stress concept: a personal account. *Psychoneuroendocrinology, 32*, S3–S9.

Lesch, K.P. (2005). Alcohol dependence and gene x environment interaction in emotion regulation: is serotonin the link? *European Journal of Pharmacology, 526*, 113–124.

Levav, I., Kohn, R., Iscovich, J., Abramson, J.H., Tsai, W.Y., & Vigdorovich, D. (2000). Cancer incidence and survival following bereavement. *American Journal of Public Health, 90*, 1601–1607.

Leventhal, J., Meyer, D., & Nerenz, D. (1980). The common-sense representation of illness danger. In S. Rachman (Ed.), *Medical psychology.* New York: Pergamon. Pp. 27–30.

Leventhal, H., Meyer, D., & Nerenz, D.R. (1985). The commonsense model of self-regulation of health and illness. In L.D. Cameron and H. Leventhal (Eds), *The self-regulation of health and illness behaviour.* London: Routledge. Pp. 42–65.

Leventhal, H., & Nerenz, D.R. (1985). The assessment of illness cognition. In P. Karoly (Ed.), *Measurement strategies in health psychology.* New York: Wiley. Pp. 517–554.

Levine, S., & Ursin, H. (1991). What is stress? In M.R. Brown, G.F. Koob, & C. Rivier (Eds), *Stress: neurobiology and neuroendocrinology.* New York: Marcel Dekker. Pp. 1–21.

Levy, S.M., Heberman, R.B., Lippman, M., & Dangelo, T. (1987). Correlation of stress factors with sustained depression of natural killer cell activity and predicted prognosis in patients with breast cancer. *Journal of Clinical Oncology, 5*, 348–353.

Levy, S.M., Heberman, R.B., Lippman, M., Dangelo, T., & Lee, J. (1991). Immunological and psychosocial predictors of disease recurrence in patients with early stage breast cancer. *Behavioral Medicine, 17*, 67–75.

Levy, S.M., Heberman, R.B., Whiteside, T., Sanzo, K., Le, J., & Kirkwood, J. (1990). Perceived social support and tumor estrogen/progesterone receptor status as predictors of natural killer cell activity in breast cancer patients. *Psychosomatic Medicine, 52*, 73–85.

Levy, S.M., Herberman, R.B., Maluish, A.M., Schlien, B., & Lippman, M. (1985). Prognostic risk assessment in primary breast cancer by behavioral and immunological parameters. *Health Psychology, 4*, 99–113.

Lewandowski, W. (2004). Psychological factors in chronic pain: a worthwhile undertaking for nursing? *Archives of Psychiatric Nursing, 18*, 97–105.

Lindley, S.E., Carlson, E.B., & Benoit, M. (2004). Basal and dexamethasone suppressed salivary cortisol concentrations in a community sample of patients with posttraumatic stress disorder, *Biological Psychiatry, 55*, 940–945.

Linton, S.J., & Hallden, K. (1997). Risk factors and the natural course of acute and recurrent musculoskeletal pain: developing a screening instrument. *Proceedings of the 8th World Congress on Pain, 8*, 527–536.

Lipowski, Z.J. (1984). What does the word 'psychosomatic' really mean? A historical and semantic inquiry. *Psychosomatic Medicine, 46*, 153–171.

Livingston, G., & Cooper, C. (2004). User and carer involvement in mental health training. *Advances in Psychiatric Treatment, 10*, 85–92.

Loeser, J.D., & Melzack, R. (1999). Pain: an overview. *The Lancet, 353*, 1607–1609.

Longmore, R.J., & Worrell, M. (2007). Do we need to challenge thought in cognitive behaviour therapy? *Clinical Psychology Review, 27,* 173–187.

Lorig, K., Gonzalez, V., & Laurent, D. (1997). The expert patients program chronic disease self-management course: leader's manual. Palo Alto, CA: Stanford Patient Education Research Center.

Lorig, T.S. (2009). What was the question? fMRI and inference in psychophysiology. *International Journal of Psychophysiology, 73,* 17–21.

Lucas, R.E., Clark, A.E., Georgellis, Y., & Diener, E. (2004). Unemployment alters the set point for life satisfaction. *Psychological Science, 15,* 8–13.

Lucini, D., Cannone, V., Malacarne, M., Bruno, D., Beltrami, S., Pizzinelli, P., Piazza, E., Di Fede, G., & Pagani, M. (2008). Evidence of autonomic dysregulation in otherwise healthy cancer caregivers: a possible link with health hazard. *European Journal of Cancer, 44,* 2437–2443.

Lundberg, U., & Frankenhaeuser, M. (1980). Pituitary–adrenal and sympathetic–adrenal correlates of distress and effort. *Journal of Psychosomatic Research, 24,* 125–130.

Lutgendorf, S.K., & Costanzo, E. (2003). Psychoneuroimmunology and health psychology: an integrative model. *Brain, Behavior and Immunity, 17,* 225–315.

Luz, C., Dornelles, F., Preissler, T., Collaziol, D., da Cruz, I., Moises, C., & Bauer, M.E. (2003). Impact of psychological and endocrine factors on cytokine production of healthy elderly people. *Mechanisms of Ageing and Development, 124,* 887–895.

Lykken, D., & Tellegen, A. (1996). Happiness is a stochastic phenomenon. *Psychological Science, 7,* 186–189.

Mackie, J.L. (1965). Causes and conditions. *American Philosophical Quarterly, 2,* 245–264.

Mackie, J.L. (1974). *The cement of the universe: a study of causation.* Oxford: Oxford University Press.

MacKinnon, D.P. (2008). *Introduction to statistical mediation analysis.* New York: Taylor & Francis.

MacKinnon, D.P., & Luecken, L.J. (2008). How and for whom? Mediation and moderation in health psychology. *Health Psychology, 27,* S99–S100.

Maier, S.F., & Seligman, M.E.P. (1976). Learned helplessness: theory and evidence. *Journal of Experimental Psychology, 105,* 3–46.

Maier, S.F., & Watkins, L.R. (1998). Cytokines for psychologists: implications of bidirectional immune-to-brain communication for understanding behavior, mood, and cognition. *Psychological Review, 105,* 83–107.

Maier, S.F., & Watkins, L.R. (2003). Immune-to-central nervous system communication and its role in modulating pain and cognition: implications for cancer and cancer treatment. *Brain, Behavior and Immunity, 17,* S125–S131.

Maigne, J.-Y., & Vautravers, P. (2003). Mechanism of action of spinal manipulative therapy. *Joint Bone Spine, 70,* 336–341.

Manchikanti, L. (2008). Evidence-based medicine, systematic reviews and guidelines in interventional pain management, part I: introduction and general considerations. *Pain Physician, 11,* 161–186.

Marmot, M. (2006). Health in an unequal world. *The Lancet, 368,* 2081–2094.

Marmot, M., Bosma, H., Hemingway, H., Brunner, E., & Stansfeld, S. (1997). Contribution of job control and other risk factors to social variations in coronary heart disease incidence. *The Lancet, 350,* 235–239.

Marmot, M.G., Davey Smith, G., Stansfeld, S.A., Patel, C., North, F., Head, J., White, I., Brunner, E., & Feeney, A. (1991). Health inequalities among British civil servants: the Whitehall II study. *The Lancet, 1991,* 1387–1393.

Marmot, M.G., & Shipley, M.J. (1996). Do socioeconomic differences in mortality persist after retirement? Twenty-five year follow-up of civil servants from the first Whitehall study. *British Medical Journal, 313,* 1177–1180.

Marmot, M.G., Shipley, M.J., & Rose, G. (1984). Inequalities in death: specific explanations of a general pattern. *The Lancet, 1,* 1003–1006.

Martikainen, P., Stansfeld, S., Hemingway, H., & Marmot, M. (1999). Determinants of socioeconomic differences in change in physical and mental functioning. *Social Science & Medicine, 49,* 499–507.

Mason, J.W. (1968). A review of psychoendocrine research on the pituitary–adrenal cortical system. *Psychosomatic Medicine, 30,* 575–607.

Matarazzo, J.D. (1982). Behavioral health's challenge to academic, scientific, and professional psychology. *American Psychologist, 37,* 1–14.

McBeth, J., & Cordingley, L. (2009). Current issues and new direction in psychology and health: epidemiology and health psychology – please bridge the gap. *Psychology & Health, 24,* 861–865.

McCaffery, J.M., Frasure-Smith, N., Dube, M.-P., Theroux, P., Rouleau, G.A., Dun, Q., & Lesperance, F. (2006). Common genetic vulnerability to depressive symptoms and coronary artery disease: a review and development of candidate genes related to inflammation and serotonin. *Psychosomatic Medicine, 68,* 187–200.

McCaffery, M. (1968). *Nursing practice theories related to cognition, bodily pain and main environment interactions.* Los Angeles, CA: University of California at LA Students Store.

McCann, J.J., Hebert, L.E., Blenias, J.L., Morris, M.C., & Evans, D.A. (2004). Predictors of beginning and ending caregiving during a 3-year period in a biracial community population of older adults. *American Journal of Public Health, 94,* 1800–1806.

McCracken, L.M., Carson, J.W., Eccleston, C., & Keefe, F.J. (2004). Acceptance and change in the context of chronic pain. *Pain, 109*, 4–7.

McDougall, S.J., Widdop, R.E., & Lawrence, A.J. (2005). Central autonomic integration of psychological stressors: focus on cardiovascular modulation. *Autonomic Neuroscience – Basic and Clinical, 123*, 1–11.

McEwen, B.S. (1998). Stress, adaptation, and disease: allostasis and allostatic load. *Annals of the New York Academy of Sciences, 840*, 33–44.

McEwen, B.S. (2000). Allostasis and allostatic load: implications for neuropsychopharmacology. *Neuropsychopharmacology, 22*, 108–124.

McEwen, B.S., & Sapolsky, R.M. (1995). Stress and cognitive function. *Current Opinion in Neurobiology, 5*, 205–216.

McEwen, B.S., & Seeman, T. (1999). Protective and damaging effects of mediators of stress: elaborating and testing the concepts of allostasis and allostatic load. *Annals of the New York Academy of Sciences, 896*, 30–47.

McEwen, B.S., & Stellar, E. (1993). Stress and the individual: mechanisms leading to disease. *Archives of Internal Medicine, 153*, 2093–2101.

McEwen, B.S., & Wingfield, J.C. (2003). The concept of allostasis in biology and biomedicine. *Hormones and Behavior, 43*, 2–15.

McMinn, M.R., Buchanan, T., Ellens, B.M., & Ryan, M.K. (1999). Technology, professional practice, and ethics: survey findings and implications. *Professional Psychology: Research and Practice, 30*, 165–172.

McNair, D.M., Lorr, M., & Droppelman, L.F. (1971). *Manual for the profile of mood states*. San Diego, CA: Educational and Industrial Testing Service.

Meads, C., Lyons, A., & Carroll, D. (2003). The impact of the emotional disclosure intervention on physical and psychological health: a systematic review (Report number 43). Birmingham: WMHTAC, Department of Public Health and Epidemiology, University of Birmingham.

Meiser, B. (2005). Psychological impact of genetic testing for cancer susceptibility: an update of the literature. *Psycho-Oncology, 14*, 1060–1074.

Meiser, B., & Dunn, S. (2000). Psychological impact of genetic testing for Huntington's disease: an update of the literature. *Journal of Neurology, Neurosurgery and Psychiatry, 69*, 575–578.

Melzack, R. (1975). McGill pain questionnaire: major properties and scoring methods. *Pain, 1*, 277–299.

Melzack, R. (1987). The short form McGill pain questionnaire. *Pain, 30*, 191–197.

Melzack, R. (1999). From the gate to the neuromatrix. *Pain, S6*, S121–S126.

Melzack, R., & Wall, P.D. (1965). Pain mechanisms: a new theory. *Science, 150*, 971–979.

MENCAP (2007). *Death by indifference*. London: Mencap. Available online at: www.mencap.org.uk/document.asp?id=284

Merskey, H.M., & Bogduk, N. (1994). *Classification of chronic pain* (2nd ed). Seattle, WA: IASP Press.

Meyerson, B.A., & Linderoth, B. (2006). Mode of action of spinal cord stimulation in neuropathic pain. *Journal of Pain and Symptom Management, 31*, S6–S12.

Michie, S., & Abraham, C. (2004). Identifying techniques that promote health behaviour change: evidence based or evidence inspired? *Psychology & Health, 19*, 29–49.

Michie, S., Bobrow, M., & Marteau, T.M. (2001). Predictive genetic testing in children and adults: a study of emotional impact. *Journal of Medical Genetics, 38*, 519–526.

Michie, S., Johnston, M., Francis, J., Hardeman, W., & Eccles, M. (2008). From theory to intervention: mapping theoretically derived behavioral determinants to behaviour change techniques. *Applied Psychology: An International Review, 57*, 660–680.

Michie, S., Miles, J., & Weinman, J. (2003). Patient-centredness in chronic illness: what is it and does it matter? *Patient Education and Counselling, 51*, 197–206.

Michie, S., Smith, J.A., Senior, V., & Marteau, T.M. (2003). Understanding why negative genetic test results sometimes fail to reassure. *American Journal of Medical Genetics, 119A*, 340–347.

Michie, S., Weinman, J., Miller, J., Collins, V., Halliday, J., & Marteau, T.M. (2002). Predictive genetic testing: high risk expectation in the face of low risk information. *Journal of Behavioral Medicine, 25*, 33–50.

Miller, C., & Newton, S.E. (2006). Pain perception and expression: the influence of gender, personal self-efficacy and lifespan socialisation. *Pain Management Nursing, 7*, 148–152.

Miller, G.A., Elbert, T., Sutton, B.P., & Heller, W. (2007). Innovative clinical assessment technologies: challenges and opportunities in neuroimaging. *Psychological Assessment, 19*, 58–73.

Miller, T.Q., Smith, T.W., Turner, C.W., Guijarro, M.L., & Hallet, A.J. (1996). Meta-analytic review of research on hostility and physical health. *Psychological Bulletin, 119*, 322–348.

Millian, M.J. (1986). Multiple opioid systems and pain. *Pain, 27*, 303–347.

Mitchell, K.J. (2007). The genetics of brain wiring: from molecule to mind. *PLoS Biology, 5*, 0690–0692.

Moher, D., Schulz, K.F., & Altman, D.G. (2001). The CONSORT statement: revised recommendations for improving the quality of reports of parallel group randomised trials. *The Lancet, 357*, 1191–1194.

Morwitz, V.G., Johnson, E., Schmittlein, D. (1993). Does measuring intent change behaviour? *Journal of Consumer Research, 20*, 46–61.

Mossman, T.R., & Coffman, R.L. (1989). Th1 and Th2 cells. Different patterns of lymphokine secretion. *Annual Review of Immunology, 7*, 145–173.

Mueller, N. (1999). Overview of the epidemiology of malignancy in immune deficiency. *Journal of Acquired Immune Deficiency Syndromes, 21*, S5–S10.

Mullis, R., Hay, E., & Lewis, M. (2005). Outcome in low back pain: what matters to the patients? *Rheumatology, 44*, I160–I160.

Muraven, M., & Baumeister, R.F. (2000). Self-regulation and depletion of limited resources: does self-control resemble a muscle? *Psychological Bulletin, 126*, 24–259.

Mustanski, B.S., Viken, R.J., Kaprio, J., & Rose, R.J. (2003). Genetic influence on the association between personality risk factors and alcohol use and abuse. *Journal of Abnormal Psychology, 112*, 282–289.

Nakamura, J., & Csikszentmihalyi, M. (2002). The concept of flow. In C.R. Snyder & S.L. Lopez (Eds), *Handbook of positive psychology*. New York: Oxford University Press.

National Audit Office (2007). Improving services and support for people with dementia. London: National Audit Office. Available online at www.nao.org.uk/publications/0607/support_for_people_with_dement.aspx

National Heart Lung and Blood Institute (2009). What is Atherosclerosis? Available online at: http://www.nhlbi.nih.gov/health/dci/Diseases/Atherosclerosis/Atherosclerosis_WhatIs.html

Neuman, Y. (2004). What does pain signify? A hypothesis concerning pain, the immune system and unconscious pain experience under general anaesthesia. *Medical Hypotheses, 63*, 1051–1053.

Nicassio, P.M., Meyerowitz, B.E., & Kerns, R.D. (2004). The future of health psychology interventions. *Health Psychology, 23*, 132–137.

Nicholas, M.K. (2007). The pain self-efficacy questionnaire: taking pain into account. *European Journal of Pain, 11*, 153–163.

Nickelson, D.W. (1996). Behavioral telehealth: emerging practice, research, and policy opportunities. *Behavioral Sciences & the Law, 14*, 443–457.

Nosek, B.A., Banaji, M.R., & Greenwald, A.G. (2002). E-research: ethics, security, design, and control in psychological research on the internet. *Journal of Social Issues, 58*, 161–176.

O'Donovan, A., Lin, J., Dhabhar, F.S., Wolkowitz, O., Tillie, J.M., Blackburn, E., & Epel, E. (2009). Pessimism correlates with leukocyte telomere shortness and elevated interleukin-6 in post-menopausal women. *Brain, Behavior and Immunity, 23*, 446–449.

O'Reilly, D., Connolly, S., Rosato, M., & Patterson, C. (2008). Is caring associated with an increased risk of mortality? A longitudinal study. *Social Science & Medicine, 67*, 1282–1290.

Ogden, J. (2003). Some problems with social cognition models: a pragmatic and conceptual analysis. *Health Psychology, 23*, 424–428.

Owen, D., Andrews, M.H., & Matthews, S.G. (2005). Maternal adversity, glucocorticoids and programming of neuroendocrine function and behaviour. *Neuroscience and Biobehavioral Reviews, 29*, 209–226.

Pacheco-Lopez, G., Engler, H., Niemi, M.-B., & Schedlowski, M. (2006). Expectations and associations that heal: immunomodulatory placebo effects and its neurobiology. *Brain, Behavior and Immunity, 5*, 430–446.

Patenaude, A.F., Guttmacher, A.E., & Collins, F.S. (2002). Genetic testing and psychology: new roles, new responsibilities. *American Psychologist, 57*, 271–282.

Pavlov, I.P. (1927). *Conditioned reflexes: an investigation of the physiological activity of the cerebral cortex. translated and edited by G. V. Anrep.* London: Oxford University Press.

Pawelec, G., Barnett, Y., Forsey, R., Frasca, D., Globerson, A., McLeod, J., Caruso, C., Franceschi, C., Fulop, T., Gupta, S., Mariani, E., Mocchegiani, E., & Solana, R. (2002). T cells and aging: January 2002 update. *Frontiers in Bioscience, 7*, D1056–D1183.

Pederson-Fischer, A., Zachariae, R., & Bovbjerg-Howard, D. (2009). Psychological stress and antibody response to influenza vaccination: a meta-analysis. *Brain, Behavior and Immunity, 23*, 427–433.

Peel, N.M., McClure, R.J., & Bartlett, H.P. (2005). Behavioral determinants of healthy aging. *American Journal of Preventive Medicine, 28*, 298–304.

Pennebaker, J.W., & Beall, S.K. (1986). Confronting a traumatic event: toward an understanding of inhibition and disease. *Journal of Abnormal Psychology, 95*, 274–281.

Perkins, F.M., & Kehlet, H. (2000). Chronic pain as an outcome of surgery. *Anesthesiology, 93*, 1123–1133.

Peterson, C. (1988). Explanatory style as a risk factor for illness. *Cognitive Therapy and Research, 12*, 119–132.

Petrie, K.J., Cameron, L., Ellis, C.J., Buick, D., & Weinman, J. (2002). Changing illness perceptions after myocardial infarction: an early intervention randomized controlled trial. *Psychosomatic Medicine, 64*, 580–586.

Petticrew, M., Bell, R., & Hunter, D. (2002). Influence of psychological coping on survival and recurrence in people with cancer: systematic review. *British Medical Journal, 325*, 1066–1069.

Peyrot, M., & Rubin, R.R. (2007). Behavioral and psychosocial interventions in diabetes: a conceptual review. *Diabetes Care, 30*, 2433–2440.

Piasecki, T.M., Hufford, M.R., Solhan, M., & Trull, T.J. (2007). Assessing clients in their natural environments with electronic diaries: rationale, benefits, limitations, and barriers. *Psychological Assessment, 19*, 25–43.

Pinquart, M., & Sorensen, S. (2007). Correlates of physical health of informal caregivers: a meta-analysis. *The*

Journals of Gerontology, Series B, Psychological Sciences and Social Sciences, 62, 126–137.

Plante, T.G., Aldridge, A., Su, D., Bogden, R., Belo, M., & Kahn, K. (2003). Does virtual reality enhance the management of stress when paired with exercise? An exploratory study. *International Journal of Stress Management, 10,* 203–216.

Pleuvry, B.J. (2005). Opioid mechanisms and opioid drugs. *Anaesthesia and Intensive Care Medicine, 6,* 30–34.

Plomin, R. (2000). Behavioural genetics in the 21st century. *International Journal of Behavioral Development, 24,* 30–34.

Plomin, R. (2002). Individual differences research in a postgenomic era. *Personality and Individual Differences, 33,* 909–920.

Plomin, R., Pedersen, N.L., Lichtenstein, P., McClearn, G.E., & Nesselroade, J.R. (1990). Genetic influence on life events during the last half of the life span. *Psychology and Aging, 5,* 25–30.

Porteous, J.W. (2004). We still fail to account for Mendel's observations. *Theoretical Biology and Medical Modelling, 1,* 1–4.

Porter, R.S. (2007). What is referred pain? *Merck manual of medical information – home edition.* Retrieved 2nd May 2008, from: http://www.merck.com/mmhe

Prochaska, J.O., & DiClemente, C.C. (1983). Stages and processes of self-change of smoking: toward an integrative model of change. *Journal of Consulting and Clinical Psychology, 51,* 390–395.

Ranger, M., Johnston, C.C., & Anand, K.J.S. (2007). Current controversies regarding pain assessment in neonates. *Seminars in Perinatology, 31,* 283–288.

Ray, R., Schnoll, R.A., & Lerman, C. (2007). Pharmacogenetics and smoking cessation with nicotine replacement therapy. *CNS Drugs, 2,* 525–533.

Reibel, D.K., Greeson, J.M., Brainard, G.C., & Rosenzweig, S. (2001). Mindfulness-based stress reduction and health-related quality of life in a heterogeneous patient population. *General Hospital Psychiatry, 23,* 183–192.

Reiner, R. (2008). Integrating a portable biofeedback device into clinical practice for patients with anxiety disorders: results of a pilot study. *Applied Psychophysiological Biofeedback, 33,* 55–61.

Reis, H.T., Sheldon, K.M., Gable, S.L., Roscoe, J., & Ryan, R.M. (2000). Daily well-being: the role of autonomy, competence, and relatedness. *Personality and Social Psychology Bulletin, 26,* 419–435.

Risch, N. (2001). The genetic epidemiology of cancer: interpreting family and twin studies and their implications for molecular genetic approaches. *Cancer Epidemiology, Biomarkers and Prevention, 10,* 733–741.

Risch, N., Herrell, R., Lehner, T., Liang, K.-Y., Eaves, L., Hoh, J., Griem, A., Kovacs, M., Ott, J., & Merikangas, K.R. (2009). Interaction between the serotonin transporter gene (5-HTTLPR), stressful life events, and risk of depression: a meta-analysis. *Journal of the American Medical Association, 301,* 2462–2471.

Robinson, P., Gregg, J., Dahl, J., & Lundgren, T. (2004). ACT in medical settings. In S. Hayes & K. Strosahl (Eds), *Acceptance and commitment therapy: a practical guide.* New York: Springer. Pp. 295–314.

Roger, D. (1998). Stress, health and personality: a new perspective. *Complementary Therapies in Nursing and Midwifery, 4,* 50–53.

Rose, R.J. (2005). Prenatal programming of behavior: a twin-study perspective. *Neuroscience & Biobehavioral Reviews, 29,* 321–327.

Rosenstiel, A.K., & Keefe, F.J. (1983). The use of coping strategies in chronic low back pain patients: relationship to patient characteristics and current adjustment. *Pain, 17,* 33–44.

Rotter, J.B. (1966). Generalized expectancies for internal versus external control of reinforcement. *Psychological Monographs: General & Applied, 80,* 1–28.

Roy-Byrne, P.P., Davidson, K.W., Kessler, R.C., Asmundson, G.J.G., Goodwin, R.D., Kubzansky, L., Lydiard, R.B., Massie, M.J., Katon, W., Laden, S.K., & Stein, M.B. (2008). Anxiety disorders and comorbid medical illness. *General Hospital Psychiatry, 30,* 208–225.

Rudell, K., & Diefenbach, M.A. (2008). Current issues and new directions in psychology and health: culture and health psychology. Why health psychologists should care about culture. *Psychology & Health, 23,* 387–390.

Russo, C.M., & Brose, W.G. (1998). Chronic pain. *Annual Review of Medicine, 49,* 123–133.

Rutter, M. (2007). Proceeding from observed correlation to causal inference: the use of natural experiments. *Perspectives on Psychological Science, 2,* 377–395.

Ryan, R.M., & Deci, E.L. (2000). Self-determination theory and the facilitation of intrinsic motivation, social development, and well-being. *American Psychologist, 55,* 68–78.

Ryan, R.M., & Deci, E.L. (2001). On happiness and human potentials: a review of research on hedonic and eudaimonic well-being. *Annual Review of Psychology, 52,* 141–166.

Ryff, C.D. (1989). Happiness is everything, or is it? Explorations on the meaning of psychological well-being. *Journal of Personality and Social Psychology, 57,* 1069–1081.

Ryff, C.D., & Singer, B. (2000). Interpersonal flourishing: a positive health agenda for the new millennium. *Personality and Social Psychology Review, 4,* 30–44.

Ryff, C.D., Singer, B., & Love, G.D. (2004). Positive health: connecting well-being with biology. *Philosophical Transactions of the Royal Society of Biological Sciences, 359,* 1383–1394.

Saab, P.G., McCalla, J.R., Coons, H.L., Christensen, A.J., Kaplan, R., Bennett-Johnson, S., Ackerman, M.D., Stepanski, E., Krantz, D.S., & Melamed, B. (2004).

Technological and medical advances: implications for health psychology. *Health Psychology, 23*, 142–146.

Salanova, M., Bakker, A.B., & Llorens, S. (2006). Flow at work: evidence for an upward spiral of personal and organizational resources. *Journal of Happiness Studies, 7*, 1–22.

Salzman, C., & Shader, R.I. (1978). Depression in the elderly: I: Relationship between depression, psychologic defense mechanisms and physical illness. *Journal of the American Geriatics Society, 26*, 253–260.

Sapolsky, R. (1999). Stress and your shrinking brain. *Discover Magazine, 20*, 116–122.

Sapolsky, R.M. (2002). *Why zebras don't get ulcers: guide to stress, stress-related disease and coping*. New York: Henry Holt & Company.

Schedlowski, M., & Tewes, U. (1999). *Psychoneuroimmunology: an interdisciplinary introduction*. New York: Kluwer.

Scheier, M.F., & Carver, C.S. (1987). Dispositional optimism and physical well-being: the influence of generalized outcome expectancies on health. *Journal of Personality, 55*, 169–210.

Scheier, M.F., & Carver, C.S. (1992). Effects of optimism on psychological and physical well-being: theoretical overview and empirical update. *Cognitive Perspectives in Health Psychology, 16*, 201–228.

Schmutte, P.S., & Ryff, C.D. (1997). Personality and well-being: re-examining methods and meanings. *Journal of Personality and Social Psychology, 73*, 549–559.

Schott, G.D. (2004). Communicating the experience of pain: the role of analogy. *Pain, 108*, 209–212.

Schulz, R., & Sherwood, P.R. (2008). Physical and mental health effects of family caregiving. *American Journal of Nursing, 108*, 23–27.

Schwartz, G.E., & Weiss, S.M. (1977). What is behavioral medicine? *Psychosomatic Medicine, 39*, 377–381.

Seckl, J.R. (2001). Glucocorticoid programming of the fetus: adult phenotypes and molecular mechanisms. *Molecular and Cellular Endocrinology, 185*, 61–71.

Seckl, J.R., & Meaney, M.J. (2004). Glucocorticoid programming. In R. Yehuda & B. McEwen (Eds), *Biobehavioral stress response: protective and damaging effects*. New York: New York Academy of Sciences. Pp. 63–84.

Seeman, T.E., Crimmins, E., Huang, M.-H., Singer, B., Bucur, A., Gruenewald, T., Berkman, L.F., & Reuben, D.B. (2004). Cumulative biological risk and socioeconomic differences in mortality: MacArthur studies of successful aging. *Social Science & Medicine, 58*, 1985–1997.

Seeman, T.E., Dubin, L.F., & Seeman, M. (2003). Religiosity/spirituality and health: a critical review of the evidence for biological pathways. *American Psychologist, 58*, 53–63.

Segerstrom, S.C. (2003). Individual differences, immunity, and cancer: lessons from personality psychology. *Brain, Behavior and Immunity, 17*, S92–S97.

Segerstrom, S.C., Taylor, S.E., Kemeny, M.E., & Fahey, J.L. (1998). Optimism is associated with mood, coping and immune change in response to stress. *Journal of Personality and Social Psychology, 74*, 1646–1655.

Seligman, M.E.P. (1975). *Helplessness: on depression, development and death*. New York: W.H. Freeman.

Seligman, M.E.P., & Csikszentmihalyi, M. (2000). Positive psychology: an introduction. *American Psychologist, 55*, 5–14.

Selye, H. (1956). *The stress of life*. New York: McGraw-Hill.

Sheldon, K.M., Ryan, R.M., & Reis, H.T. (1996). What makes for a good day? Competence and autonomy in the day and in the person. *Personality and Social Psychology Bulletin, 22*, 1270–1279.

Sherman, R.A. (1994). What do we really know about phantom limb pain? *Pain Reviews, 1*, 261–274.

Shiloh, S., Ben-Sinai, R., & Keinan, G. (1999). Effects of controllability, predictability and information seeking style on interest in predictive genetic testing. *Personality and Social Psychology Bulletin, 25*, 1187–1195.

Siegrist, J., & Marmot, M. (2006). *Social inequalities in health: new evidence and policy implications*. Oxford: Oxford University Press.

Slagboom, P.E., & Meulenbelt, I. (2002). Organisation of the human genome and our tools for identifying disease genes. *Biological Psychology, 61*, 11–31.

Sloan, R.P., Bagiella, E., Shapiro, P.A., Kuhl, J.P., Chernikhove, D., Berg, J., & Myers, M.M. (2001). Hostility, gender, and cardiac autonomic control. *Psychosomatic Medicine, 63*, 434–440.

Sluka, K.A., & Walsh, D. (2003). Transcutaneous electrical nerve stimulation: basic science mechanisms and clinical effectiveness. *Journal of Pain, 4*, 109–112.

Sluzki, C.E. (2000). Patients, clients, consumers: the politics of words. *Family, Systems and Health, 18*, 347–352.

Smyth, J.M. (1998). Written emotional expression: effect sizes, outcome types, and moderating variables. *Journal of Consulting and Clinical Psychology, 66*, 174–184.

Smyth, J.M., & Pennebaker, J.W. (2008). Exploring the boundary conditions of expressive writing: in search of the right recipe. *British Journal of Health Psychology, 13*, 1–7.

Sobal, J., & Stunkard, A.J. (1989). Socioeconomic status and obesity: a review of the literature. *Psychological Bulletin, 105*, 260–275.

Solomon, G.F., & Moos, R. (1964). Emotions, immunity and disease. *Archives of General Psychiatry, 11*, 657–674.

Somerfield, M.R., & McCrae, R.R. (2000). Stress and coping research: methodological challenges, theoretical advances and clinical applications. *American Psychologist, 55*, 620–625.

Spiegel, D., & Giese-Davis, J. (2003). Depression and cancer: mechanisms and disease progression. *Biological Psychiatry, 54,* 269–282.

Spolentini, I., Gianni, W., Repetto, L., Bria, P., Caltagirone, C., Bossu, P., & Spalletta, G. (2008). Depression and cancer: an unexplored and unresolved emergent issue in elderly patients. *Critical Reviews in Oncology/Hematology, 65,* 143–155.

Sprott, D.E., Spangenberg, E.R., Block, L.G., Fitzsimons, G.J., Morwitz, V.G., & Williams, P. (2006). The question behaviour effect: what we know and where we go from here. *Social Influence, 1,* 128–137.

Stam, R. (2007). PTSD and stress sensitisation: a tale of brain and body. Part 1: Human studies. *Neuroscience & Biobehavioral Reviews, 4,* 530–557.

Stanton, A.L., Danoff-Burg, S., Sworowski, L.A., Collins, C.A., Branstetter, A.D., Rodriguez-Hanley, A., Kirk, S.B., & Austenfeld, J.L. (2002). Randomized, controlled trial of written emotional expression and benefit finding in breast cancer patients. *Journal of Clinical Oncology, 20,* 4160–4168.

Steptoe, A., Feldman, P.J., Kunz, S., Owen, N., Willemsen, G., & Marmot, M. (2002). Stress responsivity and socioeconomic status: a mechanism for increased cardiovascular disease risk? *European Heart Journal, 23,* 1757–1763.

Steptoe, A., Gibson, E.L., Hammer, M., & Wardle, J. (2007). Neuroendocrine and cardiovascular correlates of positive affect measured by ecological momentary assessment and by questionnaire. *Psychoneuroendocrinology, 32,* 56–64.

Steptoe, A., & Marmot, M. (2004). Socioeconomic status and coronary heart disease: a psychobiological perspective. *Population and Development Review, 30,* 133–150.

Steptoe, A., Owen, N., Kunz-Ebrecht, S., & Mohamed-Ali, V. (2002). Inflammatory cytokines, socioeconomic status, and acute stress responsivity. *Brain, Behavior and Immunity, 16,* 774–784.

Sterling, P., & Eyer, J. (1988). Allostasis: a new paradigm to explain arousal pathology. In S. Fisher & J. Reason (Eds), *Handbook of life stress, cognition and health.* Oxford: John Wiley. Pp. 629–649.

Stone, A.A., Broderick, J.E., Schwartz, J.E., Shiffman, S.S., Litcher-Kelly, L., & Calvanese, P. (2003). Intensive momentary reporting of pain with an electronic diary: reactivity, compliance, and patient satisfaction. *Pain, 104,* 343–351.

Straub, R.H., Miller, L.E., Scholmerich, & Zietz, B. (2000). Cytokines and hormones as possible links between endocrinosenescence and immunosenescence. *Journal of Neuroimmunology, 109,* 10–15.

Stroebe, W., Stroebe, M., Abakoumkin, G., & Schut, H. (1996). The role of loneliness and social support in adjustment to loss: a test of attachment versus stress theory. *Journal of Personality and Social Psychology, 70,* 1241–1249.

Strong, J., Unruh, A.M., Wright, A., & Baxter, G.D. (2002). *Pain: a textbook for therapists.* London: Elsevier.

Suchman, A.L. (2005). The current state of the biopsychosocial approach. *Families, Systems & Health, 23,* 450–452.

Sullivan, M.J.L., Tripp, D., & Santor, D. (2000). Gender differences in pain and pain behavior: the role of catastrophizing. *Cognitive Therapy and Research, 24,* 121–134.

Suls, J., & Rothman, A. (2004). Evolution of the biopsychosocial model: prospects and challenges for health psychology. *Health Psychology, 23,* 119–125.

Summers, S. (2000). Evidence-based practice part 1: pain definitions, pathophysiologic mechanisms and theories. *Journal of PeriAnesthesia Nursing, 15,* 357–365.

Szanton, S.L., Gill, J.M., & Allen, J.K. (2005). Allostatic load: a mechanism of socioeconomic health disparities? *Biological Research for Nursing, 7,* 7–15.

Targonski, P.V., Jacobson, R.M., & Poland, G.A. (2007). Immunosenescence: role and measurement in influenza vaccine response among the elderly. *Vaccine, 25,* 3066–3069.

Taylor, S.E., Repetti, R.L., & Seeman, T. (1997). Health psychology: what is an unhealthy environment and how does it get under the skin? *Annual Review of Psychology, 48,* 411–447.

Tellegen, A., Lykken, D.T., Bouchard, T.J., Wilcox, K.J., Segal, N.L., & Rich, S. (1988). Personality similarity in twins reared apart and together. *Journal of Personality and Social Psychology, 54,* 1031–1039.

Tennen, H., & Affleck, G. (1999). Finding benefits in adversity. In C.R. Synder (Ed.), *Coping: the psychology of what works.* New York: Oxford University. Press. Pp. 279–304.

Tewes, U., & Schedlowski M. (1999). Psychological methods. In M. Schedlowski & U. Tewes (Eds), *Psychoneuroimmunology: an interdisciplinary introduction.* New York: Plenum. Pp. 113–124.

Theunissen, N.C., de Ridder, D.T.D., Bensing, J.M., & Rutten, G.E.H.M. (2003). Manipulation of patient provider interaction: discussing illness representations or action plans concerning adherence. *Patient Education and Counseling, 51,* 247–258.

Thomas, L. (1959). Discussion. In H.S. Lawrence (Ed.), *Cellular and humoral aspects of the hypersensitivity states.* New York: Hoeber-Harper. Pp. 529–532.

Thomas, P. (2008). Psychosocial and economic issues related to physical health in psychiatric illness. *European Neuropsychopharmacology, 18,* S115–S120.

Thorn, B.E., Boothby, J.L., & Sullivan, M.J.L. (2002). Targeted treatment of catastrophizing for the management of chronic pain. *Cognitive and Behavioral Practice, 9,* 127–138.

Tilbrook, H. (2008). Patients' preferences within randomised trials: systematic review and patient level meta-analysis. *British Medical Journal, 337*, a1864.

Trout, K.K. (2004). The neuromatrix theory of pain: implications for selected nonpharmacologic methods of pain relief. *Journal of Midwifery and Women's Health, 49*, 482–488.

Tschuschke, V., Hertenstein, B., Arnold, R., Bunjes, D., Denzinger, R., & Kaechele, H. (2001). Associations between coping and survival time of adult leukemia patients receiving allogenic bone marrow transplantation: results of a prospective study. *Journal of Psychosomatic Research, 50*, 277–285.

Tschuschke, V. (2002). Wrong conclusions drawn from insufficient research. *BMJ Rapid Response.* Retrieved 12th July 2010, from: http://www.bmj.com/cgi/eletters /325/7372/1066#118779

Tugade, M.M., & Fredrickson, B.L. (2004). Resilient individuals use positive emotions to bounce back from negative emotional experiences. *Journal of Personality and Social Psychology, 86*, 320–333.

Turk, D.C., & Okifuji, A. (2002). Psychological factors in chronic pain: evolution and revolution. *Journal of Consulting and Clinical Psychology, 70*, 678–690.

Turner, J.A., Holtzman, S., & Mancl, L. (2007). Mediators, moderators, and predictors of therapeutic change in cognitive behavioral therapy for chronic pain. *Pain, 127*, 276–286.

Uher, R., & McGuffin (2010) The moderation by the serotonin transporter gene of environmental adversity in the etiology of depression: 2009 update. *Molecular Psychiatry, 15*, 18–22.

Uhl, G.R. (2006). Molecular genetics of addiction vulnerability. *Journal of the American Society for Experimental Neurotherapeutics, 3*, 295–301.

United Nations (2002). Report of the second world assembly on ageing. Blue Ridge Summit, PA: United Nations, Department of General Assembly Affairs and Conference Services.

Ursin, H. (1998). The psychology in psychoneuroendocrinology. *Psychoneuroendocrinology, 23*, 555–570.

Ursin, H., & Eriksen, H.R. (2004). The cognitive activation theory of stress. *Psychoneuroendocrinology, 29*, 567–592.

US National Library of Medicine (2010). Handbook: help me understand genetics. Bethesda, MD: US National Library of Medicine. Available online at: http://ghr.nlm.nih.gov/handbook/illustrations

Van Dam, H.A., van der Horst, F.G., Knoops, L., Ryckman, R.M., Crebolder, H.F.J.M., & van den Borne, B.H.W. (2005). Social support in diabetes: a systematic review of controlled intervention studies. *Patient Education and Counseling, 59*, 1–12.

Van den Boer, H.M.A., & Maat-Kievit, A.A. (2001). The whole truth and nothing but the truth, but what is the truth? *Journal of Medical Genetics, 38*, 39–42.

VandenBos, G.R., & Williams, S. (2000). The internet versus the telephone: what is telehealth anyway? *Professional Psychology: Research and Practice, 31*, 490–492.

Veatch, R.M. (1981). The medical model: its nature and problems. In A.L. Caplan, H.T. Engelhardt & J.J. McCartney (Eds), *Concepts of health and disease: interdisciplinary perspectives.* Reading, MA: Addison-Wesley. Pp. 523–544.

Vellas, B.J., Albarede, J., & Garry, P.J. (1992). Diseases and aging: patterns of morbidity with age: relationship between aging and age-associated diseases. *American Journal of Clinical Nutrition, 55*, 1225S–1230S.

Verbrugge, L.M., Reoma, J.M., & Gruber-Baldini, A.L. (1994). Short-term dynamics of disability and well-being. *Journal of Health and Social Behavior, 35*, 97–117.

Vernon, H., Humphreys, K., & Hagino, C. (2007). Chronic mechanical neck pain in adults treated by manual therapy: a systematic review of change scores in randomized clinical trials. *Journal of Manipulative and Physiological Therapeutics, 30*, 215–227.

Vicenzino, B., & Wright, A. (2002). Physical treatments. In J. Strong, A.M. Unruh, A. Wright & G.D. Baxter (Eds), *Pain: a textbook for therapists.* London: Elsevier. Pp. 87–206.

Villani, D., & Riva, G. (2008). Presence and relaxation: a preliminary controlled study. *PsychNology, 6*, 7–25.

Villani, D., Riva, F., & Riva, G. (2007). New technologies for relaxation: the role of presence. *International Journal of Stress Management, 14*, 260–274.

Vissoci, R.E.M., Nunes, S.O.V., & Morimoto, H.K. (2004). Stress, depression, the immune system and cancer. *The Lancet Oncology, 5*, 617–625.

Volkow, N.D., & Li, T.-K. (2005). Drugs and alcohol: treating and preventing abuse, addiction and their medical consequences. *Pharmacology & Therapeutics, 108*, 3–17.

Volkow, N., & Li, T.K. (2005a). The neuroscience of addiction. *Nature Neuroscience, 8*, 1429–1430.

Von Korff, M., & Miglioretti, D.L. (2005). A prognostic approach to defining chronic pain. *Pain, 117*, 304–313.

Waddell, G., Newton, M., Henderson, I., Somerville, D., & Main, C.J. (1993). A fear avoidance beliefs questionnaire (FABQ) and the role of fear avoidance beliefs in chronic low back pain disability. *Pain, 52*, 157–168.

Waddington, C.H. (1957). *The Strategy of the Genes.* London: Allen & Unwin.

Wager, T.D., & Nitschke, J.B. (2005). Placebo effects in the brain: linking mental and physiological processes. *Brain, Behavior and Immunity, 19*, 281–282.

Watson, D., Clark, L.A., & Tellegen, A. (1988). Development and validation of brief measures of positive and negative affect: the PANAS scales. *Journal of Personality and Social Psychology, 54*, 1063–1070.

Watson, M. (2002). Influence of psychological coping on survival and recurrence: a response to the systematic review. *BMJ Rapid Response*. Retrieved 12th July 2010, from: http://www.bmj.com/cgi/eletters/325/7372/1066#118779

Watson, M., Haviland, J., Greer, S., Davidson, J., & Bliss, J. (1999). Influence of psychological response on survival in breast cancer: a population-based cohort study. *The Lancet, 354*, 1331–1336.

Weinman, J., Petrie, K.J., Moss-Morris, R., & Horne, R. (1996). The Illness Perception Questionnaire: a new method for assessing illness perceptions. *Psychology and Health, 11*, 431–445.

West, R. (2006). *Theory of Addiction*. London: Blackwell.

Williams, D.E., & Thompson, J.K. (1993). Biology and behavior: a set-point hypothesis of psychological functioning. *Behavior Modification, 17*, 43–57.

Wilson, P., Kendall, S., & Brooks, F. (2005). Patient empowerment in primary care: an evaluation of the expert patient. Hatfield: CRIPACC, University of Hertfordshire.

World Health Organisation (1946). Preamble to the constitution of the World Health Organisation as adopted by the International Health Conference, New York, 19–22 June, 1946, signed on 22nd July 1946 by the representatives of 61 States (Official Records of the World Health Organisation, no. 2, p. 100) and entered into force on 7th April 1948.

World Health Organisation (2003). Global strategy on diet, physical activity and health fact sheet. Geneva: WHO.

World Health Organisation (2004). Global immunisation data. Geneva: WHO.

World Health Organisation (2005). Chronic diseases and their common risk factors fact sheet. Geneva: WHO.

Wright, A., Benson, H., & O'Callaghan, J. (2002). Pharmacology of pain management. In J. Strong, A.M. Unruh, A. Wright & G.D. Baxter (Eds), *Pain: a textbook for therapists*. London: Elsevier. Pp. 307–324.

Yehuda, R. (2002). Current status of cortisol findings in post-traumatic stress disorder. *Psychiatric Clinics of North America, 25*, 341–368.

Young Casey, C., Greenberg, M.A., Nicassio, P.M., Harpin, R.E., & Hubbard, D. (2008). Transition from acute to chronic pain and disability: a model including cognitive, affective, and trauma factors. *Pain, 134*, 69–79.

Yunus, M.B. (2007). Role of central sensitization in symptoms beyond muscle pain and the evaluation of a patient with widespread pain. *Best Practice & Research in Clinical Rheumatology, 2*, 48–497.

Zimmerman, C., & Tansella, M. (1996). Psychosocial factors and physical illness in primary care: promoting the biopsychosocial model in medical practice. *Journal of Psychosomatic Research, 40*, 351–358.

Zou, Y., Sfeir, A., Gryaznov, S.M., Shay, J.W., & Wright, W.E. (2004). Does a sentinel or a subset of short telomeres determine replicative senescence? *Molecular Biology of the Cell, 15*, 3709–3718.

INDEX